COUNTRY COOKING . . .

California Style

California Farm Bureau Women
1601 Exposition Boulevard
Sacramento, California 95815

1st printing 1981 5,000 copies
2nd printing 1984 3,000 copies

International Standard Book Number 0-939114-12-7

Printed in the United States of America

Wimmer Brothers Fine Printing and Lithography
Memphis, Tennessee, 38118
"Cookbooks of Distinction"™

COOKBOOK COMMITTEE

California State Women's Committee

Pauline Bennett
Gertrude Brandenberg
Judi Buchinger
Barbara Chrisman
Marge Clark
Pauline Failla
Josephine Gowan
Jane Henning
Charlotte Humphrey
Violet Jensen
Candy Jones
Onalee Koster
Dede Mariani
Kathie Merwin
Lea Moxon
Eda Muller
Mona Pankey
Sally Parks
Lynnel Pollock
Susan Righetti
Jan Schmidl
Jean Siebe
Lorraine Valine

Kim Watson, Program Director, CFBF

ACKNOWLEDGEMENT

The Farm Bureau Women of California are responsible for the multitude of superb recipes contained in this book. These are their recipes, proven again and again in their own kitchens to be the best way of utilizing our numerous agricultural products.

Special thanks goes to the Women's State Committee for organizing and proofreading "Country Cooking".

A book is just a compilation of words until the special touches are added. We feel that our book has certainly been elevated above the ordinary with the beautiful artwork by Onalee Koster, a member of our Women's Executive and State Committees. Thank you for sharing with us your wonderful talents.

The cover design is a picture of California poppies, our state flower, and always a bright spot along rural roads in the springtime. The photograph is by Frederick Geiser, Jr.

FOREWORD

California agriculture is considered one of the most diversified in the world, with no one crop dominating the farm economy. Some two hundred crops are recognized in the state. The top commodities are cattle and calves, milk and cream, cotton, grapes, hay, almonds, tomatoes, nursery products, lettuce, and eggs and chickens. California farmers harvest close to fifty million tons of commodities annually.

California's position as the nation's leading farm state is made possible largely by her abundant resources. Of a total land area of 100 million acres, 33 million acres are used for farming. Much of this is devoted to pasture and rangeland. Most of the crop production comes from 9 million irrigated acres.

Water is the lifeblood of California agriculture. The annual rainfall varies from a high of 60 inches per year in the far northern part of the state to a low of less than 3 inches in the south. California's water storage and transport system makes it possible to use this water for the optimum benefit of crop production.

The farm people themselves are California's most important resource. Each year California farmers, making use of new developments in research and technology, feed more people by increasing their yields and bringing more land into production.

The final outcome of the harvest is, of course, measured in the repast on the dining table. While California certainly produces quantities of agricultural products, quality is also present—in the product itself and in its preparation for our partaking. California cooks know how to best utilize the state's products.

Through this cookbook we hope to share with you some of the most delectable ways of using our farm products. Each cook who has submitted a recipe is well-versed in the preparation of that commodity. We hope you will enjoy reading "Country Cooking" and will find many recipes that will become a standard in your kitchens just as they have provided sustenance and enjoyment for California farmers.

Lynnel Pollock
Chairman
California Farm Bureau Women

DEDICATION

This book is dedicated to the farmers of California who through their resourcefulness, ingenuity and perseverance have provided us with a bountiful harvest. More than mere sustenance, you have given us the reason to pursue our culinary endeavors, and, therefore, the purpose for compiling this book . . .

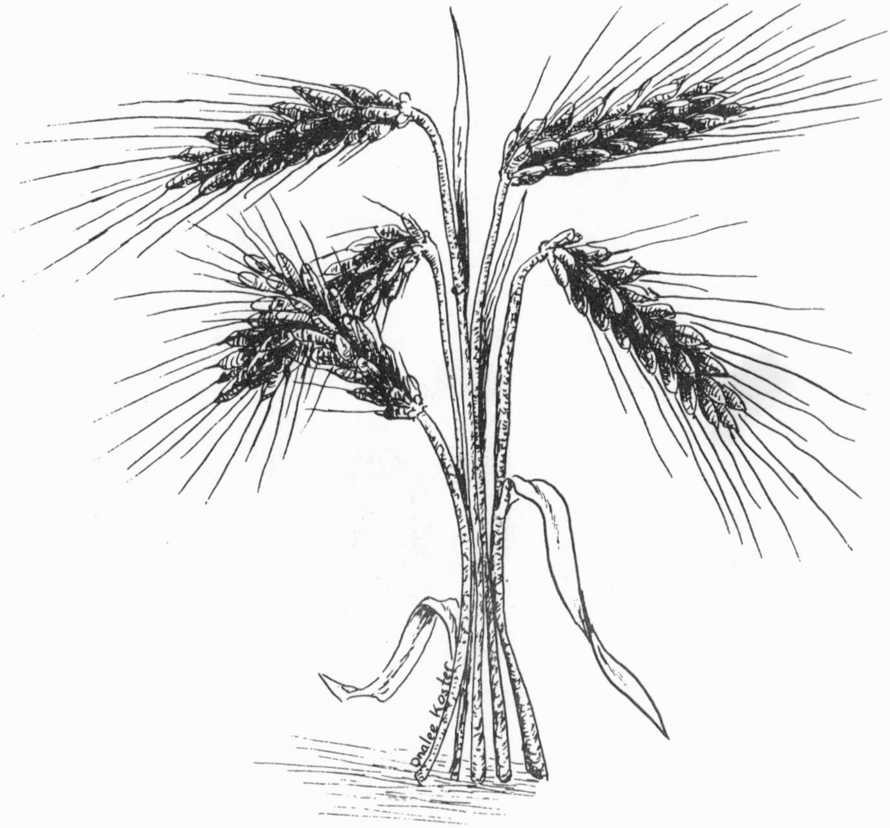
Onalee Koster

TABLE OF CONTENTS

EARLY CALIFORNIA COOKING

Historical California of the 1700's: guitars strumming softly, candlelight flickering against the adobe walls of the hacienda, and a table laden with a bountiful meal provided by the fertile fields of the rancho. The first to settle California's fertile valleys were the Spaniards with their own unique customs, including their magnificent culinary seasonings.

One hundred years later: pick-axes striking rock, mules struggling up steep mountainsides laden with supplies and the trans-continental railroad starts winding through the Sierra Nevada Mountains. Much of the work-force is provided by Chinese laborers. They come to California by the thousands, bringing with them their customs, including their methods of food preparation and exquisite tastes.

This is our heritage; first the Spanish settlers and later the Chinese who contributed immensely to California's culinary excellence.

Through the years, recipes were handed down to the next generation, and today California has a potpourri of exciting, taste-tantalizing dishes. The recipes have been adapted to today's products and methods of cooking, but the unique flavor and style remains to be enjoyed by all.

Early California Cooking

. . . spanish and oriental

HOT CHILI SALSA

1 pound onions
2 pounds hot chilies (jalapeño peppers)
5 pounds tomatoes
3 teaspoons salt
½ teaspoon pepper
¾ to 1 cup vinegar
2 teaspoons fresh oregano, chopped fine
1 teaspoon fresh sweet basil, chopped fine

Peel and wash onions; chop or grind. Wash chilies, remove seeds and chop or grind. Wash tomatoes, peel, if desired, chop or grind. Mix all vegetables and add salt, pepper, vinegar and spices. Simmer 10 minutes. Pack in clean hot jars. Seal. Process for 15 minutes in hot water bath. Wear rubber gloves when preparing hot chilies.
Marie McDermott
San Luis Obispo County

HOT TOMATO SALSA

1 pound can whole tomatoes
1 medium red onion, cut in four pieces
1 teaspoon salt or to taste
2 cloves garlic, minced
2 whole jalapeño peppers (more if desired hotter)

Place 2 tomatoes and all of juice in blender together with onion, salt, peppers and garlic. Blend on high speed for 30 seconds. Add remaining can of tomatoes and blend just until mixed, 15-20 seconds. *Do not over blend.* This salsa will have tiny chunks of tomatoes and onion. Yield: 1 quart. Use on tacos or as a dip.
Note: Store in refrigerator and it improves with age.
Sandra Schirmer
Yolo County

HOT MEXICAN DIP

1 pound Velveeta cheese, cut into cubes
1 can chili without beans
1 small can diced green chili peppers
1 bunch green onions, chopped

Preheat oven to 350 degrees. Mix Velveeta, chili, green chili peppers and onions in casserole dish. Bake for 1 hour. Serve warm with corn chips.
Linda James
Sacramento County

CHILI APPETIZERS

½ cup butter
10 eggs
½ cup flour
1 teaspoon baking powder
Dash salt
2 4-ounce cans diced chilies
1 pint small curd cottage cheese
1 pound Jack cheese, shredded

Preheat oven to 350 degrees. Melt butter in a 13 x 9 x 2-inch glass baking dish. Beat eggs lightly in a large bowl; add flour, baking powder, salt and blend. Add rest of ingredients, turn into baking dish. Bake for 15 minutes; reduce heat to 325 degrees, baking an additional 35-45 minutes until eggs are set and brown. Cut into squares.
Note: Can be made ahead of time and warmed when served. May also be served for a breakfast meal.
Bernice Greer
Sonoma County

LIZ'S STOCKTON CHEESE SQUARES

1 pound extra-sharp Cheddar cheese
1 pound Jack cheese
2 4-ounce cans Ortega diced green chilies
6 eggs

Preheat oven to 350 degrees. Grate cheeses and mix together. Put half into a 9-inch x 13-inch pan. Sprinkle chilies over the cheeses then put the other half of cheese over the chilies. Beat eggs together and pour over all. Bake 45 minutes. Cut into squares when cool.
VadaRae Ohm
San Joaquin County

SOUTH OF THE BORDER HORS D'OEUVRES

5 eggs
¼ cup flour
¼ teaspoon salt
¼ cup butter or margarine, melted
½ teaspoon baking powder
1 8-ounce can diced Ortega chilies
½ pound Jack cheese, shredded
½ pint cottage cheese

Preheat oven to 400 degrees. Beat eggs until foamy. Add flour, salt, melted butter and baking powder, mixing well. Blend in the chilies and cheeses and mix well together. Pour into 8 x 11-inch glass baking dish and bake for 10 minutes. Turn oven down to 350 degrees and bake for an additional 15 minutes. Cool for at least 5 minutes. Cut into bite-size pieces.
Carmen Mitosinka
Imperial County

ALBONDIGA SOUP (MEXICAN MEATBALL SOUP)

2 onions, diced
3 tablespoons bacon drippings
1 16-ounce can tomatoes, chopped (fresh are better)
1 4-ounce can chopped green chilies
1 quart beef broth or brown stock
¼ teaspoon cumin powder
Fresh cilantro leaves or ½ teaspoon ground coriander
Salt and pepper to taste
3 raw tortillas
1 pound extra lean ground beef
1 egg
2 cloves garlic, crushed
¼ teaspoon cumin powder
Salt and pepper to taste

In skillet sauté diced onions with the bacon drippings. Put onions in large pot and add chopped tomatoes, green chilies, beef stock, cumin powder, cut-up cilantro leaves, and salt and pepper to taste. Cook at least 30 minutes, adding more stock as necessary for a good pot of soup.
Cut tortillas into tiny slivers. Work into ground meat with the egg, garlic, cumin powder, and salt and pepper. Shape into tiny balls, about the size of a small marble. Drop into soup and when they float, soup is ready to serve.
Note: This soup freezes well. Serves 4-6 people.
Mable Herburger
Tuolumne County

SOUTHERN CALIFORNIA SCRAMBLE

2 corn tortillas cut into one-inch squares
2 tablespoons vegetable oil
2 green onions, chopped
2 tablespoons chopped Ortega green chili peppers
3 eggs, slightly beaten
Salt and pepper to taste

Fry tortillas in oil until crisp but not brown. Add green onions and chili peppers; stir to mix well with tortillas. Add eggs and scramble until desired consistency. Season to taste. Serves two.
Chonita Hinojosa
Imperial County

CHILI RELLENO CASSEROLE

Sour dough bread
Butter
2 cups Cheddar cheese, shredded
2 cups Monterey Jack cheese, shredded
1 7-ounce can Ortega green chilies
6 eggs
2 cups milk
2 teaspoons paprika
1 teaspoon salt
½ teaspoon oregano
½ teaspoon pepper
¼ teaspoon garlic powder
¼ teaspoon dry mustard

Preheat oven to 325 degrees. Butter trimmed sour dough bread; place buttered side down in 7 x 4-inch pan. Sprinkle shredded cheeses evenly over bread. Chop green chilies and spread over cheese mixture. In separate bowl mix eggs, milk and seasonings. Beat until well blended. Pour over bread, cheese and chili mixture. Cover with foil and let chill overnight. Bake uncovered about 50 minutes. Let stand 10 minutes before serving.
Jo Steffanic
Plumas County

TOMATOES A QUESO

4 medium onions, thinly sliced
3 tablespoons butter
5 or 6 large tomatoes, thickly sliced
1½ cups sharp Cheddar cheese, grated
1 cup bread crumbs
¼ teaspoon salt
1 teaspoon paprika
2 eggs, beaten
1 cup sour cream

Preheat oven to 375 degrees. In a 10-inch skillet sauté the onions in the butter for 5 minutes over medium heat, not browning them. Grease a deep 2-quart casserole and arrange a layer of tomatoes on the bottom. Sprinkle some cheese on top, followed by some bread crumbs, onion, salt and paprika. Repeat layers until all these ingredients are used, ending with cheese. In a small mixing bowl beat together the eggs and sour cream until smooth. Pour the sour cream sauce over the casserole and sprinkle with salt and paprika to add color. Cover and bake for 30 minutes, then uncover and bake 15 minutes longer or until puffed and brown.
Sheila Fry
Kern County

THE SOUTH PLACER EGG RANCHER SPECIAL

2 corn tortillas per serving
1 tablespoon butter
2 eggs
2 slices Monterey Jack cheese
Green chile salsa

Allow 2 corn tortillas per serving, add 1 tablespoon butter. Heat butter in pan slightly larger than tortillas. Fry tortillas on both sides. Place 1 tortilla in pan and add 2 slices Monterey Jack cheese. Beat 2 eggs; pour over cheese. Place other tortilla on top. Press top tortilla down around sides to seal well. Fry over medium heat. With large spatula, turn the whole thing over . . . *very carefully!* It is ready to serve when egg is set well. Serve with green chile salsa.
Iris Sippola
Placer County

EARLY CALIFORNIA TACO SALAD

1 head iceberg lettuce, shredded
1 grated carrot
½ cup grated Jack and Cheddar cheese
1 small can sliced black olives
2 medium tomatoes, chopped
1 pound ground beef
1 package taco seasoning mix
1 regular size package taco chips
Italian salad dressing

Combine first five ingredients. Brown meat and add taco seasoning. *Before serving:* Toss lettuce mixture and meat mixture with 1 regular size package taco chips. Pour Italian salad dressing or thinned guacamole dressing over salad while tossing. Serves 8-10.
Valerie Holcomb-Lane
Siskiyou County

SPANISH STYLE ZUCCHINI

1 pound ground beef
½ cup onion, chopped
¼ teaspoon garlic salt (or garlic clove)
1½ pounds zucchini squash, sliced (about 5 cups)
½ teaspoon salt
¼ teaspoon ground cumin
¼ teaspoon pepper
1 12-ounce can tomato sauce or 1 15-ounce can tomato sauce with tomato tidbits
1 12-ounce can mexicorn

Sauté ground beef, onion and garlic in a 10-inch skillet until meat is well-browned. Add zucchini squash, salt, cumin and pepper. Cook mixture over medium heat, stirring occasionally, for 3 to 5 minutes. Add tomato sauce and mexicorn. Bring to a boil, reduce heat. Cover. Simmer for 10 minutes or until zucchini is tender. If mixture is too thick, add a little water. Makes six servings.
Dolores Barandas
Sacramento County

MEATBALLS IN SPANISH GRAVY

Meatballs:

2 pounds ground beef
½ pound ground pork
1 small onion, minced
2 cloves garlic, minced
⅛ cup parsley, minced
1 egg
½ teaspoon chili powder
Salt and pepper to taste
2 tablespoons olive oil

Mix ground beef, ground pork, onion, garlic, parsley, egg, ½ teaspoon chili powder and salt and pepper. Form into small meatballs—the size of a quarter. Brown in heavy skillet with 2 tablespoons olive oil, and set aside.

Gravy:

½ cup olive oil
¾ cup flour
3 teaspoons chili powder
2 cups cold water
½ teaspoon cumin
¼ teaspoon oregano
¼ teaspoon marjoram
1 beef broth packet (or cube)
Salt and pepper to taste
Added water if needed

Heat ½ cup olive oil in heavy skillet and stir in flour with wire whip. Add 3 teaspoons chili powder and brown slightly. Add cold water and blend. Add cumin, oregano, marjoram, beef broth, salt and pepper. Add more water if needed to desired consistency. Add meatballs to gravy and let simmer for 15 to 20 minutes, stirring lightly with a spatula so meatballs will not break up.
Note: Delicious served with white or brown rice. Also, potatoes or noodles go well with this too.
Marge Kiriluk
Tuolumne County

SOUR CREAM ENCHILADAS

2 cans cream of chicken soup
1 pint sour cream
2 cans (small) green chilies, chopped
2 bunches green onions, chopped
1 pound Monterey Jack cheese, shredded
1 pound Cheddar cheese, shredded
2 dozen flour tortillas

Preheat oven to 300 degrees. Mix together the 2 cans of chicken soup and sour cream. Then mix together the green chilies and green onions. Then mix together the two cheeses. Put equal amounts (1 heaping teaspoon) of each of these three mixtures on each tortilla, roll and place in greased pan. Pour over top the remainder of soup and sour cream mix; then sprinkle with a little cheese. Bake for 20 to 30 minutes.
Liz Biller
Marin County

CHICKEN TORTILLA CASSEROLE

1 chicken, boiled and boned
6 corn tortillas
1 onion, chopped
1 7-ounce can pitted olives, drained
1 cup chicken broth
1 can cream of mushroom soup
1 can cream of chicken soup
1 can Gebhardt's Chili (hot dog sauce)
½ 8-ounce can Ortega Chile Salsa
1 cup Cheddar cheese, grated
1 cup Monterey Jack cheese, grated

Preheat oven to 375 degrees. Lay pieces of chicken in casserole, add broken pieces of tortilla. Add layer of grated onion and pitted olives. Add broth, soups and chili sauces which have been blended together. Top with Cheddar and Monterey cheese. Bake until hot and bubbly, about 30 minutes.
Lorraine Valine
Sacramento County

SUNSHINE CHICKEN TORTILLA BAKE

2 whole chicken breasts (or 1 chicken)
1 dozen corn tortillas
½ or less can Ortega green chilies
1 can mushroom soup
1 can chicken soup
1 cup broth
¾ pound Cheddar cheese, grated

Preheat oven to 350 degrees. Boil chicken; cut in pieces. Break up tortillas and lay on bottom of 9 x 12-inch baking dish. Cut chilies in small pieces; mix broth and soups together with chilies. Lay chicken pieces on top of tortilla pieces, then pour the soup mixture over that. Bake for ½ hour. The last 10 minutes put grated cheese on top and continue baking.
Jan Cox
Shasta County

EARLY CALIFORNIA CHILI CASSEROLE

18 California chilies (Anaheims), roasted and peeled
2½ cups Bisquick or other baking mix
3 eggs, separated
1½ cups milk
1 pound Monterey Jack cheese
1 large onion
2 tablespoons butter or margarine
2 tablespoons Parmesan cheese

To Roast Chilies:
Place on baking sheet under broiler, broil until skin blisters on top side. Turn, and blister; continue turning and blistering until all sides are well blistered. Now place chilies in a heavy paper bag and close, and let steam at least 15 minutes. Now remove and peel, then remove seeds and rinse.

Preheat oven to 350 degrees. Beat together baking mix, milk and egg yolks, reserving whites. Beat whites of eggs until stiff, and fold into batter. Butter generously a 9½ x 13-inch baking pan. Pour a third of the batter into pan. Slice cheese into 18 sticks, and insert a stick into each chile. Place stuffed chiles in two rows in pan. Dice onion, and sauté in butter until clear but not browned. Pour onion over chiles. Pour remainder of batter over onions and chilies. Sprinkle Parmesan over batter. Bake for 30 minutes, or until golden brown.
Note: To make a heartier dish, ½ pound ground round may be sautéed, drained, and added after the diced onion.
Betty Middlecamp
San Luis Obispo County

TAMALE LOAF OLÉ

½ cup salad oil
3 tablespoons margarine
2 onions, chopped finely
2 cloves garlic, minced
1 cup tomatoes
1 cup corn
2 tablespoons chili powder
1½ cups corn meal
3 eggs, beaten
1 cup milk
½ cup olives
1 tablespoon salt
1 pound ground beef, cooked

Preheat oven to 350 degrees. Cook onions and garlic in the oil and butter for 15 minutes in large skillet. Add the tomatoes and corn. Dissolve chili powder in a little water, and add it to the above. Add corn meal, eggs, milk, olives, salt, and meat; cook 15 minutes more. Place in a greased casserole and bake 30 minutes in oven. Serves 10 to 12.

Inez Borror
Tehama County

CALIFORNIA TAMALE LOAF

½ cup vegetable oil
3 teaspoons butter
1 medium onion
2 cloves garlic
2 pounds ground beef
1 can whole kernel corn, drained
1 can pitted black olives, drained
1 16-ounce can stewed tomatoes
1½ cups yellow corn meal
3 eggs, lightly beaten
1½ cups milk
3 to 6 teaspoons chili powder
1 teaspoon salt
½ teaspoon black pepper

Preheat oven to 350 degrees. Heat cooking oil and butter in a large skillet. Add the onion, garlic and ground beef and brown well. To this mixture, add the corn, olives and tomatoes. In separate bowl, mix the corn meal, eggs, milk, chili powder, salt and pepper and blend together. Add to meat mixture. Place in large casserole and bake uncovered for 30 minutes. Serve with green salad. Will serve 14.

Rivon Nilson
Imperial County

TAMALE PIE

1 pound ground beef
1 onion, chopped
1 teaspoon salt
2 tablespoons chili powder
1 can tomatoes, or 2 small cans tomato sauce
1 small can pitted ripe olives, drained
1 can whole kernel corn, undrained
½ to ¾ cup corn meal
½ cup grated cheese
2 strips of bacon

Heat oven to 350 degrees. In large skillet, brown the meat with the onions, salt and chili powder. Add the tomatoes, olives, corn, cornmeal and cheese. Stir all ingredients together. Pour into a casserole and top with 2 strips of bacon. Bake for 35 minutes.
Margaret Hager
San Luis Obispo County

MOCK ENCHILADA

3 onions, chopped
3 cloves garlic, chopped fine
¼ cup vegetable oil
2 pounds ground beef
¼ cup flour
½ teaspoon oregano
3 small cans of chopped olives
3 cans enchilada sauce
1 46-ounce can tomato juice
1½ pounds cheese, grated
1 large package crackers

Preheat oven to 350 degrees. Sauté onions and garlic in oil until tender. Add beef and cook well. Add flour, oregano, olives, enchilada sauce and tomato juice. Arrange a layer of crackers on bottom of buttered loaf pan. Spread a layer of meat mixture, then sprinkle on cheese. Repeat layers 3 more times, ending with the cheese. Refrigerate for 24 hours. Bake for 45 minutes. Yield: 20 servings.
Joan Dutil
Calaveras County

LAYERED ENCHILADA PIE

2 tablespoons butter or margarine
1 pound ground beef
1 medium onion, chopped
1 tablespoon chili powder
1 teaspoon salt
¼ teaspoon pepper
1 4½-ounce can chopped olives
1 8-ounce can tomato sauce
6 corn tortillas
2 cups sharp Cheddar cheese, grated
⅔ cup water

Preheat oven at 400 degrees. Brown ground beef and onion in butter or margarine. Add seasonings, olives and tomato sauce. In round 2-quart casserole, alternate layers of tortillas, meat sauce and cheese, reserving enough cheese for last layer. Pour water into casserole and top with reserved cheese. Cover and bake for 30 minutes.

Edna Whittenburg
San Luis Obispo County

CHILI RELLEÑOS CASSEROLE WITH MEAT

1 pound ground beef
½ cup onion, chopped
½ teaspoon salt
¼ teaspoon pepper
2 cans (4 ounces) green Ortega chilies, cut in half crosswise and seeded
1½ cups sharp Cheddar cheese, shredded
1½ cups milk
¼ cup all-purpose flour
½ teaspoon salt
⅛ teaspoon pepper
4 eggs, beaten
3-4 drops bottled hot pepper sauce

Preheat oven to 350 degrees. In skillet, brown beef and onion. Drain off fat. Sprinkle meat with the first ½ teaspoon salt and ¼ teaspoon pepper. Place half of the chilies in 10 x 6 x 1½-inch baking dish; sprinkle with cheese, top with meat mixture. Arrange remaining chilies over meat. Combine remaining ingredients; beat until smooth. Pour over meat-chili mixture. Bake for 45-50 minutes, or until knife inserted just off center comes out clean. Let cool 5 minutes; cut in squares to serve. Makes 6 servings.

Yvonne Baker
Kings County

BEEF ENCHILADA OLÉ

1 pound ground beef
1 cup water
1 teaspoon oregano
1 teaspoon cumin
½ teaspoon garlic powder
1 teaspoon salt
½ teaspoon pepper
1 package flour tortillas
1 pound Longhorn or Jack cheese, grated
1 bunch green onions, chopped

Sauce:

2 tablespoons cooking oil
2 tablespoons flour
1 small can Las Palmas red chili sauce
1 can water
1 tablespoon sugar
1 tablespoon vinegar
1 teaspoon cumin
1 teaspoon oregano

Preheat oven to 350 degrees. Brown meat, add 1 cup water and seasonings. Simmer for 20 minutes. Combine all ingredients for sauce and heat to boiling. Dip each tortilla in sauce, place meat mixture and spoonful of cheese in center. Roll and place in flat ovenproof dish. Pour remaining sauce over. Sprinkle remaining cheese and the green onions over top. Bake for 30 minutes.
Vi Pharaoh
Placer County

LAYERED ENCHILADAS

1 pound ground beef
1 onion, chopped
1 clove garlic, minced
½ teaspoon salt
¼ teaspoon pepper
1 tablespoon chili powder
1 4½-ounce can chopped ripe olives
2 8-ounce cans tomato sauce
6 corn tortillas
½ pound sharp Cheddar cheese, grated (about 2 cups)

Preheat oven to 350 degrees. Brown meat, onion and garlic on medium heat, drain. Add salt, pepper, chili powder, olives and tomato sauce; simmer for 10 minutes. In a round, 2-quart casserole, alternate layers of whole tortillas, meat sauce and cheese, ending with cheese. Cover and bake for 25 to 30 minutes.
Note: I like to add refried beans before meat sauce.
Linda James
Sacramento County

EASY MEXICAN CASSEROLE

1½ pounds ground meat
1 small onion, chopped
1 small can chopped black olives
1 package taco seasoning mix
3 small cans tomato sauce
½ pint small curd cottage cheese
½ pint sour cream
1 package tortilla chips
Monterey Jack cheese, grated

Preheat oven to 375 degrees. Sauté ground meat, add onion, black olives, taco seasoning mix and tomato sauce. Combine cottage cheese and sour cream and set aside. Crush tortilla chips to form crust in a 2-quart casserole dish. Cover with meat mixture. Spoon over creamy mixture, cover with grated Jack cheese. Layer meat and creamy mixture until ingredients are all gone. Top with thick layer Jack cheese. Heat in oven 30 to 40 minutes or until bubbly.
Linda James
Sacramento County

SOUTH OF THE BORDER ENCHILADA PIE

1 pound ground beef
1 medium onion, chopped
1 clove garlic, minced (optional)
2 tablespoons butter
1 teaspoon salt
¼ teaspoon pepper
1 tablespoon chili powder (optional)
1 4½-ounce can chopped ripe olives
1 8-ounce can tomato sauce
6 corn tortillas, lightly buttered
2 cups sharp Cheddar cheese, shredded (about ½ pound)
⅔ cup water

Preheat oven to 400 degrees. Brown ground beef, onion and garlic in butter. Add salt, pepper, chili powder, olives and tomato sauce and simmer for one minute. In a round 2-quart casserole, alternate layers of buttered tortillas, meat sauce and 1½ cups of the shredded cheese. Sprinkle ½ cup of shredded cheese on the top tortilla. Carefully pour the water, at edge, into bottom of casserole. Cover. Bake for 30 minutes. Makes 4 servings.
Note: Casserole can be made ahead and frozen, but do not add the water until you are ready to bake.
Juanita Hershey
Kern County

JULIE'S TACOS

2 pounds ground round
Seasoning salt to taste
2 cans Ortega Chili Salsa
1 or 2 cups frozen hash brown potatoes
Taco shells
Cheddar cheese, grated
Sour cream
Lettuce, shredded
1 small can El Patio Chili Sauce

Brown the ground round and season with season salt. Drain the excess fat but do not completely drain all. Add the chili salsa and the potatoes and let simmer until the potatoes are tender. Fill taco shells with meat mixture, add cheese, teaspoon sour cream and then lettuce. If you desire a bit more tang, add the El Patio Sauce.
Julie Wood
Sacramento County

MEXICAN BEEFIES

5 pounds chuck roast (T-bone, blade-bone in), roasted in a 200 degree oven covered (no seasoning) for 12 hours
3 tablespoons fat from drippings
3 large onions, chopped
1 4-ounce can chopped green chilies
2 7-ounce cans chili salsa
¼ teaspoon garlic powder
4 tablespoons flour
4 teaspoons salt
1 teaspoon ground cumin
Skimmed meat juices
Flour tortillas
Lettuce
Tomatoes
Guacamole
Sour cream
Olives
Picante (Rosarita) sauce

Shred roast into small pieces; set aside. In a large fry pan put 3 tablespoons fat, add chopped onions, sauté until clear. Add next 6 ingredients. Cook for 1 minute. Add juices and meat; heat through. At this point you have a basic meat mixture. You can freeze or refrigerate or continue ahead for Mexican Beefies.
Put enough oil to cover bottom of fry pan ¼ inch deep. Heat to medium heat. Put ¼ cup meat mixture in middle of tortilla. Fold up to make rectangle. Fry until golden brown on both sides. Place on bed of shredded lettuce, garnish with tomatoes, olives, guacamole, sour cream. Serve with picante sauce. Serves at least 10.
Ann Dutra
Siskiyou County

LOMPOC BEEF CHILI

¾ pound dried pinto beans
3 1-pound cans tomatoes
2½ tablespoons vegetable oil
4 large onions, chopped (5 cups)
3 cloves garlic, minced
½ cup fresh parsley, minced
½ cup butter or margarine
5 pounds ground beef chuck
1 cup red wine
2 tablespoons salt
1 tablespoon sugar
1½ teaspoons pepper
1½ teaspoons ground cumin

Wash beans. Cook beans in a large kettle with water to cover. Simmer about 45 minutes or until soft. Add tomatoes and simmer 5 minutes. Set aside. Sauté onions and cook until soft in the vegetable oil. Add garlic and parsley. Melt margarine or butter in a large skillet. Add beef and lightly brown. Add beef mixture to beans. Stir in remaining ingredients. Cover and simmer 1 hour. Remove cover and cook 30 minutes longer. Skim fat from top and serve. Makes 8-12 servings.
Joan Scolari
Santa Barbara County

FAMOUS MEXICAN DISH

1½ pounds ground beef
1 small onion, chopped
1 package taco seasoning mix
1 cup water
½ cup bottled taco sauce
10 corn tortillas cut into triangles
2 10-ounce packages frozen chopped spinach
3 cups Jack cheese, shredded
½ pound cooked ham strips
1 cup sour cream

Preheat oven to 375 degrees. Brown beef and onion in a skillet and stir in taco mix and water. Cover and simmer 10 minutes. In a 3-quart casserole pour ½ taco sauce (bottled). Place ½ tortilla strips in pan and coat with sauce. Spread strips to overlap. Cook spinach and set aside. Press all water out of spinach. Stir ½ spinach into beef mixture. Then take beef and spinach mixture and pour over taco strips. Sprinkle with ½ of the cheese. Cover with rest of tortilla strips (making sure overlapping); spread over rest of taco sauce. Place ham on top; spread with sour cream. Scatter rest of spinach and top with rest of cheese. Bake for 50 minutes, covering for first 25 minutes. Serves 6-8.
Mona Pankey
Kern County

RANCHO ENCHILADAS

1 pound ground beef
1 teaspoon oregano
1 teaspoon chili powder
2 12-ounce cans of Las Palmas Enchilada Sauce
1 package medium-size flour tortillas
1 medium onion, chopped
1 8-ounce package mild Cheddar cheese, grated
1 can black olives

Preheat oven to 350 degrees. Brown meat, add oregano and chili powder. Set aside. Heat enchilada sauce and dip 6 tortillas in sauce. Lay them in a 9 x 13-inch casserole dish. Spread hamburger, chopped onion, cheese (save out ¼ cup cheese) and ¾ can of olives over the tortillas. Dip 6 more tortillas and cover the hamburger, onion and cheese. Pour remaining enchilada sauce over the layers in dish. Sprinkle with remaining ¼ cup cheese and dot with remaining ¼ can of olives. Bake for approximately ½ hour.
Marlene Righetti
San Luis Obispo County

MEXICAN LASAGNA

1½ pounds ground beef
1 small onion, chopped
½ cup black olives, chopped
1 package taco seasoning mix
3 small cans tomato sauce
½ pint cottage cheese
½ pint sour cream
1 9-ounce package tortilla chips
Jack cheese, grated

Preheat oven to 375 degrees. Sauté ground beef. Add onion, olives, taco seasoning mix and tomato sauce. Combine cottage cheese and sour cream. Set aside. Crush tortilla chips to form crust in a 2-quart casserole. Cover with one half of meat mixture. Spoon over one half sour cream mixture. Cover with grated cheese. Layer again with remaining mixtures and cheese. Bake for 30 minutes or until bubbly.
Christine Van Steyn
Sacramento County

COTTAGE CHEESE CHILI BAKE

1 cup small curd cottage cheese
½ cup milk
2 eggs
¼ cup flour
⅛ teaspoon salt
½ teaspoon oregano
¼ teaspoon basil
8 ounces Monterey Jack cheese, grated
1 4-ounce can diced green chilies

Preheat oven to 400 degrees. Combine cottage cheese, milk, eggs, flour, and salt in blender. Whirl until smooth. Stir in oregano and basil. Pour half the mixture into a greased 8-inch baking dish. Cover with half of cheese. Sprinkle with chilies and cover with remaining cottage cheese mixture. Sprinkle with remaining cheese. Bake for 30 minutes or until light brown. Serves 4.

Lorri Frandsen
San Diego County

BEEF CHOW MEIN

1 cup cooked beef, diced
½ cup onion, sliced
2 tablespoons cooking oil
1½ cups celery, sliced
2 beef bouillon cubes, dissolved in ½ cup boiling water
1 16-ounce can mixed chop suey vegetables
3 tablespoons cornstarch, dissolved in 3 tablespoons water
1 teaspoon brown sugar
½ teaspoon pepper
2 tablespoons soy sauce, mixed with 3 tablespoons water

In a medium size saucepan, brown meat and onion in oil. Add celery and dissolved beef cubes. Cover and boil 5 minutes. Add chop suey vegetables. Combine cornstarch with brown sugar, pepper, and soy sauce. Add to meat and cook over low heat until mixture thickens and clears. Serve over crisp chow mein noodles or hot rice.

Rozilla Ashurst
Imperial County

BEEF, ONION AND TOMATO ORIENTAL

1 pound beef round or flank steak
3 medium-sized firm tomatoes
2 small yellow onions
1 medium green pepper
2 teaspoons cornstarch
½ teaspoon salt
1 tablespoon soy sauce
¼ cup water
1 teaspoon cooking oil
3 tablespoons cooking oil
1 slice fresh ginger root, minced

Cut beef across grain into strips about ⅛-inch thick, and ½ by 2-inches. Cut tomatoes and onions in ½-inch wedges; cut green pepper in uniform pieces about the size of other vegetables. Keep each separate until ready to add. Combine cornstarch, salt, soy sauce, water and 1 teaspoon oil; set aside. Heat wok, add 3 tablespoons oil to wok and preheat 5 minutes. Add minced ginger and beef when hot. Stir fry until meat is browned. Add onion, stir fry 1 minute longer, add green pepper and stir fry until onions are transparent. Stir cornstarch mixture before adding to wok, stir in cornstarch mixture, cook 1 minute; add tomatoes and cook 1 minute longer or until sauce is clear. Serve immediately with cooked rice. Serves 3 or 4.
Note: Electric skillet can be used in place of wok.
Charlotte Goulding
Modoc County

CHINESE PEPPER STEAK

1 pound round steak
2 tablespoons salad oil
Salt and pepper to taste
1 medium onion, chopped
1 clove garlic, minced
½ cup celery, sliced
1 cup mushrooms, sliced
2 small zucchini, sliced
½ green pepper, diced
1 bouillon cube
1 cup tomatoes, chopped
1½ tablespoons cornstarch
2 tablespoons soy sauce
¼ cup cold water

Cut steak into thin strips, about 2 inches long. In large skillet brown meat in oil. Season with salt and pepper. Add vegetables and continue cooking until soft, stirring frequently. Add bouillon and tomatoes; cover and simmer about 15 minutes. Mix cornstarch and soy sauce with water. Stir into meat mixture to thicken. Serve over hot California rice.
Lynnel Pollock
Yolo County

CANTONESE TOMATO BEEF

½ pound beef
3 tablespoons soy sauce
¼ teaspoon sugar
1 tablespoon wine (optional)
Dash pepper
4 teaspoons cornstarch
2 stalks green onion, diced
2 tomatoes
2 stalks celery
1 green pepper
1 small onion
6 tablespoons oil
1 piece ginger, crushed
1 clove garlic, crushed
½ teaspoon salt
1 cup water
¼ teaspoon Accent

Slice beef thin and soak in soy sauce, sugar, wine, pepper, green onions, and 3 teaspoons cornstarch for 15 minutes. Cut tomatoes, celery, green pepper, and onion into 1-inch squares. Heat 3 tablespoons oil in pan and brown ginger and garlic lightly. Add beef, stirring rapidly and cooking to medium rareness. Remove from pan. Add rest of oil in pan and fry onion, green pepper, and celery for a minute, or so. Add beef and tomatoes and stir for another minute. Add mixture of salt, water, Accent, and 1 teaspoon cornstarch; bring to a boil. Add green onions as garnish and serve over steamed rice.
Anita Chan
Santa Clara County

VICTORVILLE'S CHINESE HASH

1 pound ground beef
1 medium onion, chopped
1 cup celery, chopped
1 10-ounce can cream of mushroom soup
1 10-ounce can cream of chicken soup
1 small can water chestnuts, sliced
½ cup raw rice
2 tablespoons soy sauce
1½ cups water
1 5½-ounce can chow mein noodles

Preheat oven to 350 degrees. Brown the meat and drain off the fat. Mix meat and all the other ingredients except noodles in a 2-quart casserole dish. Bake for 1 hour. Top with noodles the last 15 minutes of baking time. Put soy sauce on the table for those who desire it.
Carolyn Lounsbury
San Bernardino County

ORIENTAL BEEF AND ASPARAGUS

1 pound lean beef steak, preferably sirloin
3 tablespoons sesame oil
1 tablespoon sesame seeds
1 teaspoon minced fresh ginger root
18 large asparagus spears, cut into 1½-inch lengths
2 medium onions, cut into thin wedges
2 cups water
2 cups fresh mushrooms, thickly sliced
½ cup soy sauce
2 tablespoons cornstarch

Cut meat into thin 2-inch length strips. In an electric or large skillet brown meat in oil, along with the sesame seeds and ginger root. Add asparagus, onions and ½ cup of the water. Stir well and cover. Cook at medium heat (350 degrees) for 10 minutes. Turn heat down to simmer. Add mushrooms and a little more water if necessary. Simmer for 5 more minutes. Combine remaining water, soy sauce and cornstarch; add to skillet. Cook until slightly thickened, stir occasionally. Serve immediately over rice. Serves 4 generously.
Note: You may substitute 3 cups of cut broccoli for asparagus.
Mary Brandenberg
Imperial County

CHINESE HAWAIIAN SPARE RIBS

3 to 4 pounds pork spare ribs
½ teaspoon pepper
½ teaspoon ginger
1 teaspoon salt
1 teaspoon paprika
1 teaspoon celery salt
1 teaspoon chili powder
1 cup brown sugar
1 can tomato soup
½ can vinegar

Cut ribs into individual pieces. Mix dry ingredients together. With fingers rub on all sides of ribs. Set side by side on edge in 11 x 16-inch pan. Broil approximately 15 minutes on each side. Mix tomato soup and vinegar together and pour over ribs. Bake for 40 minutes at 350 degree. Spoon sauce over ribs occasionally during baking. Remove ribs from sauce. Skim grease from sauce and serve with rice.
Margaret Vandegrift
San Luis Obispo County

ORIENTAL BEEF AND VEGETABLE SKILLET

1 pound sirloin steak, 1-inch thick
2 tablespoons hot cooking oil
1 pint fresh mushrooms, sliced
1 5-ounce can bamboo shoots, drained
1 5-ounce can water chestnuts, drained and sliced
1 medium onion, cut in wedges
1 stalk celery, cut into 1-inch pieces
½ large green pepper, cut into pieces
1 tablespoon sugar
1 cup beef broth
1 tablespoon cornstarch
¼ cup soy sauce
2 tablespoons water

Partially freeze meat, then slice in thin strips. Brown meat, half at a time, in hot oil in skillet (electric skillet works best for this recipe). Add mushrooms, bamboo shoots, water chestnuts, onion, celery, green pepper, sugar and beef broth to skillet. Cover and simmer 5 minutes. Blend cornstarch, soy sauce and water. Stir into meat mixture. Cook and stir till thickened. Serve with rice, if desired. Makes 3-4 servings.
Betty Bergman
Kern County

CHICKEN CHOW MEIN NOODLE CASSEROLE

1½ pounds chicken breasts
2 green onions, chopped
1 green pepper, thinly sliced (small)
6 medium fresh mushrooms
2 tablespoons margarine
1 10-ounce package frozen carrots and peas, cooked
2 tablespoons mayonnaise
2 10¾-ounce cans cream of chicken soup
1 5-ounce can chow mein noodles

Preheat oven to 350 degrees. Boil or pressure cook chicken breasts until tender. Dice. Fry green onions, green pepper, and mushrooms in margarine until wilted. Combine cooked vegetables with cooked carrots and peas and diced chicken breasts. Add 2 tablespoons mayonnaise. Add cream of chicken soup. Sprinkle one half of the noodles on bottom of greased or buttered 11¾ x 7½-inch casserole. Pour in the chicken mixture. Sprinkle the remaining noodles on top. Bake for 15 minutes to warm through.
Florence Drury
San Joaquin County

VALLEY MANDARIN CHICKEN WITH WALNUTS

1½ pounds chicken breasts, skinned and boned
3 tablespoons soy sauce
2 tablespoons cornstarch
2 tablespoons dry sherry
1 teaspoon grated ginger root
1 teaspoon sugar
½ teaspoon salt
1 teaspoon Chinese Five Spices
½ teaspoon crushed Chinese red pepper
2 tablespoons cooking oil
2 medium-sized green peppers, cut into ¾-inch pieces
4 green onions, bias-sliced into 1-inch lengths
1 cup walnut halves
1 8-ounce can water chestnuts, sliced

Cut chicken into 1-inch pieces. Set aside. Blend soy sauce, cornstarch, dry sherry, ginger root, sugar, salt and spices. Set aside. Preheat a wok or large skillet over high heat; add cooking oil. Stir fry green pepper and green onion until tender. Remove from skillet and set aside. Add walnuts and water chestnuts to oil and stir fry until walnuts are golden. Remove and set aside. Stir fry ½ the chicken at a time in hot fat for 2 minutes or until pieces are white in color. Return all chicken to pan, add soy mixture and cook until thickened. Stir in vegetables and nuts, cook 1 minute more. Serve at once with hot cooked rice. Makes 4 to 6 servings.
Darlene Shubert
Kings County

FRIED RICE ORIENTAL

2 tablespoons onion, chopped
½ cup canned mushrooms, drained
1 cup cooked chicken, pork or ham, chopped
2 tablespoons oil
4 cups cold cooked rice
2 tablespoons soy sauce
1 egg, well beaten
2 tablespoons parsley, minced
⅛ teaspoon pepper

Sauté onion, mushrooms and meat(s) in oil in large skillet until tender. Add rice and soy sauce. Cook over low heat 5 to 10 minutes stirring occasionally with a fork. Add egg, parsley and pepper. Cook over low heat 5 minutes stirring constantly with a fork. If desired, add additional soy sauce.
Rachel Moore
Placer County

SWEET AND SOUR VENISON CHOPS

4 thick venison chops
1 teaspoon salt
½ teaspoon pepper
¼ cup flour
3 tablespoons shortening
1 cup pineapple juice
⅓ cup vinegar
1 cup pineapple chunks
½ large green pepper, cut into thin slices
¼ cup water
2 tablespoons cornstarch
¼ cup brown sugar

Cut venison chops into 1-inch cubes. Dredge with flour to which the salt and pepper have been added. Brown the meat in the shortening. After the meat has been browned, add the pineapple juice and vinegar. Cook slowly for 45 to 60 minutes, or until meat is tender. Then add the pineapple chunks and the green pepper and cook over low heat for fifteen minutes more. Then add the water to which has been added the cornstarch and sugar. Cook slowly until thickened. Serves two or three people.
Olive Beamer
Trinity County

BEEF FRIED RICE

2 cups water
¼ teaspoon salt
3 tablespoons butter or margarine, divided
2¼ cups minute rice
2 eggs, lightly beaten
3 tablespoons vegetable oil
¾ cup scallions, chopped
1 cup chuck roast, cooked and ground
1 large stalk celery, sliced
1 small can water chestnuts, sliced
1 small can mushrooms
2 tablespoons soy sauce
½ teaspoon sugar
¼ teaspoon monosodium glutamate (optional)
½ teaspoon salt

In a small saucepan bring 2 cups water, salt and 1 tablespoon butter to a boil. Stir in rice, remove from heat, cover and let stand 5 minutes, then refrigerate. Heat 2 tablespoons butter or margarine in a small skillet, add eggs and scramble lightly. Remove and set aside. Heat the 3 tablespoons of oil in a heavy skillet and fry the scallions and ground meat. After a few minutes, add celery, water chestnuts, mushrooms and cold rice, stirring constantly. Season with soy sauce, sugar, salt, and monosodium glutamate. Add scrambled eggs. Serve immediately.
Dorothy Marie Baker
San Diego County

COOKING WITH WINE

The Spanish mission fathers brought wine grapes to California over two centuries ago for use in Sacramental wine. Grape production has since become one of the top four agricultural crops in California with last year's crush totaling over 2.9 million tons. California has been called a "Paradise for the vine" due to long, warm, normally rainless growing seasons, low humidity, and mild winters. The climatic variations between California's viticultural districts provides the consumer with a wide selection of wine from which to choose.

Many of the grapes used for California wine production are the same varieties as those grown in the famous European wine areas. In addition to excellent "premium" wines such as Pinot Noir, Chardonnay or Cabernet Sauvignon, California's "everyday" table wines such as Chablis, Rosé, or Burgundy are said to be among the best in the world. Whether used as a component in cooking or a beverage enjoyed with food, California wine, with its consistent quality and value, enhances any meal.

Cooking With Wine

. . . wining and dining

ITALIAN GARBANZOS

1 15-ounce can drained Garbanzo beans
½ cup red wine vinegar
4 tablespoons salad oil
1 teaspoon salt
1 teaspoon sugar
¼ teaspoon oregano
Dash of pepper
3 tablespoons chopped onion
1 tablespoon parsley
1 small garlic clove (minced)

Mix all of the ingredients together in a bowl. Chill several hours. Serve as an appetizer or a salad ingredient.
Alice Kneeland
Humboldt County

ALL-PURPOSE MARINADE SAUCE

1 cup California sherry wine
1 cup soy sauce
⅓ cup olive oil
2 cloves garlic, crushed
2-inch piece ginger root, grated
¼ cup lemon juice

Mix all ingredients together. Use to marinate meat before broiling or barbecuing. This is especially good for venison, beef and chicken.
Note: ½ teaspoon powdered ginger may be substituted for the ginger root.
Herbert Pollock
Yolo County

FRENCH TARRAGON VINEGAR DRESSING

1 quart white or wine vinegar
1 handful of French tarragon leaves (not crushed)

Put the French tarragon leaves loosely into a quart bottle. Pour the vinegar over the leaves to fill the bottle. Cap the bottle and let stand at room temperature for 2 to 3 months.
Marqus Martin
Sonoma County

TUOLUMNE OVEN-BAKED STEW

1 pound stew meat
1 onion, chopped fine
1 10¾-ounce can bouillon soup
½ cup Burgundy wine
¼ cup bread crumbs
¼ cup flour

Preheat oven to 350 degrees. Put stew meat in a medium-sized casserole. Sprinkle onion over the meat and add the bouillon soup and wine. Sprinkle the bread crumbs and flour on top. Cover and bake in the oven for 1½ hours or until the meat is done.

Note: Onion soup can be used in place of the bouillon, and any dry wine for the Burgundy. Serves 4.

Lila Jury
Tuolumne County

BEEF BURGUNDY

2 pounds chuck, cut into 1-inch cubes
2 tablespoons butter or margarine
¼ cup sherry
½ pound mushrooms, quartered
6 tablespoons flour
2 tablespoons catsup
2 teaspoons bottled brown gravy sauce (A-1 sauce)
2 cups water or stock
2 cups Burgundy wine
1 bay leaf
1 teaspoon fines herbs (herb seasoning)
Salt and pepper to taste
1 can (or 1 pound) small, whole onions, drained

Brown the beef in butter or margarine. Pour sherry over the beef, then remove from pan with slotted spoon. Add mushrooms to pan and cook for 1 minute. Stir in flour, catsup, gravy sauce and water. Cook, stirring until mixture begins to boil. Return meat to pan and add 1 cup of Burgundy and remaining seasoning. Place onions on top of meat, so they will hold their shape. Cover pan and simmer 2 to 2½ hours, until meat is tender, adding remaining cup of Burgundy as needed. Serves 6.

Note: Mashed potatoes or crusty French bread should be served in order to absorb the extra gravy. Rice does nicely, also.

Lorraine Valine
Sacramento County

CROCK POT BEEF BURGUNDY

3 pounds beef, cubed (chuck or round)
2 10¾-ounce cans mushroom soup
½ cup Burgundy (or Rosé)
1 envelope of dry onion soup mix

Put all ingredients in crock pot and cook for 5 hours or more.
Will Pierce
Marin County

"DADDY'S GOOD SPAGHETTI SAUCE"

1½ pounds ground beef
1 medium onion, chopped
½ pound fresh mushrooms, chopped
2 tablespoons butter
1½ teaspoons garlic salt
2 tablespoons olive oil
2 tablespoons Italian seasoning
1-2 cups Burgundy wine (California Wine, please!)
1 pinch sage
2 15-ounce cans tomato sauce
2 6-ounce cans tomato paste

Cook ground beef, drain off fat. Sauté onions and mushrooms in butter. Add remaining ingredients to the ground beef. Add sautéed onions and mushrooms to ground beef mixture and simmer for 1½ hours. Serves 6-8.
John Baranek
Sacramento County

EASY BAKED CHICKEN

2 broiling chickens, split in halves
½ cup butter or margarine
½ cup California Sauterne, Chablis or other white dinner wine
1 teaspoon salt
¼ teaspoon pepper
½ teaspoon dried tarragon
2 teaspoons cornstarch

Preheat oven to 325 degrees. Put cnickens in shallow baking pan, skin side up. Melt butter; add wine, salt, pepper, tarragon. Spoon a little over chicken. Bake in moderately slow oven about 1 to 1¼ hours, basting often with sauce. When chicken is tender and brown, pour off sauce and heat to boiling. Stir in cornstarch mixed with a little cold water; boil 1 or 2 minutes, stirring constantly. Spoon over chicken.
Jean Siebe
Solano County

EL MIRASOL CHICKEN

1 cut-up frying chicken
2 cups cooked brown rice
1 10¾-ounce can cream of mushroom soup
1 4-ounce can (½ cup) sliced or chopped ripe olives
1 teaspoon poultry seasoning
¼ teaspoon black pepper
Paprika for garnish
½ cup Sherry wine
Parsley sprigs

Preheat oven to 375 degrees. Place pieces of chicken in large baking dish 13 x 9-inches. Bake for 45 minutes. Combine soup, rice, olives, seasonings and wine around the cooked chicken. Sprinkle paprika on top, bake for 15 more minutes. Garnish with fresh green parsley sprigs.
Lola Lee Turner
Tehama County

GAME HEN TAIWAN

4 Rock Cornish hens
¼ cup salad oil
½ cup dry sherry
⅓ cup soy sauce
½ cup walnut halves
2 large onions, sliced
2 green peppers, sliced
½ pound mushrooms, sliced
2 tablespoons cornstarch
4 tablespoons cold water

Preheat oven to 350 degrees. Thaw hens, if frozen. Remove giblets and make 1 cup stock. Brown birds in hot oil and place in baking dish. Add giblet broth, sherry and soy sauce. Cover and bake for one hour. Brown walnuts in the same oil and remove. Sauté remaining ingredients. Drain liquid from hens and add to vegetables, cook until tender. Thicken sauce with cornstarch dissolved in cold water. Pour over hens. Sprinkle with fried walnuts. Serves 4.
Lorraine Valine
Sacramento County

BIRDS CHASSEUR

2 pheasants, 3 to 4 pounds each, cut in pieces
½ cup flour
½ teaspoon salt
¼ teaspoon pepper
1 teaspoon paprika
¼ cup salad oil
½ cup brandy
1 large clove garlic, minced
½ teaspoon thyme
¼ teaspoon seasoned salt
1 10½-ounce can cream of mushroom soup
1 4-ounce can mushrooms
½ cup milk
½ cup dry sherry
Chopped parsley

Wash pheasant pieces and pat dry. Combine flour, salt, pepper and paprika. Dredge bird parts in flour mixture, shake off excess. Heat oil in a deep electric frying pan, set at 375 degrees. Add pheasant parts, a few at a time, and cook until browned on all sides. Remove pieces when browned and set aside. Pour off and discard any fat. Add brandy to pan, bring to a boil and cook for 1 minute. Add the garlic, thyme, and seasoned salt. Mix the soup, mushrooms and their liquid, milk and sherry. Pour into pan and stir well. Return bird parts to pan, cover and simmer until tender. About 1½ hours. Remove parts to serving dish and sprinkle with parsley. Skim fat and use liquid in pan for gravy.
Cynthia Salman
Sacramento County

BRAISED PHEASANT IN WINE

1 pheasant
½ cup flour
1 teaspoon salt
¼ teaspoon pepper
¼ teaspoon celery salt
½ teaspoon paprika
Garlic and onion seasoning to taste
3 tablespoons butter
3 tablespoons dry white wine
3 tablespoons water

Clean, wash and dry the pheasant. Section it. Prepare bag containing flour, salt, pepper, celery salt, paprika and garlic and onion seasoning. Place pheasant pieces in bag and shake until well covered. In heavy skillet, melt butter and bring to medium heat. Brown pheasant. Add wine and water to pheasant; cover and cook over low heat until tender, 45 to 60 minutes. Remove cover last 10 minutes to crisp.
Note: Soaking overnight in baking soda and water will draw the wild taste from the pheasant. If frozen, can be soaked while thawing.
Anne Wanner
Sacramento County

"PHEASANT ALA DELTA"

¾ cup Good Seasons Salad Dressing
½ cup dry sherry or any white wine
1 pheasant, cut into pieces
Seasoned flour
3 tablespoons butter
1 bell pepper, chopped
½ medium onion, chopped
½ cup orange juice

Preheat oven to 325 degrees. Marinate cut-up pheasant with Good Seasons Salad Dressing and wine for about 3 hours. Dust pheasant in the seasoned flour and brown in a skillet. Retain the marinade. Meanwhile, sauté the green pepper and onion in the butter. Place pheasant in a glass baking dish and put the pepper and onion over the top of the pheasant. Put the marinade back over the pheasant. Bake for 45 to 50 minutes. Occasionally baste with the orange juice. Serves 4 to 5.
Catherine Baranek
Sacramento County

CALIFORNIA SCALLOPS AND SHRIMP

⅓ cup dry white wine
2 tablespoons chopped green onion
½ pound scallops, cut into small pieces
¼ pound medium-sized uncooked shrimp
1 cup sliced fresh mushrooms
3 tablespoons butter
3 tablespoons flour
½ teaspoon salt
1½ cups light cream
2 tablespoons chopped parsley
½ cup grated Jack cheese

Preheat oven to 350 degrees. In a 1½-quart saucepan, combine wine, onion, scallops, shrimp, and mushrooms. Cover and simmer 5 minutes. Meanwhile, melt butter in skillet. Stir in flour and salt. Pour in light cream; cook, stirring constantly, until thickened. Add parsley; then scallops-shrimp mixture. Pour into 6 individual custard cups and sprinkle with cheese. Place into oven and heat for 10 to 15 minutes, or until cheese melts. Serves 6.
Cheryl Snow
Kern County

WINE WATERMELON PUNCH

1 large watermelon (approximately 25 pounds)
2 bottles (750 ml each) dry white wine
¾ cup kirsch or other cherry liqueur
12 to 14-inch straws (optional)

Select a melon about 20-inches long with a flat base. The day before serving, cut an 8-inch oval section, making a sawtooth edge, out of the top of the melon. Remove cut portion and reserve. Using a long-handled spoon, scoop out all pulp; remove seeds. Place about ¼ of the pulp in a blender container or food processor; cover and blend until pureed. Repeat with remaining pulp. Place melon shell on tray. Return puree to melon shell (should have about 12 cups puree); add the wine and kirsch. Replace cut portion of melon; refrigerate overnight. To serve, remove cut portion of melon and ladle punch into cups, or use a skewer to make ¼-inch round holes for straws around the top half of the melon at just above the liquid level. Insert straws, replace cut portion of melon, and allow guests to help themselves. Makes 20 cups.
Kathy Parker
Kern County

HOLIDAY PUMPKIN PIE

2 cups canned pumpkin
1 can Eagle Brand sweetened condensed milk
1 egg
½ teaspoon salt
½ teaspoon cinnamon
¼ teaspoon nutmeg
¼ teaspoon ginger
½ cup hot water
½ cup Sherry
1 9-inch unbaked pastry shell

Preheat oven to 375 degrees. Combine pumpkin, condensed milk, egg, salt, spices, water and Sherry in large bowl. Beat vigorously until well-blended. Pour into unbaked pie shell. Bake for 45 to 55 minutes. Let cool. Serve with whipped cream.
Adrienne Lanza
Solano County

PEACHES CHABLIS

1½ cups California Chablis wine
½ cup sugar
¼ teaspoon nutmeg
1 stick cinnamon
4 whole cloves
8 fresh peaches, sliced

Mix together first five ingredients. Peel and slice peaches. Pour mixture over peaches and chill in refrigerator at least four hours before serving.
Lynnel Pollock
Yolo County

OLIE'S WINE COOLER

1 gallon Vin Rosé Wine, chilled
2 cans (6 ounces each) frozen lemonade
3 quarts club soda, chilled

Combine ingredients in punch bowl. Serves 25.
Linda Jensen
Fresno County

BARBECUE

With California's mild climate, cooking out-of-doors has always been an enjoyable aspect of California living. Whether it is hot dogs cooked over a campfire by a mountain stream or a gourmet repast sizzling on a gas-fired bar-b-que, food always seems to taste better outside. There is a myriad of ways to cook out-of-doors, and we hope the recipes and helpful hints in this section will give you some new ideas.

Barbecue

. . . cooking out-of-doors

HOW-DO BARBECUE!

Steaks
Chops
Hamburger
Frankfurters
Smoked sausage links
Chicken halves or quarters

Roasts
Bone-in beef
Lamb
Pork
Ham, Canadian bacon
Chickens, small turkeys

STEAKS: SIRLOIN is best suited to serve a crowd. Cut 2-inches thick it can easily be sliced for sandwiches. OTHER STEAKS: Cut 1½-inches thick and barbecue 8-10 minutes per side. PORTERHOUSE, 9-13 minutes per side. TENDERLOIN OF BEEF, barbecue whole tenderloin 15 to 18 minutes per side, turning once—can serve rare, medium and well-done sections from one piece. T-BONE, 9-13 minutes per side. CHOPS, cut 1 to 1½-inches thick, cut small slit in meat to check for doneness (as with steaks), 9-13 minutes per side. Hamburgers, frankfurters, smoked sausage links or fully-cooked specialty sausages are good for grilling. Chicken halves or quarters are also. If using a rotisserie, boneless roasts, bone-in ribs of beef, lamb or pork or loin roasts can be balanced on a spit. A well-tied canned ham or Canadian-style bacon are easy to barbecue. Chickens and small turkeys are good rotisserie favorites.
Note: In general, all roasts and steak tender enough for oven roasting or broiling may be cooked over charcoal too. Less tender cuts can be barbecued satisfactorily when marinades or meat tenderizers are used correctly.
Pauline Bennett
Tuolumne County

TERIYAKI MARINADE

½ cup soy sauce
2 tablespoons sugar
1 garlic clove, minced
1 2-inch piece of ginger root, grated

Mix all ingredients. This marinade is especially good for lean beef. Meat should remain in mixture at least 30 minutes, but no longer than 8 hours. Note: Marinade may be kept in refrigerator for up to one month and used again.
Cyndy Mickelsen
Sacramento County

BARBECUED SHORT RIBS

4 pounds beef short ribs with the excess fat trimmed off
Salt and pepper to taste
⅓ cup catsup
2 tablespoons molasses
1 tablespoon lemon juice
2 teaspoons dry mustard
¼ teaspoon chili powder
Dash garlic powder

Early in the day, place short ribs in a Dutch oven and season with salt and pepper. Add enough water to cover and simmer until tender, about 2 hours. Drain. Meanwhile, combine the catsup, molasses, lemon juice, dry mustard, chili powder, and garlic powder. Set aside.
About 30 minutes before serving time, brush ribs with the above sauce. Broil them 4 to 5 inches from the heat for 15 minutes, turning over and brushing again with the sauce. Serves 4. They can be broiled in the oven or grilled over hot coals.
Note: The briquets need to burn 30 to 40 minutes and when they are coated with gray ash, they are ready. Knock off the gray ash with tongs or rake from time to time so that the coals can burn properly. If you cannot use an electric starter, use liquid starter. But NEVER start a fire with gasoline or kerosene, or add the liquid starter after the coals are burning!
Pauline Bennett
Tuolumne County

CAMPERS SPECIAL

- ½ cup salad oil
- 4 large cloves garlic, finely chopped
- 1 cup catsup
- ½ cup A-1 sauce
- 1 teaspoon salt
- 1 teaspoon coarse ground pepper
- 1 teaspoon dry mustard
- 5 teaspoons brown sugar
- ¼ cup wine vinegar
- 5 to 6 pound chuck roast, bone in, cut at least 2-inches thick
- 2 large onions, sliced ½-inch thick
- 6 potatoes, peeled and cut in half
- 12 medium-sized carrots, cut in half lengthwise

Combine salad oil, garlic, catsup, A-1 sauce, salt, ground pepper, dry mustard, brown sugar, and vinegar in saucepan. Bring to a slow boil over low heat and remove when heated.

Spread barbecue sauce on both sides of roast and barbecue over a medium charcoal fire for 15 minutes on each side. Put onion slices on sheet of aluminum foil (large enough for wrapping roast and vegetables with a generous double fold on top). On top of onions, put roast, spreading more barbecue sauce on roast. Put split potatoes and carrots on roast and then fold aluminum foil on top to seal contents and prevent steam from escaping. Place foil-wrapped meat and vegetables on barbecue grill and leave for 2 hours. Serves 6.

Note: Coals are ready when covered with ash and glowing in center. HAND TEST by holding hand over coals with palm down and near the grid level for . . . 4-5 seconds: coals are medium, 300 degrees . . . 3-4 seconds: coals are hot, 350 degrees . . . less than 3 seconds: coals are hot, 400 degrees.

Pauline Bennett
Tuolumne County

GRILLED MARINATED STEAK

1 large onion, chopped
1 cup cooking oil
½ cup dry red wine
¼ cup lemon juice
1 teaspoon salt
2 cloves garlic, minced
1 bay leaf
6 peppercorns
3½ pounds London broil steak (or round)

In a large screw jar, combine the chopped onion, cooking oil, red wine, lemon juice, salt, minced garlic, bay leaf, and peppercorns. Shake well and let stand at room temperature for 2 hours, shaking occasionally. Place beef in a shallow pan and pour marinade over and marinate meat at least one hour. While meat is marinating, prepare grill for barbecuing and light the briquets at least 45 minutes before serving time. Grill steak over hot coals to desired doneness and serve on warm plates. Serves 6-8.
Note: This can be broiled as well as grilled. You can prevent steaks from curling while on the grill or broiling by making diagonal slashes at 2-inch intervals in fat along the outer edge of the steak.
Nancy Rosasco
Tuolumne County

STEAK A LA ROQUEFORT

1 clove garlic, minced
¼ cup butter or margarine, softened
¾ cup Roquefort cheese, crumbled
Dash Worcestershire sauce
2 pounds porterhouse or sirloin steak
Salt and pepper to taste

Prepare grill; if using charcoal briquets start fire at least 30-40 minutes before placing meat on grill.
While grill is heating, combine garlic, butter, Roquefort cheese, and Worcestershire sauce. Place meat on grill and broil over hot coals, seasoning both sides with salt and pepper until desired doneness. Three minutes before steak is finished, top meat with the cheese mixture, spreading evenly over meat. Serves 4 to 6.
Note: When turning thin pieces of food such as steaks or chicken, use tongs rather than a fork, which may pierce the meat and allow juices to escape. Also, when barbecuing, heat may be increased by fanning the ashes off the coals. It may be decreased by sprinkling water on the coals. Briquet heating time may vary due to weather and number of briquets used or how spread out.
Pauline Bennett
Tuolumne County

MOTHER LODE AFTER-THE-GAME FAVORITE BARBECUE

2 pounds lean ground beef
1 onion, chopped
1 green pepper, chopped
2 teaspoons salt
2 eggs
1 8-ounce can tomato sauce
1 teaspoon oregano or Italian seasoning
2 cups fine bread crumbs or cracker crumbs
1 cup water

Mix ground beef, onion, green pepper, salt, eggs, tomato sauce, oregano or Italian Seasoning, bread or cracker crumbs, and water. Cover and store in refrigerator.

Have on hand:

2 loaves French bread
3 large tomatoes cut in thin slices
12 ounces Cheddar cheese, grated

After the game, split the French loaves in half lengthwise. Spread the beef mixture on each of the four loaf pieces and place on baking sheets. Heat oven to broil. Broil 9 inches from heat for 10-12 minutes until meat mixture is done. Remove from broiler and cover with tomato slices and grated Cheddar cheese. Return to hot oven for 3 minutes, watching carefully. When cheese has melted, cut loaf in generous chunks and serve hot. Yield: 12-15 servings.
Note: Good served with onion slices, celery sticks, additional small tomatoes and carrot curls.
Mary Baker
Tuolumne County

BARBECUED PORK CHOPS

6 pork chops, 1-inch thick
1 8-ounce can tomato sauce
½ cup catsup
1 teaspoon Worcestershire sauce
½ teaspoon onion salt
½ teaspoon liquid smoke

In heavy skillet, brown chops in small amount shortening. Pour off fat. Season with salt and pepper. For sauce, combine tomato sauce, catsup, Worcestershire, onion salt, and liquid smoke; pour over chops. Cover and simmer till tender, about 1 hour, turning occasionally. Serves 6.
Virginia Adamek
Imperial County

SIERRA YOUNG COWHANDS' SUPER BARBECUE BEEF BUN

2 pounds lean ground chuck beef
4 tablespoons margarine or butter
1 cup onion, chopped
1 cup green pepper, chopped
1 cup celery, chopped
1 8-ounce can tomato sauce
1 clove garlic, minced
1½ teaspoons salt
3 tablespoons vinegar
2 tablespoons brown sugar
1 teaspoon chili powder
1 teaspoon oregano or Italian seasoning
1½ to 2 cups water

Heat a large flat-bottomed pan. Add ground beef and margarine, break up beef and brown. Add the onion, green pepper, celery, tomato sauce, minced garlic, salt, vinegar, brown sugar, chili powder, oregano or Italian seasoning, and water. Mix well. Cover pan and reduce heat and let simmer for 40 minutes. Stir and adjust amount of liquid as cooking progresses.

Have ready:

8 sliced, toasted hamburger buns
3 large tomatoes, thinly sliced
2 onions, sliced
Toothpicks
16 ripe olives

Serve over lower half of bun. Cover with tomato slice and/or sliced onion. Top with upper half of toasted bun. Spear bun with long toothpick topped with two olives.
Note: It is nice to surround the bun with celery leaves and carrot sticks.
Mary Baker
Tuolumne County

CHÉRI-GLAZED PORK

6 pork chops, 1 side meaty spareribs, or 6 pork steaks
Salt and pepper to taste
1 8-ounce can tomato sauce
½ cup California sherry
¼ cup honey
2 tablespoons onion, minced
1 clove garlic, minced (optional)
¼ teaspoon Worcestershire sauce

Sprinkle meat with salt and pepper. Place in shallow baking pan and bake in hot oven (400 degrees) for 40 minutes. Drain off fat. Combine remaining ingredients; pour over the meat. Bake 1 hour longer in moderate oven (350 degrees) or until tender. If desired, meat can be barbecued over low coals, brushing on the same sauce to glaze.
Tressa Connor
Yolo County

COUNTRY-STYLE RIBS

Salted water
4 pounds country-style pork ribs, cut into serving-size pieces
1 tablespoon butter or margarine
1 clove garlic, crushed
½ cup catsup
⅓ cup chili sauce
2 tablespoons brown sugar
2 tablespoons onion, chopped
1 tablespoon Worcestershire sauce
1 tablespoon prepared mustard
1 teaspoon celery seed
¼ teaspoon salt
Dash bottled hot pepper sauce
3 thin lemon slices

In a large kettle, simmer the ribs in enough salted water to cover. It will take about one hour. In saucepan, melt butter, add garlic and cook 5 minutes. Add catsup, chili sauce, brown sugar, onion, Worcestershire sauce, prepared mustard, celery seed, salt, hot pepper sauce and lemon slices. Bring to a boil. Drain ribs. Grill over a medium heat (coals) about 10 minutes on each side, brushing often with the sauce till well coated. (If ribs are chilled before grilling, cook 15 to 18 minutes on each side.) Makes 6 to 8 servings.
Note: Some charcoal fires are hotter than others. Heat will vary with the individual fire. Size of fire bowl, amount of charcoal used, placement of briquets, the distance from the top of coals to the food will all affect the degree of heat. For this reason, recipe timings are really guidelines. Also, foods such as pork and chicken must reach higher internal temperatures and require longer barbecuing than beef or lamb. Larger or chunkier pieces need more time, too.
Pauline Bennett
Tuolumne County

SHORELINE RANCH BBQ BUTTERFLY LEG'O'LAMB

1 large onion, chopped
1 clove garlic, crushed
½ cup parsley, chopped
2 teaspoons Fines Herbes
1 cup red wine
½ cup salad oil
1 teaspoon salt
½ teaspoon freshly ground pepper
1 leg of lamb (5-6 pounds) boned, or butterflied, laying flat

In a large bowl, combine everything but lamb, thus making the marinade. Add lamb, coating it thoroughly, and chill (preferably overnight), turning occasionally. Cook on barbecue rack over hot coals, or a Farberware grill, basting frequently with the marinade. Usual cooking time is about one hour.
Bob Parks
Marin County

BARBECUED LAMB RIBLETS

2 rib sections breast of lamb cut in 2 rib portions
Salt and pepper
Smoked salt
4 medium onions
1 lemon, thinly sliced
1 cup catsup
1 cup water
½ cup vinegar
2 tablespoons sugar
4 teaspoons Worcestershire sauce
Several dashes Tabasco sauce
2 teaspoons dry mustard
1 clove garlic, mashed
2 teaspoons salt

Preheat oven to 400 degrees. Brown lamb on both sides. Drain fat and arrange lamb in roaster with tight-fitting cover. Sprinkle lightly with salt and pepper and bit of smoke salt, if desired. Tuck between lamb pieces onion and lemon slices. Reduce heat to 325 degrees, cover and bake 1½ hours or until tender. Spoon over sauce made of catsup, water, vinegar, sugar, Worcestershire sauce, Tabasco sauce, dry mustard and garlic crushed with salt. Baste 2-3 times during baking, adding more water if necessary. Uncover and bake 15-20 minutes more. Serve with butter-tossed spaghetti and Parmesan cheese and mixed vegetable salad.
Note: Can be grilled by first pre-cooking in simmering water for about 1 hour. Drain and set aside. Later, finish by placing on properly heated grill and brushing with the sauce as you turn them over. Or lay raw ribs on grill at least 6 inches above glowing coals. Grill very slowly, turning often for about 1 hour, or until tender. Then start brushing with the sauce.
Pauline Bennett
Tuolumne County

BARBECUED FRANKS

1 onion, chopped
3 tablespoons oil
1 tablespoon sugar
1 teaspoon dry mustard
1 teaspoon paprika
½ cup catsup
½ cup water
¼ cup vinegar
1 tablespoon Worcestershire sauce
Drop Tabasco sauce
Salt and pepper to taste
8 to 12 frankfurters
8 to 12 frankfurter buns

Preheat grill with briquets until coals are covered with gray ash and glowing coals underneath. Meanwhile, in a small pan sauté onion in oil. Add sugar, dry mustard, paprika, catsup, water, vinegar, Worcestershire sauce, Tabasco sauce, and salt and pepper. Bring to a boil and boil 2-3 minutes. Set aside. Remove gray ash from coals. Split frankfurters in half and place cut side down on grill. Baste well with sauce, turn over and baste until nicely browned. Serve with frankfurter buns. Serves 8 to 12.
Note: Sauce that is left can be kept in refrigerator for future use. Also, wiping the grill with oil before barbecuing will make it easier to clean at clean-up time!
These can be broiled in a 350 degree oven for 20-30 minutes, basting often.
Pauline Bennett
Tuolumne County

TURKEY SHISH-KA-BOBS

½ cup brown sugar
½ cup soy sauce
½ cup salad oil
½ cup catsup
½ cup pineapple juice
Breast of raw turkey
Salt and pepper to taste
1 bell pepper, cut in 1-inch pieces
1 small can pineapple chunks
12 cherry tomatoes
12 mushrooms
1 onion, cut in 1-inch pieces

Combine the first five ingredients for marinade sauce. Cut turkey meat into bite size pieces. Season with salt and pepper. Marinate several hours or overnight in above marinade. Skewer with green pepper, pineapple chunks, cherry tomatoes, mushrooms and onions. Barbecue until done—approximately 15 minutes.
Elsie Steinwandt
Placer County

CHICKEN-ON-THE-GRILL

1 cup catsup
¼ cup vinegar
¼ cup water
2 tablespoons prepared mustard
1 teaspoon salt
½ teaspoon oregano, crumbled
2 cloves garlic, crushed
2½ to 3 pound broiler chicken, cut into pieces

Prepare grill and light briquets 40 to 45 minutes before grilling chicken. In a medium sized bowl, mix the catsup, vinegar, water, prepared mustard, salt, oregano, and garlic. Set aside, until coals are ready. Lightly oil grill. Baste chicken pieces and place on grill, turning chicken about every 10 minutes and basting as you turn them. Over a medium heat, it will take about one hour depending on how large the pieces are. When it is no longer pink, it is done.

Note: This can be baked in the oven by placing chicken pieces in a pan and cover with the sauce. Cover pan with foil and bake about 30 minutes in a 375 degree oven. Remove cover and bake 20 to 30 minutes longer, basting and turning a few times.

Use very thick basting sauces or sauces containing sugar only over a low fire or during the last half hour of cooking as they burn easily!

Pauline Bennett
Tuolumne County

MEATS

Cattle, sheep and hogs are all produced to a large extent in California. Cattle and calf production is the number one commodity in the state. A familiar sight in the rolling foothills is an open field dotted with grazing cattle or sheep.

The meat course is usually the focal point of any dinner. When your family and friends gather and tantalizing smells come from the kitchen, the cook must be able to come forth with a dish that satisfies all that has been anticipated.

We hope that the recipes in this section will provide you with many enjoyable meals.

Meats

. . . marvelous meats

COWBOY HORS D'OEUVRES (BEEF JERKY)

4 pounds very lean boneless beef
2 tablespoons water
1 teaspoon liquid smoke
¼ cup seasoning salt
Pepper, if desired

Chill meat in freezer until extra firm.
Remove from freezer and cut away any connective tissue and gristle, and trim off all the fat. Slice the meat into long strips, ¼ to ⅛-inch thick. Combine the remaining ingredients and pour over the meat in a large bowl, being sure all meat pieces are covered. Cover tightly and refrigerate overnight. Heat oven to 150 degrees.
Remove the meat strips and pat dry with paper towels. Stretch the meat strips across clean oven racks. Allow the meat to touch but do not overlap. Arrange the racks so there is at least 4 inches from top element and 4 inches from bottom element. Bake for 6 hours.
Anne Willard
Tehama County

ALL BEEF SALAMI ROLLS

5 pounds ground beef
¼ cup liquid smoke
¼ cup curing salt
¼ cup red wine
¼ cup brown sugar
Garlic salt
Hot pepper flakes
Ground cumin
Curry powder

Place all ingredients in a large bowl and mix thoroughly, adding as much of the seasonings as you want for your own special taste. Cover and refrigerate for 24 hours.
Preheat oven to 225 degrees.
Remove mixture from refrigerator and divide into four equal portions. Roll each portion by hand on a hard surface, to form stick-like rolls. Wrap rolled sticks in clean meat netting to hold its shape. Place on roasting rack and bake for 4 hours. To serve, slice and heat in skillet or microwave oven. Makes delicious sandwiches or just plain good snacking.
Barbara Pacheco
Tulare County

CRANBERRY MEATBALLS

1 16-ounce can jellied cranberry sauce
1 12-ounce bottle of red chili sauce
1 cup water
1 pound ground beef
⅔ cup bread or cracker crumbs
1½ teaspoons dehydrated onion
Salt and pepper to taste

Simmer cranberry sauce, chili sauce and water for 15 minutes. Mix ground beef, cracker crumbs, onion and salt and pepper together and shape into small balls. Add meatballs to sauce and continue to simmer for 3 minutes. Note: Shape meat into larger meatballs and simmer for 5 to 7 minutes. Serve over hot noodles or rice for main dinner dish.
Juanita Hershey
Kern County

SPICY CALIFORNIA MEATBALLS

1½ pounds ground beef
¾ pound pork sausage, ground fine
1 egg, slightly beaten
½ cup cracker crumbs
1 small onion, chopped
¾ teaspoon seasoned salt
½ teaspoon pepper
¼ teaspoon oregano
½ teaspoon parsley
¼ cup warm milk
1 medium bell pepper, chopped
16 ounces chunk pineapple
2 16-ounce bottles Heinz barbecue sauce with onions

Preheat oven to 350 degrees. Combine ground beef and sausage in large bowl. In separate bowl mix together egg, cracker crumbs, onion and spices. Add to meat mixture and work in the hands. Mix in enough warm milk so that mixture holds together well. Form into cocktail-size meat balls. Arrange on cooky sheets and bake for 25 minutes. Place the baked meatballs into a crockpot. Add bell pepper, pineapple chunks with juice, and barbecue sauce. Stir together and heat on high for 1 hour. Let simmer on low while serving. Makes 60.
Laurel Blankenship
Tulare County

CZECH LIVER DUMPLINGS

½ pound beef liver
2 tablespoons margarine
2 tablespoons onion, finely chopped
1½ teaspoons parsley, finely chopped
¾ cup fine dry bread crumbs
3 tablespoons water
¼ teaspoon salt
1 egg
1 envelope spring vegetable soup mix

Remove tough membrane from liver. Chop liver very fine. Melt margarine in skillet; add onion and parsley and cook over low heat, stirring frequently, until onion is golden brown. Mix vegetables, bread crumbs, water, salt and pepper with chopped liver. Beat egg; blend into liver mixture. Shape into 1-inch balls; drop into boiling soup made with favorite recipe or a packaged mix. Cover; boil gently 8 minutes.
This recipe makes 24 dumplings.
Mary Falls
Fresno County

HUMBOLDT OVEN STEW

3 pounds stew meat
3 tablespoons flour
1 tablespoon sugar
3 potatoes, halved
3 onions, halved or quartered
1 cup tomatoes
1 cup water
3 large carrots
3 stalks celery in large chunks
Salt and pepper to taste
¼ teaspoon rosemary
¼ teaspoon sweet basil

Preheat oven at 325 degrees. Mix all the ingredients in large roaster. Bake for three hours. Stir 2 or 3 times only. Serves 8.
Note: If you desire more gravy add a little more water or tomatoes. This recipe is good warmed over, also as a take out dish. If cooking for an extra large crowd, just double recipe.
Pam Giacomini
Humboldt County

HAMBURGER SOUP

2 pounds ground beef
2 tablespoons oil
½ teaspoon salt
¼ teaspoon each of pepper, oregano, basil
⅛ teaspoon seasoned salt
1 package onion soup mix
6 cups boiling water
1 8-ounce can tomato sauce
1 tablespoon soy sauce
1 cup chopped celery
1 cup chopped carrots
⅓ cup dried yellow split peas
1 cup elbow macaroni

In saucepan (with tight-fitting lid) brown meat in oil. Add seasoning and soup mix. Stir in water, tomato sauce and soy sauce. Cover and simmer for 15 minutes. Add vegetables and peas and cook 30 minutes. Add macaroni and simmer 30 minutes longer, adding water or beef broth if necessary. Sprinkle with Parmesan cheese if desired.
Millie Pedrazzini
Humboldt County

ADD-TO-STEW

Large jar or can marinara sauce
2 pounds ground beef
1 can consommé
6 carrots, sliced
1 onion, chopped

Preheat oven to 350 degrees. Brown meat. Add marinara sauce and consommé. Mix well. Add vegetables and pour into casserole dish. Bake about 1 hour or until vegetables are tender.
Note: Any other vegetables can be added for variety.
Sharon Azevedo
Solano County

SPICY BEEF SALAD

1 cup cooked roast beef, cubed
1 cup celery, chopped
1 cup carrots, grated
1 teaspoon onion, grated
½ cup mayonnaise
¼ teaspoon salt
¾ teaspoon prepared mustard
¼ teaspoon prepared horseradish
1 cup packaged shoestring potatoes

Combine meat with celery, carrots, and onion. Mix mayonnaise with salt, mustard, and horseradish. Add to meat mixture. Just before serving, add potatoes. Spoon into lettuce cups and serve at once while potatoes are still crisp.
Pat Rose
Imperial County

BEEF 'N' BARLEY

1 teaspoon butter
¾ cup onion, chopped
1 cup pearl barley
1 10¾-ounce can cream of mushroom soup
1 4-ounce can mushrooms
1 teaspoon salt
1 4-ounce can diced pimientos
1 teaspoon Worcestershire sauce
4 cups water
2 tablespoons shortening
½ cup bread crumbs
1 tablespoon sesame seeds
½ teaspoon paprika
2 pounds tenderloin steak, cut in strips

Preheat oven to 350 degrees. Sauté butter, onions and barley in skillet until brown. Add 2 cups water, cover and simmer 15 minutes. Add soup, mushrooms, ½ teaspoon salt, pimiento, Worcestershire sauce and 2 cups water. Melt 2 tablespoons shortening in skillet. Combine bread crumbs, sesame seeds, ½ teaspoon salt and paprika in plastic bag, coat meat with bread crumb mixture and brown in shortening. Add to barley mixture. Pour into 3-quart casserole, cover and place in oven. Bake 1¼ hours.
Lynn Schluter
Modoc County

BEER BAKED STEAK

2 pounds round steak
½ clove garlic
Flour
¼ cup shortening
1½ teaspoons salt
⅛ teaspoon pepper
½ cup chopped onions
1 cup tomato sauce
½ cup light beer

Preheat oven to 325 degrees. Rub the steak with garlic. Pound flour into both sides of steak with the edge of a plate or metal tenderizer. Cut meat into serving size pieces. Brown on one side in melted shortening. Turn, season with salt and pepper, and add chopped onions. Sauté until onions are brown. Add tomato sauce and beer. Cover tightly and bake in a slow oven for two hours; uncover during last hour of baking. Turn meat occasionally and add more beer or a little hot water if it becomes dry. Serves 8.

Note: A family favorite—meat is so tender you can cut it with a fork.

Lynn Peters
Siskiyou County

BEEF WITH CAULIFLOWER

1 pound boneless round steak, cut ½-inch thick and tenderized
2 tablespoons butter or margarine
1 green pepper, cut into ¾-inch pieces
1 clove garlic, minced
1 small head cauliflower, separated into flowerettes
¼ cup soy sauce
2 tablespoons cornstarch
½ teaspoon sugar
1½ cups beef broth
1 cup green onions with tops, sliced

Cut steak into ½-inch squares. Brown in butter or margarine, about 4 minutes. Add pepper, garlic, soy sauce and cauliflower. Cover pan and simmer until vegetables are fork tender. Blend together the cornstarch and sugar, add the beef broth and onions. Cook, stirring constantly until thickened. Serve with steamed rice. Serves 6.

Emily Jorstad
Placer County

RUTH'S SPANISH STEAK

1 flank steak, scored
1 whole lemon, diced
1 medium onion, chopped
1 4-ounce can Ortega diced chilies
1 14-ounce bottle tomato ketchup
2 tablespoons water

Preheat oven to 375 degrees. Place steak in a 7 by 11-inch baking dish. Layer remaining ingredients evenly over steak. Cover with aluminum foil. Bake for one hour or until steak is tender.
Note: Leftover sauce is good on hot dogs.
Pat Merwin
Yolo County

FLANK STEAK ONION STYLE

1 full flank steak
1 package dry onion soup mix
½ cup water

Preheat oven to 350 degrees. Place steak in center of double layer of foil. Sprinkle with dry onion soup mix. Pour the water around the edges of the steak. Wrap up tightly, making sure all edges are sealed. Place on a cookie sheet and bake for 1 to 1½ hours.
Pam Dillon
Humboldt County

CREOLE STEAK

1 full round steak
Flour
1 onion, chopped
1 green pepper, chopped (optional)
1 7½-ounce can Nalley's Mushroom Sauce
2 7½-ounce cans mushrooms
Garlic salt to taste
¼ teaspoon sweet basil
¼ teaspoon cumin powder
¼ teaspoon allspice
Bacon grease or shortening

Preheat oven to 350 degrees. Cut round steak into serving size pieces, pound with flour and brown in bacon grease. Remove meat and saute onions. Combine green pepper, mushrooms, mushroom sauce, tomato sauce and spices. Put meat and onions in casserole, pour sauce mixture over them. Bake for at least 1 hour.
Cyndy Mickelsen
Sacramento County

BEEF STEAK POTATO SCALLOP

1 pound beef round steak, cut 1-inch thick
3 tablespoons shortening
3 small onions, thinly sliced
3 tablespoons flour
1½ teaspoons salt
¼ teaspoon pepper
¼ teaspoon thyme
¼ teaspoon garlic powder
2 cups water
3 medium potatoes, pared and thinly sliced
½ teaspoon salt
1 teaspoon paprika

Heat oven to 350 degree. Cut meat into 1-inch cubes and coat generously with flour. Melt shortening in large skillet; brown meat on all sides. Add onion and cook while stirring until onion is tender. Pour into ungreased 2-quart casserole and sprinkle with 3 tablespoons flour, salt, pepper, thyme and garlic. Pour water over the mixture and cover. Bake 45-60 minutes or until meat is tender. Increase oven temperature to 450 degree. Arrange potatoes on meat mixture. Sprinkle with salt and paprika. Bake uncovered 30 minutes longer or until potatoes are tender. Makes 6 servings.
Clare Weeks
Imperial County

CARRIBBEAN BEEF

2 pounds round steak
2 cloves garlic, mashed
1 tablespoon coarse black pepper
1 tablespoon oregano
½ teaspoon salt
2 tablespoons vegetable oil
1 tablespoon wine vinegar
3 cups water
1 pound fresh carrots
½ teaspoon salt
⅔ cup brown sugar
2 tablespoons raisins
1 1-pound can small white onions
6 tablespoons cornstarch
½ cup sherry

Mix garlic, pepper, oregano, salt, oil and vinegar. Spread on both sides of meat. Cover with foil and marinate overnight. Put 2 additional tablespoons vegetable oil in Dutch oven. Make slits in meat to prevent curling. Brown well on both sides. Add three cups water and cook for 1½ hours at medium heat. Peel and cut carrots in ½-inch rounds. Add carrots, salt, brown sugar and raisins to the meat and cook another ½ hour. Add onions and cook for another ½ hour or until meat is tender. Remove meat to a hot platter. Mix sherry and corn starch and stir in gravy of meat. Cook until slightly thickened. Serves 4.
Mary Dalaria
San Diego County

CORNISH PASTY PIE

2½ cups flour
1 teaspoon salt
¾ cup shortening
2 tablespoons vegetable oil
⅓ cup water
1 pound round steak, cut into small cubes
1 onion, chopped fine
1 turnip, chopped fine
4 large potatoes, diced
1 tablespoon dried parsley leaves
1½ teaspoons salt
½ teaspoon pepper
1 egg yolk, slightly beaten
Parsley

Preheat oven to 375 degrees. Sift together flour and salt. Cut in shortening and oil, then add water, mixing well until it sticks together. Divide dough into four balls. Roll out on lightly floured surface to fit 2 8-inch pie pans, leaving 2 balls for top crusts. Mix together the steak cubes, onion, turnip, potatoes, parsley, salt and pepper. Add more potatoes if necessary to fill pie pan. Cover with top crust and seal edges, but do not prick top crust. Spread beaten egg yolk over top crust and sprinkle with a little parsley. Bake for 1 hour. Test for doneness by inserting a fork or sharp knife into potatoes. Serve hot with or without your favorite gravy. Serves 10 to 12 people.
Note: This may be prepared several hours in advance and placed in the freezer immediately to avoid a soggy crust. Move pies directly from freezer to oven and allow 30 minutes extra baking time.
Annalie Hodge
Tuolumne County

HUNGARIAN GOULASH

1 pound bacon
1 full round steak cut into 1-inch cubes
1 large onion, chopped
2 tablespoons paprika
3 tablespoons caraway seeds
¼ teaspoon salt
1 10½-ounce can beef broth
½ cup sherry
Potatoes cut into 1-inch cubes to equal amount of meat
1 pint sour cream

Cook bacon until crisp and crumble. Brown meat and onion in bacon grease. Add paprika, caraway seeds, salt, broth and sherry. Simmer until meat is tender. Add potatoes and continue to simmer until they are done. Add bacon. Slowly add sour cream. Bring to serving temperature over low heat. Serve.
Robyn Payne
Sacramento County

ITALIAN BEEF PARMIGIANA

1 cup bread crumbs
¾ cup grated Parmesan cheese
¼ teaspoon garlic powder
2 eggs
3 tablespoons milk
2 pounds beef round steak, ½-inch thick pounded until thin and cut into pieces
⅓ cup olive oil
1 medium onion, chopped
2 cups tomato juice or 1 can (16-ounce) whole tomatoes
1 6-ounce can tomato paste
1 teaspoon salt
1 teaspoon sweet basil leaves (more if desired)
½ teaspoon oregano leaves (more if desired)
¼ teaspoon pepper
⅛ teaspoon garlic powder
8 ounces Mozzarella cheese, sliced thin
Parsley to garnish

Combine the bread crumbs, Parmesan cheese, and garlic powder. In a separate dish beat the eggs with the milk. Dip pieces of steak into the crumb, then egg, and again into the crumb mixture to coat the meat. In a large skillet brown meat on both sides in the olive oil. Remove and place meat in a shallow 13 x 9-inch baking dish, retaining drippings in skillet. Preheat oven to 350 degrees. While heating, cook onion in oil drippings in skillet. When soft add the tomato juice, tomato paste, salt, sweet basil leaves, oregano leaves, pepper and garlic powder. Simmer 5 to 15 minutes. Pour over meat and cover tightly, baking in the oven for 45 minutes. Remove from oven and place cheese slices over top. Continue baking, uncovered, about 15 minutes. Garnish with parsley.
Note: 1 jar (16-ounce) Italian cooking sauce may be substituted for the sauce mixture.
Pauline Bennett
Tuolumne County

POCKET STEAKS

4 steak filets cut 2-inches thick, top sirloin is best
8 fresh or frozen oysters
¼ teaspoon salt
¼ teaspoon pepper
2 tablespoons butter
1 tablespoon vegetable oil
4 tablespoons butter, melted
1 tablespoon fresh parsley, finely chopped

Cut a pocket in the steak filets about 2-inches long and 2½-inches deep. Sprinkle oysters with salt and pepper. Insert 2 oysters into each steak pocket, and close with skewers. Sprinkle outside of steaks with small amount of pepper. In a heavy skillet, melt 2 tablespoons butter, add vegetable oil, using a very high heat. When foam begins to subside, add the steaks and brown them quickly for 1 or 2 minutes on each side. Continue cooking steaks, turning them often so that a crust does not build up. Cook for 8 to 10 minutes. Remove from skillet and place on heated plates. Pour melted butter and parsley over steaks just before serving.
Nancy Claverie
Imperial County

SOUR CREAM BEEF CASSEROLE WITH DUMPLINGS

⅓ cup flour
1 teaspoon paprika
2½-pound boneless round or chuck
¼ cup cooking oil
1 16-ounce can small onions, with liquid
1 10¾-ounce can condensed cream of chicken soup or condensed cream of mushroom soup
1 cup dairy sour cream
Dumplings

Preheat oven to 350 degrees. Mix flour and paprika. Cut meat into 1½-inch cubes and coat meat with flour mixture and brown on all sides in cooking oil in medium skillet. Remove meat to 2-quart casserole. Combine onion and onion liquid, soup, and sour cream in a saucepan. Heat just to boiling and pour over meat. Bake uncovered 45 minutes. Reduce oven heat to 325 degrees and top casserole with dumplings. Bake 25 minutes or until golden brown.
Kathy Brandenberg
Imperial County

STEAK A'LA OLIVES & SHERRY

2 pounds round steak, cut into serving size pieces
2 medium onions, sliced
1 large garlic clove, minced
1 can condensed cream of celery soup
½ cup dry sherry
½ cup liquid from stuffed green olives
2 medium tomatoes, cut in wedges
⅓ cup green olives, sliced
Cooked egg noodles

Brown the meat on both sides. Add onions and garlic and simmer until tender, approximately 2½ hours. During last ten minutes, stir in the olives, tomatoes, wine and olive juice. Serve over egg noodles. Serves 4 to 6.
Emily Jorstad
Placer County

SWISS STEAK

¾ cup flour
2 teaspoons salt
¼ teaspoon pepper
2 pounds round steak, cut ¾-inch thick
3 tablespoons shortening
1 onion, thinly sliced
1 can cream of mushroom soup
1 can water

Combine flour, salt and pepper. Cut steak into individual serving pieces. Pound as much of the flour mixture as possible into the steak. Brown in hot shortening. Add the onion, then the soup mixed with water. Cook in pressure cooker at 10 pounds pressure for 25 minutes. Or cook in Dutch oven or heavy skillet for 1 hour or until tender. Serves 6 to 8.
Marjorie Clarke
Plumas County

CHUCKWAGON SWISS STEAK

1 tablespoon flour
¾ teaspoon salt
Generous dash of pepper
1 pound lean beef bottom round steak, cut into four slices
1 tablespoon butter or margarine
1 16-ounce can tomatoes
1½ cups sliced onions
⅓ cup celery, diced
1 clove garlic, crushed
½ teaspoon sugar

Combine flour, salt and pepper; pound into meat. In Dutch oven or large heavy skillet, melt butter or margarine over medium heat. Add meat and brown on both sides, about 5 minutes. Add remaining ingredients. Reduce heat, cover and simmer, stirring occasionally until beef is tender. About one hour. Makes 4 servings.
Venita Pitkin
Tehama County

OVEN BEEF BURGUNDY

4 tablespoons soy sauce
4 tablespoons flour
¼ teaspoon pepper
½ teaspoon marjoram
½ teaspoon thyme
1 teaspoon salt
2 pounds beef stew meat
6 carrots, cut in chunks
2 large onions, thinly sliced
1 cup celery, thinly sliced
2 cloves garlic, minced
1 cup red wine
1 can onion soup
1 can water
1 cup mushrooms, sliced

Preheat oven to 325 degrees. Blend soy sauce and flour with the seasonings in a 3-quart baking dish. Cut meat into 1½-inch cubes, and coat well with the flour mixture. Add carrots, onions, celery, garlic and liquids to the coated milk. Stir gently to mix. Cover tightly, place in oven and cook for 1 hour. Add mushrooms, stir gently, cover and bake for an additional 1½ to 2 hours or until meat is tender. Serve with hot rice. Serves 6-8.
Lorine Willard
San Luis Obispo County

INSTANT SAUERBRATEN

4 pounds beef chuck roast
¼ cup butter or margarine
1 teaspoon salt
½ teaspoon pepper
3 cups water
1½ tablespoons mixed pickling spice
1 pound onions, sliced lengthwise
1 cup ketchup
3 tablespoons brown sugar
3 tablespoons Worcestershire sauce
½ cup cider vinegar (more if you like sour taste)
3 tablespoons cornstarch

Cut beef into bite-size cubes. Brown in Dutch oven, season with salt and pepper. Add the water and mixed pickling spices (in bag). Cook at simmer 1 to 1½ hours or until tender. Add onions, ketchup, sugar and Worcestershire sauce. Cook 20 minutes. Add vinegar, simmer 10 minutes. Thicken with cornstarch dissolved in water, stirring constantly until clear. Serve over noodles, potato dumplings or mashed potatoes. Serves 8.
Marie Long
San Diego County

MARINATED PATIO ROAST

½ cup finely chopped onion
⅓ cup butter or margarine
1 cup dry white wine
2 teaspoons salt
2 tablespoons chopped parsley
1 tablespoon crushed mint leaves
6 to 8 pound boneless round rump, eye or tip roast

Sauté onion in butter until soft but not browned. Slowly stir in wine and salt. Bring to a boil, reduce heat and simmer 5 minutes. Remove from heat, add parsley and mint, mix well. Cool. Marinate roast in cooled wine mixture 2 hours in refrigerator, turning occasionally. Cook on rotisserie, basting every 30 minutes with marinade. Or it can be roasted in oven at 325 degrees for 2½ to 3 hours, basting at 30 minute intervals.
Gertie Brandenberg
Imperial County

BEEFY RIB TICKLERS

⅓ cup flour
½ teaspoon salt
⅛ teaspoon pepper
3 pounds beef short ribs
4 tablespoons vegetable oil
1 medium onion, thinly sliced
1 10¾-ounce can beef consomme
½ cup water
3 tablespoons vinegar
1 teaspoon prepared horseradish
1 bay leaf
⅛ teaspoon ground allspice
⅛ teaspoon ground cloves

Preheat oven to 350 degrees. Mix flour, salt and pepper. Coat meat with mixture. Heat 2 tablespoons of oil in skillet, brown meat well on all sides. Place in 2½-quart casserole. Add remaining 2 tablespoons oil to skillet and saute onion until tender. Stir in consomme, water, vinegar, horseradish, bay leaf, allspice and cloves, and pour over meat. Cover and bake 1¾ to 2 hours or until fork tender. Serves 4 to 6.
Shirley Davis
Tehama County

SESAME-SOY-SHORT RIBS

3 tablespoons sesame seeds
4 pounds beef short ribs, cut in 2 to 3-inch lengths
1 medium-sized onion, sliced
½ cup soy sauce
¼ cup firmly packed brown sugar (can be omitted)
1 large clove garlic, minced
¼ teaspoon each ground ginger and pepper
2 small diced hot chili peppers, seeded and crushed
1½ cups water
1 teaspoon each cornstarch and water

Preheat oven to 400 degrees. Put the sesame seed in a 4 or 5-quart kettle, one that can be used in the oven; place over medium heat until lightly browned, shaking pan often to toast evenly. Remove from heat and arrange the ribs and onion on top of the seed. Combine the soy, brown sugar, garlic, ginger, pepper, chili peppers and water; pour over the meat. Cover and bake for 2½ hours or until meat is tender when pierced. Stir well occasionally.
Lift meat to a warm serving platter; keep warm. Skim fat from pan juices. Combine cornstarch and water; stir into juices and cook, stirring until thickened; pass in a bowl. Makes 4 to 6 servings.
Note: You eliminate the task of browning the meat when you oven-cook short ribs at a high temperature.
Lynn Peters
Siskiyou County

WESTERN SHORT RIBS

6 pounds short ribs
2 pounds stew meat
1 teaspoon salt
⅛ teaspoon pepper
Garlic salt to taste
1 large onion, diced
1 8-ounce can sliced mushrooms
3 15-ounce cans stewed tomatoes
3 15-ounce cans kidney beans

Preheat oven to 350 degrees. Trim most of the fat and remove bones from short ribs. Cut meat in 1-inch cubes and brown thoroughly, using no fat. Add salt and pepper. When meat is browned, place in large deep casserole or roasting pan. Sprinkle with garlic salt. Add diced onions and mushrooms. Pour tomatoes over all. Bake for 3½ hours. Add kidney beans, stir and cover. Bake ½ hour longer.
Note: Any combination of ribs and stew meat to total 8 pounds may be used.
Nancy Barnes
Siskiyou County

QUICK BEEF STROGANOFF

½ cup onion, chopped
2 tablespoons vegetable oil
3 cups cooked beef, cubed
1 can condensed tomato soup
1 4-ounce can chopped mushrooms
1 teaspoon sugar
1 cup dairy sour cream

Sauté onion in vegetable oil in large skillet, add beef and brown lightly. Stir in tomato soup, mushrooms and liquid, and sugar. Cover. Simmer 20 minutes to blend flavors. Gently stir in sour cream and heat, being careful that the cream does not curdle. Serve hot over buttered noodles or steamed rice. Can be ready in minutes when using leftover roast beef. Makes 6 generous servings.
Shawn Brandenberg
Imperial County

BEEF PINWHEELS

2 cups packaged biscuit mix
⅔ cup milk
1 pound ground beef
2 tablespoons melted butter
3 tablespoons catsup
2 teaspoons prepared mustard
1 teaspoon instant minced onion
⅓ cup chopped celery
1 can cream of mushroom soup
½ can milk

Heat oven to 450 degrees. Mix together the biscuit mix and milk to form a soft dough. Roll out dough to form a 14-inch square. Crumble ground beef evenly over dough. Mix together the butter, catsup, mustard, onion and celery, and spread over dough. Roll up jelly roll fashion and cut into 12 slices. Place slices, cut side up on baking sheet and bake 15 minutes or until golden brown. While pinwheels are baking, mix the mushroom soup and milk and heat for gravy. Serve over the pinwheels. Serves 6.
Juanita Hershey
Kern County

BEEF TOMATO SWIRLS

2 pounds lean ground beef
2 eggs, slightly beaten
1 can condensed tomato soup
2 teaspoons salt
½ teaspoon pepper
½ cup onion, finely chopped
½ cup green pepper, chopped
1 tablespoon Worcestershire sauce
2 cups fresh bread crumbs
1½ cups Cheddar cheese, grated

Preheat oven to 350 degrees. Combine the meat with the eggs, half the tomato soup, 1 teaspoon of the salt and ⅛ teaspoon pepper. Pat the mixture out on a piece of heavy waxed paper into an oblong 15 by 8-inches. In another bowl, combine the remaining soup, salt and pepper with the onion, green pepper, Worcestershire sauce, bread crumbs and cheese. Spread evenly over the meat mixture. Roll up like a jelly roll, using the waxed paper to lift the meat. Cut into 1½-inch thick slices and arrange in a greased shallow baking dish. Bake for 45 minutes. Makes 10 to 12 slices and will serve at least 6 people.
Gertie Brandenberg
Imperial County

FORTY-NINER HAMBURGER DELIGHT

1 16-ounce package elbow macaroni
2 pounds ground beef
1 large onion, chopped
1 can mushrooms
2 cans tomato soup
1 can water
Salt
Pepper
Parsley

Preheat oven at 325 degrees. Cook macaroni and drain. Brown meat with chopped onion. Add mushroom soup, tomato soup and water. Mix and add to macaroni. Season to taste. Put in casserole dish and bake for about 25 minutes. Sprinkle with parsley.
Shirley Azevedo
Solano County

GROUND BEEF CASSEROLE

1 medium to large onion, sliced into rings
1½ pounds ground beef
¼ teaspoon oregano leaves, crushed
½ teaspoon basil leaves, crushed
1 10½-ounce can tomato soup, undiluted

Preheat oven to 375 degrees. Put onion slices on bottom of casserole dish. Save some onion rings for topping. Break ground beef into pieces, about 1½ to 2-inch in size. Sprinkle with oregano and basil, add soup over all, and decorate top with onion rings. Cover casserole with lid and bake one hour.
Note: Soup is salty because undiluted, so use salt sparingly, if at all.
Doris Dunlap
Tehama County

ONE-STEP CASSEROLE

1 pound ground beef
1 can cream of asparagus soup
1 box frozen Tater Tots
1 cup Cheddar cheese, grated

Preheat oven to 425 degrees. Crumble *raw* ground beef on bottom of casserole. Spread soup over meat. Arrange frozen Tater Tots on top of soup. Cover Tater Tots with cheese. Cook 45-60 minutes.
Note: This is easily doubled or tripled. Do Not Add Salt to The Recipe.
Robyn Payne
Sacramento County

HAMARONI CASSEROLE

1 pound ground beef
1 medium onion, chopped
1 teaspoon salt
½ teaspoon pepper
1 pound elbow macaroni
1 quart milk
4 eggs, well beaten
Grated Parmesan cheese
Butter
Cinnamon

Preheat oven to 350 degrees. Brown meat, onion, salt and pepper. Cook macaroni in salted water according to directions on package. Rinse and drain well. Add to meat mixture. Scald milk, then cool until just warm. Add beaten eggs gradually to milk. Place ½ macaroni in well buttered 9 by 14-inch shallow pan. Sprinkle generously with cheese and dot with butter. Place meat mixture on top, then add remaining macaroni, again sprinkling with cheese and butter. Now pour milk-egg mixture over all and sprinkle with a little cinnamon. Bake for 1 hour.
Mary Tonini
San Luis Obispo

HAMBURGER AND EGGPLANT SANDWICH

1 medium-sized eggplant, peeled
Flour seasoned with salt and pepper
4 tablespoons bacon fat
¾ pound ground beef
1 small onion, minced
¼ cup fine dry bread crumbs
¼ cup water
2 tablespoons chopped parsley
½ teaspoon salt
¼ teaspoon pepper
⅛ teaspoon cinnamon
Butter
1 8-ounce can tomato sauce

Cut eggplant into 8 crosswise slices. Coat on both sides in seasoned flour. In a frying pan, quickly brown eggplant slices on both sides in bacon fat. Keep warm in oven.
Combine ground beef, onion, bread crumbs, water, parsley, salt, pepper, and cinnamon. Form mixture into 4 patties, each about the size of an eggplant slice. Fry patties in a small amount of butter until crisp and brown on both sides. To serve, place a meat patty between 2 eggplant slices. Pass heated tomato sauce. Makes 4 servings.
Clare Weeks
Imperial County

MORE

- 1 16-ounce package salad macaroni
- 1 pound ground beef
- 1 onion, chopped
- 2 7½-ounce cans tomato sauce
- 1 7½-ounce can Nalley's Mushroom Sauce
- 1 15-ounce can creamed corn
- 2 3½-ounce cans chopped olives
- Garlic salt to taste
- ¼ teaspoon sweet basil
- ¼ teaspoon cumin powder
- ¼ teaspoon allspice
- Parmesan cheese

Preheat oven to 350 degrees. Cook and drain macaroni. Brown ground beef and onions. Combine tomato sauce, mushroom sauce, creamed corn and chopped olives. Add meat and onions, add spices, then pour into large casserole and stir in macaroni. Bake for 30 minutes.

Robyn Payne
Sacramento County

QUICK SKILLET

- 1 pound ground beef
- ½ cup onion, chopped
- 1 tablespoon vegetable oil
- 2 cups hot water
- 1 1-pound can tomatoes, cut into bite sized pieces
- ¼ cup Heinz 57 Sauce
- 2 teaspoons salt
- 1 teaspoon sugar
- ⅛ teaspoon pepper
- 4 ounces uncooked elbow macaroni

Brown beef and onion in oil. Drain off excess fat. Stir in water, tomatoes, sauce, salt, sugar and pepper and bring to a gentle boil. Add macaroni and mix well. Bring to a boil, then reduce heat and simmer uncovered for 15 to 20 minutes, stirring occasionally, until macaroni is tender. Garnish with parsley if desired.

Rose Claverie
Imperial County

RANCH HOUSE SUPPER CASSEROLE

3 medium onions, chopped
1 pound ground beef
½ pound pork sausage
1 cup half and half
2 teaspoons chili powder
1 can cream of mushroom soup
8 ounces canned green chilies, chopped
½ teaspoon salt
½ teaspoon oregano
1 dozen corn tortillas
2 cups cottage cheese
1 cup Jack cheese, grated
1 cup Cheddar cheese, grated

Preheat oven at 350 degrees. Brown onions, ground beef and sausage together until well cooked. Add the half and half, chili powder, soup, chilies, salt and oregano. Mix well, stirring so milk does not curdle. Cut tortillas into quarters. Arrange layers of tortillas, meat mixture and cheeses. Top the last layer with cheese. Bake for 45 minutes. Serves 12.
Margaret Hager
San Luis Obispo County

RANCHERO DELIGHT

1 pound spaghetti
2 green peppers
2 medium onions
2-3 tablespoons olive oil
½ pound ground beef
½ pound sausage
1 can tomato soup
1 can corn
1 small can mushrooms
1 tablespoon chili pepper
1½ pounds Tillamook cheese, grated

Cook spaghetti in salt water until done. Drain, run cold water over it and let stand until cold. Preheat oven to 375 degrees. Dice onions and peppers and fry in olive oil until slightly brown. Add ground beef and sausage, soup, corn, mushrooms and chili pepper. Cook until done. Put spaghetti in baking pan or bowl. Pour over hamburger mixture and mix. Cover top with grated cheese, put in oven until cheese is melted.
Venita Pitkin
Tehama County

WESTERN COMBO

1 pound ground chuck
1 medium onion, chopped
1 16-ounce can Veg-All, drained
1 can condensed tomato soup
1 4-ounce can sliced mushrooms, drained
½ teaspoon salt
¼ teaspoon pepper
1 cup cheese, grated

Preheat oven to 400 degrees. Brown together the meat and onions. Pour off excessive fat. Add drained Veg-All, soup and drained mushrooms. Place in greased casserole and sprinkle with grated cheese. Bake 20 minutes. Serves 4.

Juanita Hershey
Kern County

LASAGNE SUPERB

½ pound ground pork
½ pound ground beef
1 clove garlic, minced
1 tablespoon parsley, chopped
1 tablespoon basil
1½ teaspoons salt
1 1-pound can tomatoes
2 6-ounce cans tomato paste
10 ounces lasagne or wide noodles
2 12-ounce cartons large curd or cream style cottage cheese
2 eggs, beaten
2 teaspoons salt
½ teaspoon pepper
2 tablespoons parsley, chopped
½ cup grated Parmesan cheese
1 pound Mozzarella cheese, thinly sliced

Preheat oven to 375 degrees. Brown meats slowly, spoon off excess fat. Add next 6 ingredients to meat. Simmer, uncovered, til thick—45 minutes to 1 hour. Stir occasionally. Cook noodles in boiling salted water until tender. Rinse in cold water and drain. Combine cottage cheese with next 5 ingredients. Place ½ of noodles in 13 x 9 x 2-inch baking dish. Spread ½ of cottage cheese mixture over noodles. Add ½ of Mozzarella cheese and ½ of meat mixture. Repeat layers. Bake for 30 minutes. Let stand 10 to 15 minutes before cutting in squares. Serves 12.

Carmen Mitosinka
Imperial County

MARY'S LASAGNE

3 quarts boiling water
1 tablespoon salt
1 tablespoon cooking oil
12 ounces lasagne macaroni
2 tablespoons cooking oil
2 pounds ground beef
1 onion, diced
1 10-ounce package frozen chopped spinach
1 16-ounce can tomatoes
1 11-ounce can tomato soup
1 11-ounce can Cheddar cheese soup
1 teaspoon Italian herbs
2 teaspoons chili powder
2 tablespoons sugar
1 egg, beaten
1 tablespoon salt
1½ cups cottage cheese
1 cup Cheddar cheese, grated
Olives, if desired

In a large pan of boiling water add salt and cooking oil. Slowly add the lasagne and boil 9 minutes and drain. Set aside.

Preheat oven to 325 degrees. In a large skillet add the cooking oil and beef and onion, browning lightly. Add the spinach, tomatoes, tomato soup and cook until spinach is done. Add the Cheddar cheese soup, Italian herbs, chili powder, sugar, beaten egg, and salt and mix well. In a 9 x 3-inch oiled casserole, layer lasagne macaroni and meat mixture alternately with cottage cheese, finishing with the meat mixture on top. Bake 45 minutes. Sprinkle with grated cheese and olives and bake another 10 minutes to set. Serves 10.

Note: Can use Swiss chard for spinach and/or 1 8-ounce can tomato sauce for the tomato soup.

Mary S. Baker
Tuolumne County

SAUCY TART MEATBALLS

2 pounds ground beef
½ cup onion flakes
½ cup parsley flakes
1 tablespoon garlic powder
1½ cups cornflakes, crushed
2 eggs, slightly beaten
2 tablespoons soy sauce
1 16-ounce can cranberry sauce
1 15-ounce bottle Heinz chili sauce

Preheat oven to 350 degrees. Mix beef, onion, parsley, garlic, cornflakes, eggs and soy sauce together and shape into small balls. Place in 9 by 13 by 2-inch baking dish. Make sauce by combining the cranberry sauce and chili sauce together. Pour over meatballs and bake for 20 minutes, turning meatballs once.

Note: 1 cup of fresh onions, chopped fine, may be used instead of the onion flakes.

Lynn Peters
Siskiyou County

MEATBALLS AND BEANS

2 cups pink dried beans
Water
1 tablespoon salt
1 pound ground beef
½ pound ground pork
¾ cup rolled oats or fine dry bread crumbs
1 teaspoon salt
Pepper to taste
½ cup evaporated milk
1 medium-sized green pepper, chopped
1 medium-sized onion, sliced

Wash beans; cover with water and simmer for 2½ hours, or until tender. Just before beans are tender, add the 1 tablespoon salt. Mix together thoroughly the ground meats, rolled oats or crumbs, the 1 teaspoon salt, pepper, and evaporated milk; form into balls; add the green pepper and sliced onion. Cover and simmer for 45 minutes. Mash 1 cup of the beans and return to pan to thicken the broth. Makes 8 servings.
Verna Sunghera
Imperial County

SAVORY MEATBALLS

1½ pounds ground beef
2 tablespoons minced onions
1½ tablespoons minced green pepper
1⅓ cups fine soft bread crumbs
½ teaspoon salt
1 egg, unbeaten
3 tablespoons catsup
2½ teaspoons prepared horseradish
½ teaspoon dry mustard
½ cup milk
1 8-ounce can tomato sauce

Mix and blend together all ingredients except the tomato sauce. Heat oven to 350 degrees. While oven is heating, shape meat mixture into small balls. Place in greased 10 x 6-inch baking dish. Pour the can of tomato sauce over the top of the balls. Bake for 1 hour. Serves 6-8.
Barbara Humphrey
Tehama County

SWEDISH MEATBALLS

1 tablespoon butter
1 green pepper, chopped
1 onion, minced
1 can condensed chicken with rice soup
1 can condensed tomato soup
1 cup water or beef stock
2 slices soft white bread
¼ cup evaporated milk
1 egg, slightly beaten
1 teaspoon salt
1 pound ground beef

Melt butter in large skillet. Add the pepper and onion and cook until tender. Stir in the soup and water or beef stock. Heat to boiling, then turn down heat to simmer. Put all remaining ingredients into bowl and mix thoroughly. Shape into balls, about the size of ping pong balls. Drop balls into simmering sauce and cook slowly for 1 hour, or until sauce has cooked down enough to be thickened. Serves 6 to 8 persons.
Kathy Brandenberg
Imperial County

TEHAMA MEATBALLS

2 eggs, slightly beaten
1 cup whole milk
½ cup dry bread crumbs
1 onion, finely chopped
3 tablespoons butter or margarine
1 pound ground beef
½ pound pork, finely ground
⅛ teaspoon allspice
1 tablespoon salt
½ teaspoon pepper
2 cups boiling water
¼ cup flour

Preheat oven to 250 degrees. In large bowl, combine eggs, milk and bread crumbs. Soak for 5 minutes. In large skillet, cook onion in 2 teaspoons of the butter or margarine until tender. Add to the egg mixture. Add the meat and seasonings and mix well. Shape into 1-inch balls. Melt the remaining butter or margarine and brown the meatballs, turning occasionally. Place meatballs in a lightly greased casserole and bake for 30 minutes. Make gravy in skillet by adding ¼ cup flour to remaining fat in skillet, then add the boiling water and stir until thickened. Pour over the meatballs and keep warm until served.
Inez M. Borror
Tehama County

WESTERN MEATBALLS

- 1 10-ounce package frozen spinach
- 1 medium onion, chopped fine
- 1 clove garlic, minced
- 2 pounds ground beef
- 3 tablespoons Cheddar cheese, grated
- 2 slices bread, soaked in milk then squeezed dry
- 1 tablespoon Worcestershire sauce
- 1 teaspoon salt
- ¼ teaspoon pepper
- 2 tablespoons parsley, chopped
- 1 egg, slightly beaten
- 1 can cream of chicken soup
- ½ can water

Preheat oven to 350 degrees. Cook spinach until almost done, drain well. Add together with all other ingredients, except soup and water. Mix thoroughly and form into small balls. Roll in flour and brown in small amount of oil. Place meatballs in casserole and pour over soup and water. Bake for 45 minutes.

Betty Barnes
Siskiyou County

CARROT MEATLOAF

- 1½ pounds lean ground beef
- ½ pound ground pork
- 1 cup cooked rice
- 2 eggs, slightly beaten
- ½ teaspoon salt
- ¼ teaspoon pepper
- 2 cups grated carrot
- 1 can (6 ounces) tomato paste, plus three cans water
- 1 small onion finely chopped
- 1 clove garlic, minced
- 1 teaspoon salt
- ⅛ teaspoon pepper
- ¼ teaspoon oregano
- ¼ teaspoon basil

Preheat oven to 350 degrees. Combine the beef, pork, rice, eggs, salt, pepper and grated carrots. Mix together thoroughly. Shape into 2 loaves, and place in large baking dish. Set aside while preparing sauce.
Combine remaining ingredients together in medium sized saucepan and simmer for ten minutes. Pour over meatloaves. Place in oven and bake for one hour, basting with the sauce frequently during the baking. Makes 8 to 10 generous servings.

Karen Brinkman
Imperial County

HAM-BEEF LOAF

½ pound ham
1 small onion
1 pound ground beef
½ cup quick-cooking rolled oats
1 2-ounce can mushroom stems and pieces, drained
½ 4½-ounce can chopped ripe olives
1 egg, slightly beaten
⅔ cup evaporated milk
½ cup warm water

Preheat oven to 325 degrees. Grind ham and onion together in food chopped or blender. Add ground beef, rolled oats, mushrooms, olives, egg, and milk; mix thoroughly. Form into a loaf in baking pan, and pour the warm water over loaf. Bake for one hour and 15 minutes, basting occasionally with liquid in pan. Allow to cool about 15 minutes before slicing. Makes 6 servings.
Emily Claverie
Imperial County

MEATLOAF WITH PIQUANT SAUCE

⅔ cup dry bread crumbs
1 cup milk
1½ pounds ground beef
2 beaten eggs
¼ cup grated onions
1 teaspoon salt
1 teaspoon sage
Dash pepper

Preheat oven to 350 degrees. Soak bread crumbs in milk. Add meat, eggs, onion and seasoning; mix well. Form into loaf; place in greased baking dish. Cover with piquant sauce. Bake for 1 hour.

Piquant Sauce:

3 tablespoons brown sugar
¼ cup catsup
¼ teaspoon nutmeg
1 teaspoon dry mustard

Combine and mix ingredients. Spread over meatloaf.
Francis Mitosinka
Imperial County

STUFFED MEAT LOAF

1½ pounds lean ground beef
¾ pound ground pork
1½ teaspoons salt
¼ teaspoon pepper
1 egg
½ cup seedless raisins
4 cups toasted bread cubes
⅓ cup onion, minced
2 tablespoons parsley, minced
¼ teaspoon sage
¼ teaspoon pepper
¾ teaspoon salt
⅔ cup hot meat broth or water

Preheat oven to 350 degrees. Mix together the beef, pork, salt, pepper, and egg. On a sheet of waxed paper, pat meat mixture evenly to form a square about ½-inch thick. Toss together until well mixed, the raisins, bread, onion, parsley, sage, pepper, salt, and broth. Pat in an even layer over the meat. Roll as for jelly roll and place in a baking pan seam side down. Bake for 1½ hours. Serve sliced, hot or cold. Makes 8 servings.
Carol Anne Nero
Imperial County

ZUCCHINI MEATLOAF

2 small zucchini
2 medium-sized onions
1 tablespoon salad oil
2 medium-sized tomatoes, peeled and chopped
¼ cup milk
1 slice day-old bread, torn into small pieces
1 egg
1 teaspoon Worcestershire sauce
1 small clove garlic, mashed and minced
1 teaspoon salt
½ teaspoon pepper
1 pound ground beef
¼ pound ground pork

Heat oven to 325 degrees. Run the unpeeled zucchini and onions through the food chopper; saute in salad oil for one minute. Add tomatoes, and simmer until zucchini and onions are tender; cool. Heat milk to lukewarm, pour over bread, and let stand for 5 minutes. Beat egg, then stir into milk mixture with Worcestershire, garlic, salt, pepper, and vegetables. Combine with meat mixture and blend together thoroughly. Pack into a greased 9 by 5-inch loaf pan; let stand for at least 1 hour before baking so flavors blend. Bake in a moderately slow oven for 1½ hours. Let stand for 10 minutes before slicing. Makes 8 servings.
Alice Rice
Imperial County

EASY PIZZA

1 pound ground beef
½ cup chopped onion
¾ cup ketchup
1 teaspoon garlic powder
1 teaspoon salt
½ teaspoon pepper
1 16-ounce can stewed tomatoes
1 2½-ounce can sliced mushrooms, drained
1 2¼-ounce can sliced olives, drained
1 medium green pepper, thinly sliced
2 cups buttermilk baking mix
½ cup milk
2 cups shredded Mozzarella cheese

Preheat oven to 400 degrees. Cook ground beef over medium heat until browned; drain off fat. Stir in onion, ketchup, garlic powder, salt, pepper, stewed tomatoes, mushrooms, olives and green pepper. Simmer for 10 minutes.
Combine buttermilk baking mix and milk with a fork until it forms a soft dough. Knead the dough on a board with a little of the buttermilk baking mix or flour, for one whole minute. Roll the dough into a 14-inch circle and place on pizza pan. Pinch the edge to make a rim. Spread the meat mixture over the dough. Sprinkle on Mozzarella cheese. Bake for 20-25 minutes.
Ruth Machado
Sacramento County

COWBOY QUICHE

1 unbaked pie shell
½ pound ground beef
½ cup mayonnaise
½ cup milk
2 eggs
1 tablespoon cornstarch
1½ cups (½ pound) Swiss cheese, grated
⅓ cup green onion, sliced

Preheat oven to 350 degrees. Brown meat in skillet over medium heat. Drain fat and set aside. Blend next 4 ingredients until smooth. Stir in meat, cheese and onion. Pour into pastry shell. Bake for 35-40 minutes or until golden brown on top and knife comes out clean. Serves 4 to 6.
Judy Armstrong
Modoc County

WRANGLER PIE

½ pound ground round beef
1 tablespoon Wesson oil
1 onion, chopped
¾ cup celery, chopped
¼ green pepper, chopped
1 8-ounce can tomato sauce
½ teaspoon salt
⅛ teaspoon pepper
1 teaspoon Worcestershire sauce

1 cup sifted all-purpose flour
1½ teaspoons baking powder
½ teaspoon salt
⅙ cup Wesson oil
⅓ cup milk
1 tablespoon parsley, chopped
½ teaspoon celery seed

Preheat oven to 450 degrees. Brown meat in Wesson oil, add onion, celery and green pepper. Cook over medium heat for 5 minutes. Stir in tomato sauce, Worcestershire sauce, salt and pepper. Turn mixture into a round 8-inch ovenproof pan. Set aside. Sift together flour, baking powder and salt. Add parsley and celery seed. Measure Wesson oil and milk into a cup but do not stir. Pour over flour mixture and stir with fork until mixture cleans sides of bowl and forms a ball. Roll into an 8-inch circle and place over hot meat mixture. Bake 15 minutes. Remove from oven and let stand 5 minutes. Invert over hot serving platter. Serves 6.
Carmel Humphrey
Tehama County

ZARINA

1 pound lean ground beef
1 medium onion, diced
1 can mushroom soup
1 4-ounce can mushroom pieces

½ pint sour cream
Salt and pepper to taste

Brown beef lightly; put aside and brown onion in same pan. Add mushroom soup and mushrooms. Season to taste. Cover and simmer for 10 minutes. Fold in sour cream and simmer for 5 minutes more. Serve over noodles or rice. Makes 4 servings.
Juanita Hershey
Kern County

MAIDRITES FOR A CROWD

10 pounds hamburger
2 cans tomato soup
2 cans tomato paste
3 teaspoons dry mustard
6 teaspoons salt
6 teaspoons pepper
Onion if preferred

Brown the hamburger in a heavy skillet or Dutch oven until the meat looses its red color. Add remaining ingredients and simmer for 20 minutes. Serve on hamburger rolls. Serves 75 people.
Eloise Warren
San Luis Obispo County

HOME MADE MINCEMEAT

3 pounds beef shortribs
3 tablespoons cooled fat from beef
1 lemon
¾ cup fruit cake mix
7 medium sized apples, peeled and sliced
1 pound dark seedless raisins
¾ cup frozen orange juice concentrate
¾ cup molasses
3 tablespoons vinegar
1 teaspoon salt
1 cup sugar
½ cup water
1 teaspoon cinnamon
1 teaspoon nutmeg
1 teaspoon cloves
1 teaspoon pepper (if desired)

Boil beef shortribs one hour and cool. Cut beef to make 2 cups and add cooled fat from beef. Cut up lemon with seeds removed. Add fruit cake mix and peeled and sliced apples. Grind above ingredients using a large pan. Add raisins, orange juice concentrate, molasses, vinegar, salt, sugar, water, cinnamon, nutmeg, cloves, and pepper. Cook and stir 45 minutes over a low heat. Pour into jars and seal, or store in refrigerator. You can add more apples if desired when making pies. Makes 3 pints for 3 8-inch pies.
Mary Baker
Tuolumne County

COWBOY BEEF BROWNIES

3 eggs
1 cup sugar
½ teaspoon salt
1 teaspoon vanilla
½ cup butter or margarine
2 squares unsweetened chocolate
½ cup cooked beef, finely ground
¾ cup flour
½ teaspoon baking powder
½ cup nuts, chopped
Confectioners sugar

Preheat oven to 350 degrees. Beat eggs, sugar, salt and vanilla together until fluffy. Melt butter and chocolate together. Cool and add to egg-sugar mixture. Add ground beef and mix well. Sift flour and baking powder together and stir into beef mixture. Add nuts. Spread in a 8 by 8-inch pan which has been lined with wax paper. Bake for 35 minutes. Cool on wire rack. Sprinkle with confectioners' sugar, cut into squares and remove from pan.
Cathy MacDonnell
Modoc County

MRS. BOPEEP SPECIAL

1 pound ground lamb (lean)
1 egg, slightly beaten
½ cup bread crumbs
1 teaspoon chopped parsley
½ onion, chopped
1 teaspoon salt
1 teaspoon Worcestershire sauce
¼ teaspoon pepper
1 12-ounce bottle chili sauce
1 10-ounce jar grape jelly
1 teaspoon lemon juice
2 tablespoons brown sugar

Preheat oven to 350 degrees. Combine the top 8 ingredients. Form in balls the size of walnut . . . if used for cocktails. In saucepan stir chili sauce, grape jelly, lemon juice, brown sugar and soy sauce. Bring to boil, stirring constantly. Add meatballs to sauce, cover and simmer for 1 hour. Serve warm from chafing dish.
Alternate method: Place meatballs in pan. Cover with sauce and bake for 30 minutes at 325-350 degrees. This can be made ahead and frozen.
Jacqueline Ford
Humboldt County

SWEET 'N' SOUR LAMBBALLS . . . ALA GINA

2 pounds ground lamb
1 envelope dry onion soup mix
2 small cans tomato sauce
2 cups water
½ cup firmly packed brown sugar
Salt and pepper
1 can pineapple chunks (mint-flavored, okay)

Combine ground LAMB and onion soup mix, and let stand. Bring tomato sauce and water to boil in a large pot. Add brown sugar and salt and pepper to taste, boiling for ten minutes. Shape meat mixture into small, bite-sized balls and drop into the boiling sauce. Cook at simmer point for an hour, uncovered. Serve with toothpicks, preferably in a chafing dish. Makes forty lambballs.
Sally Parks
Marin County

GRANDMA'S LAMB STEW

3 pounds lamb stew meat
Salt and pepper to taste
1 quart water
4 cloves garlic
¼ teaspoon cinnamon
Dash of paprika
1 tablespoon chopped parsley
1 bay leaf
5 potatoes, cubed
3 large carrots
1 package frozen peas

Salt and pepper stew meat and brown in heavy pot. Add water and seasonings, simmer for 1½ hours. Add vegetables last and cook until tender.
Joan Rhodes
San Joaquin County

SWEET-SOUR LAMB CHOPS

4 lamb shoulder chops, about 1-inch thick
¼ cup brown sugar
¼ cup vinegar
½ teaspoon ground ginger
4 orange slices
4 lemon slices
1 tablespoon cornstarch

In large skillet, brown chops on both sides over low heat. Combine brown sugar, vinegar, ginger, 1 teaspoon salt, and dash pepper; pour over meat. Top each chop with an orange slice and lemon wedge. Cover; cook over low heat about 30 minutes or till chops are tender. Remove to warm platter. Pour pan juices into measuring cup; skim off fat; add water to make 1 cup. Return liquid to skillet. Blend cornstarch and 1 tablespoon cold water; stir into liquid. Cook, stirring constantly, till mixture is boiling. Serve on fluffy rice. Serves 4.
Virginia Adamek
Imperial County

SHEPHERD'S BARBECUE

3 pounds brisket or rib of lamb
1 tablespoon fat
1 large onion, thinly sliced
3 teaspoons salt
¼ teaspoon pepper
1 teaspoon paprika
½ cup catsup
⅓ cup vinegar
2 teaspoons vinegar
2 teaspoons chili powder
1 bay leaf

Cut lamb into serving size pieces. Using a 2½-quart pressure pan, brown meat on all sides in hot fat. Add sliced onion. Mix seasonings with catsup and vinegar and pour over browned meat. Cover pressure cooker, set control at 10 pounds and cook for 30 to 45 minutes after pressure is up. Reduce pressure normally. Serves 6.
Helen Bartow
Mendocino County

COUNTRY RHODES BREAST OF LAMB

1 breast of lamb
1 tablespoon cooking oil
½ teaspoon salt
½ teaspoon pepper
½ teaspoon garlic salt
¼ cup soy sauce
¼ cup brown sugar, packed firm
1 fat clove of garlic, crushed
¼ teaspoon ground ginger

Heat oven to 325 degrees. Trim off all outside fat and cut breast of lamb into ribs and pieces. Fry in cooking oil until well browned. Lift out of grease in frying pan and put in a baking dish. Salt, pepper and garlic salt should be added while cooking.
Mix together soy sauce, brown sugar, garlic, and ginger. Spoon over lamb ribs. Bake, uncovered, 25 minutes. Baste the ribs three or four times while cooking with the sauce in the bottom of the baking dish.
Joan Rhodes
San Joaquin County

BURBANK'S BBQ LAMB SHANKS

4 lamb shanks
1 medium onion, sliced
½ cup catsup
½ cup water
1 tablespoon brown sugar
1 tablespoon vinegar
1 tablespoon Worcestershire sauce
1 teaspoon salt
1 teaspoon dry mustard
¼ teaspoon pepper

Brown lamb shanks in a large skillet or Dutch oven, and then drain off fat. Combine remaining ingredients and pour over shanks. Cover and simmer, turning meat occasionally, for 1½ to 2 hours or until tender. Serve over rice or noodles. Serves 4.
Marianne Burbank
Marin County

OVEN BARBECUE LAMB RIBLETS

2 tablespoons Wesson oil
2 rib sections of breast of lamb cut in 2 rib portions
Dash of smoke salt, if desired
Salt and pepper to taste
4 medium onions, sliced
1 thinly sliced lemon
1 cup catsup
1 cup water
¼ cup vinegar
2 tablespoons sugar
4 teaspoons Worcestershire sauce
½ teaspoon Tabasco sauce
2 teaspoons dry mustard
1 minced clove of garlic
2 teaspoons salt

Preheat oven to 325 degrees. Brown rib portions on each side in oil. Drain off the fat and arrange lamb in a roaster with cover. Sprinkle with smoked salt and salt and pepper to taste.

Put sliced onions and lemon between pieces of lamb. Combine catsup, water, vinegar, sugar, Worcestershire sauce, Tabasco sauce, dry mustard, and garlic minced with the salt. Pour mixture over lamb and cover tightly. Bake for 1½ hours or until done. Spoon sauce over the lamb two or three times during baking, adding water if needed so meat does not stick to the pan. Uncover and bake 15 to 20 minutes longer.

This is delicious served with spaghetti and Parmesan cheese, and a tossed salad. 8 servings.

Note: Searing does not hold in juices. It is better to brown lamb slowly. Regardless of the cooking method, it should always be cooked at low temperature.

Pauline Bennett
Tuolumne County

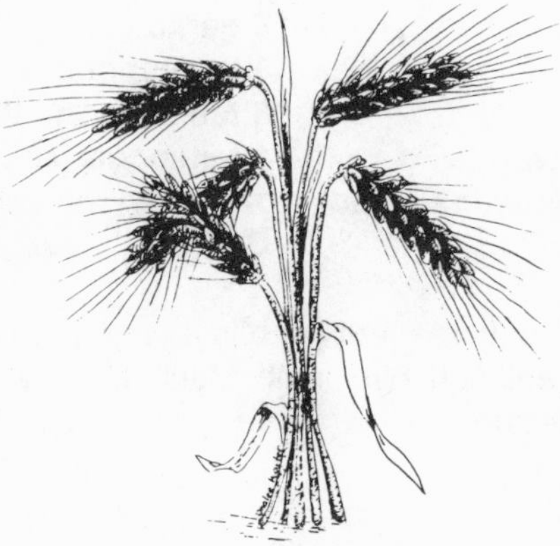

GIGOY D'AGNEAU ROTI

5 or 6 pound leg of lamb
1 garlic clove, cut in slivers
3 tablespoons vegetable oil
2 tablespoons salt
1 teaspoon black pepper
2 onions, sliced thin
2 carrots, sliced thin
1½ cups fresh or canned beef or chicken stock
½ teaspoon lemon juice

Preheat oven to 500 degrees. Insert garlic in lamb. Brush leg of lamb with oil and pat salt all over it. Insert thermometer, avoiding bone. Roast on rack uncovered and fat side up for 20 minutes. Reduce heat to 375 degrees and scatter vegetables around rack and roast another 40 to 60 minutes, or until done to your liking. (Rare: 130 to 150 degrees, well done: 150 to 160 degrees.) Place on heated platter and remove thermometer. Let rest 10 minutes before carving. Skim off fat from pan, add stock to the vegetables and boil briskly on top of stove 4 or 5 minutes, scraping in any browned bits clinging to pan. When intensity of flavor desired is reached, strain through fine sieve into saucepan, pressing down hard on the vegetables before discarding them. Remove surface fat from sauce; taste and season with lemon juice, salt and pepper. Reheat and serve with lamb.
Dorothy Farnworth
Plumas County

"MAGNIFICENT MARINADE" LEG OF LAMB

1 leg of spring lamb, cut into 2-inch squares
1 onion, chopped
1 cup olive oil
2 cups Burgundy wine
1 package Good Seasons salad dressing mix
2 bay leaves
5 garlic cloves, crushed
1 tablespoon rosemary, crushed
3 tablespoons Italian seasoning
1 teaspoon marjoram
1 tablespoon sage
Garlic salt, season to taste

Cut lamb into 2-inch squares. Put lamb in a large bowl. Mix rest of ingredients for marinade and pour over lamb. Marinate for 24 hours. Cook lamb on skewers on barbecue.
John Baranek
Sacramento County

SPANISH LAMB

2 pounds boneless lamb, cubed
¼ cup olive oil
2 medium leaks (white part), sliced
1 clove garlic, minced
1 1-pound can whole peeled tomatoes
½ cup dry white wine
1 10½-ounce can consommé or stock
1 10-ounce package frozen peas
Salt and pepper

Preheat oven to 275 degrees. In a heavy casserole, brown meat in olive oil. Add sliced leeks and cook until these are soft. Add tomatoes, garlic, wine and simmer 5 minutes. Then add consommé, salt and pepper, cover and place in the oven for 3 hours. Add peas, cover and cook another 15 minutes. Serve with hot asparagus spears. Serves 6.
California Tomato Research Institute, Inc.

RIO VISTA LAMB CASSEROLE

1 pound ground lamb
1 clove garlic, minced
½ cup finely chopped green pepper
1 medium onion, finely chopped
¼ cup finely chopped celery
¼ cup minced parsley
1 cup cooked rice
½ cup dry bread crumbs
1 teaspoon salt
¼ teaspoon pepper
1 cup chili sauce
¼ cup grated Parmesan cheese

Preheat oven to 350 degrees. Brown the lamb in a skillet over medium heat, stirring occasionally, until browned. Drain off excess drippings. Add all the remaining ingredients except Parmesan cheese and mix well. Turn into a 1½-quart casserole and sprinkle with Parmesan cheese. Bake for one hour. 4 to 6 servings.
Ed Hobbs-Brann
Solano County

CALIFORNIA PORK CHOPS AND SPUDS

4 pork chops
½ cup sour cream
1 can cream of mushroom soup
¼ cup water
2 tablespoons chopped parsley
4 cups potatoes, thinly sliced
¼ teaspoon salt
¼ teaspoon pepper

Preheat oven to 375 degrees. Brown pork chops in small amount of fat. Blend together the soup, sour cream, water and parsley. In a 2-quart casserole, alternate layers of potatoes, sprinkled with salt and pepper, and the sauce. Top with the pork chops. Bake for 1¼ hours.
Joan Scolari
Santa Barbara County

SWEET-SOUR PORK

1½ pounds boneless lean pork shoulder
½ teaspoon salt
1 tablespoon cooking oil
¾ cup water
1 13½-ounce can pineapple chunks
3 tablespoons brown sugar
¼ teaspoon ground ginger
3 tablespoons cornstarch
¼ cup cider vinegar
2 tablespoons soy sauce
1 medium green pepper, cut in 2-inch strips
1 medium onion, cut in thin slices
Hot fluffy rice

Cut pork into 2½-inch strips. Sprinkle with salt. Brown pork in hot oil in 12-inch skillet. Add water. Bring to boil, reduce heat. Cover and simmer 1 hour or until pork is tender. Drain pineapple, reserving juice. Add enough water to juice to make 1¼ cups. Combine 1¼ cups reserved pineapple liquid, brown sugar, ginger, cornstarch, vinegar, and soy sauce in bowl. Gradually stir into meat mixture. Cook until slightly thickened. Add green pepper, onion and pineapple. Cover and simmer 5 minutes. Serve over rice. Makes 4 servings.
Wilma Claverie
Imperial County

POLYNESIAN PORK

1½ pounds pork, cut into 1-inch cubes
Salt and pepper
2 tablespoons salad oil
4 teaspoons cornstarch
¾ cup vinegar
½ cup tomato catsup
1 cup brown sugar
2 tablespoons soy sauce
1 can pineapple chunks, drained
1 green pepper, diced

Season meat and brown in hot oil. Remove from skillet. Drain off excess fat. Blend cornstarch and vinegar in the skillet, then add catsup, sugar and soy sauce. Cook, stirring constantly, until thick. Add meat. Cover and simmer 30 minutes. Add pineapple chunks and green pepper, continue cooking for 10 minutes. Serve over hot rice.
California Tomato Research Institute, Inc.

LOW CALORIE SPARERIBS

3 to 4 pounds spareribs
½ cup catsup
Juice of ½ lemon

Preheat oven to 350 degrees. Bake spareribs on rack in oven for 2 hours. Pour off excess fat. Mix lemon juice and catsup. Brush mixture on ribs, return to oven. Bake at 300 degrees for ½ hour longer.
Jo Bruno
San Bernardino County

OVEN BBQ SPARERIBS

3 to 4 pounds spareribs, cut in pieces
1 lemon, sliced
1 large onion
1 cup catsup
⅓ cup Worcestershire sauce
1 teaspoon chili powder
1 teaspoon salt
2 dashes Tabasco
2 cups water

Preheat oven to 450 degrees. Place spareribs in shallow roasting pan, meaty side up. On each piece, place 1 slice lemon and 1 slice onion. Bake for 30 minutes. Combine remaining ingredients in saucepan and bring to boil. Take meat from oven and pour sauce over. Return to oven and bake at 350 degrees until tender, 45 minutes to 1 hour. Baste every 15 minutes. Serves 4.
Anna Brinkman
Imperial County

SPARERIBS WITH KRAUT

3 pounds pork spareribs
3½ cups sauerkraut
1 cup finely chopped unpared tart apple
1 cup shredded carrot
1½ cups tomato juice
2 tablespoons brown sugar
2 teaspoons caraway seed

Cut ribs in pieces; season with 2 teaspoons salt and ¼ teaspoon pepper; place in Dutch oven and brown well. Combine kraut (including liquid) with remaining ingredients; spoon over ribs. Simmer, covered, 1¾ hours or until ribs are done, basting with juices several times during the last hour. Skim off excess fat. Makes 6 servings.
Inge Brundy
Imperial County

POPE VALLEY'S PORK SAUSAGE CAKE

1½ cups brown sugar
1½ cups granulated sugar
½ cup cold coffee
1 pound seasoned pork sausage
1 pound raisins, cooked and drained
1 cup walnuts, chopped
½ cup buttermilk
½ teaspoon soda
2½ cups flour
1½ teaspoons cinnamon
1½ teaspoons nutmeg
1½ teaspoons cloves
1 8-ounce package cream cheese
1 pound powdered sugar
1 teaspoon vanilla extract

Preheat oven to 350 degrees. Mix together brown and white sugar, add coffee and sausage and mix together until well blended. Stir the soda into the buttermilk. Add buttermilk, raisins and nuts to sugar mixture. Add flour and spices, mixing well. Bake in ungreased glass pan for 30 minutes. Reduce heat to 325 degrees and bake an additional 30 minutes. Remove from oven and let cool. Beat together cream cheese, powdered sugar and vanilla until it is a good spreading consistency. Spread on cooled cake.
Betty Wilms
Napa County

SHEEPHERDER'S VEAL HUNGARIAN

2 tablespoons cooking oil
4 veal chops, about 1-inch thick
Flour to coat
Salt to taste
Pepper to taste
1 small onion, chopped
½ green pepper, diced
2 stalks celery, sliced
1 tablespoon paprika
1 cup chicken broth
½ cup white wine
1 cup sour cream

Heat oil in skillet. Dust chops with flour, salt and pepper and brown on each side. Remove to platter. In skillet, sauté onion, pepper and celery, cooking until tender but not brown. Return chops to pan. Add paprika, broth and wine. Cover and simmer 30 minutes, until chops are tender. Remove chops to platter. Stir sour cream into sauce and just bring to a boil. Pour over chops and serve.
Elinor Clow
Mendocino County

RABBIT IN WHITE WINE WITH MUSHROOMS

2½ pounds rabbit
¼ cup olive oil
1 pound small mushrooms
2 tablespoons flour
1½ cups dry white wine
8-10 small whole onions, 1½-inches in diameter
¼ cup chopped parsley
2 cloves garlic, mashed
¼ teaspoon rosemary
¼ cup butter
2 cups garlic-flavored croutons

Cut rabbit into serving size pieces and sprinkle lightly with salt. Place in a wide frying pan over medium-low heat; add olive oil and rabbit; brown rabbit well on all sides. Remove rabbit from pan and set aside.
Add mushrooms to pan, cook on medium heat, stirring until lightly browned and all juices have evaporated. Remove pan from heat, stir in flour, blend in wine, onions, parsley, garlic, and rosemary. Replace rabbit, arranging among vegetables; cover and simmer 45 minutes or until meat is tender when pierced and onions are done. Melt butter in a frying pan. Add croutons and stir until well coated and lightly toasted. Place rabbit in a shallow serving dish and garnish with toasted croutons. Serves 4.
Note: Chicken is also good in place of rabbit.
Claudia Hanna
Napa County

FISH

Fish farming is an up and coming segment of California aquaculture. Trout and catfish farms are located throughout the state. The small amount of area needed to raise fish, along with efficient feed conversion, has made fish farming a large source of high protein food. The ocean along California's coast is also being farmed. Shellfish operations, such as abalone, oyster, scallop, crab, and lobster are in the infancy stages, but show the potential to be a viable source of food production.

FOWL

California raises over 125 million chickens and over 19 million turkeys annually. Most of this done on farms in the central portion of the San Joaquin Valley. Even though California grows a large number of chickens, the number is insufficient to meet the demand from California's growing population, therefore chickens are imported from other states. Scientific research has discovered new ways of improving the feed consumption efficiency of turkeys, fryers and broilers. This has resulted in cost savings to the consumer.

EGGS

California is the largest producer of eggs in the United States, with over 38 million birds producing more than 8 billion eggs annually. Most of the egg farms are located in the northern San Joaquin Valley and Southern California. It is not uncommon to find farms with over one million egg laying hens. Eggs continue to be one of the least costly foods and highest sources of protein.

Fish, Fowl and Eggs

. . . from fin to fowl

CALIFORNIA CLAM CHOWDER

½ onion, diced
2 stalks celery, diced
2 tablespoons butter
5 small potatoes, cubed
2 6½-ounce cans minced clams with juice
1 quart milk
6 tablespoons Wondra flour
1 teaspoon each salt and Worcestershire sauce
½ teaspoon each pepper, Beau Monde seasoning, dry mustard
6 slices bacon, cut up and browned

Sauté onion and celery in butter. Add potatoes with a little water and cook until tender. Mash slightly. Add clams and milk. Make paste with Wondra flour and add to above. Add remaining ingredients except bacon to taste. Simmer for 2 minutes. Add bacon just before serving.
Note: Clams become tough when overcooked.
Caralee Scala
Siskiyou County

CREAMY CLAM CHOWDER

¼ cup butter
1 cup diced onion
½ cup sliced celery
1 4-ounce can mushroom stems & pieces
2 cups sliced or diced potatoes
2 6½-ounce cans chopped clams and juice
½ cup water
2 teaspoons salt
2 teaspoons pepper
1 pint whipping cream
4 tablespoons flour
¼ cup water

Melt butter in medium saucepan. Sauté onion and celery in butter until tender. Add drained mushrooms, potatoes, clams and juice, ½ cup water, and salt and pepper. Simmer until potatoes are tender. Combine whipping cream, flour and ¼ cup water, blending well. Add whipping cream mixture to clam mixture and simmer until thickened, stirring constantly.
Ruth Machado
Sacramento County

HUMBOLDT CRAB COBBLER

½ cup butter
½ cup green pepper, chopped
½ cup onion, chopped
1 cup flour, sifted
1 teaspoon dry mustard
½ teaspoon Accent
1 cup milk
1 cup American cheese, shredded
2 cups crabmeat (Dungeness preferred)
1½ cups tomatoes, drained
½ teaspoon salt
2 teaspoons Worcestershire sauce

Preheat oven to 450 degrees. In top of double boiler, melt butter. Add green pepper and onion, cook until tender, about 10 minutes. Blend in flour, dry mustard, Accent and salt. Stir in milk and cheese. Cook, stirring constantly, until cheese is melted and mixture is very thick. Add crabmeat, tomatoes and Worcestershire sauce. Mix well and put into a greased casserole dish.

Cheese biscuit topping:

½ cup flour
2 teaspoons baking powder
½ teaspoon salt
¼ cup American cheese, shredded
2 tablespoons shortening
½ cup milk

Prepare topping. Sift flour, baking powder and salt into bowl. Add cheese, cut in shortening. Add milk and mix only until all flour is moistened. Drop by rounded teaspoonsful on top of hot crabmeat mixture. Bake 20 to 25 minutes.

Dona DePaoli
Humboldt County

BATTLE CREEK SMOKED TROUT OMELET

1 tablespoon butter or margarine
2 tablespoons scallions, chopped
¼ cup mushrooms, sliced
¼ cup smoked trout, boned, crumbled
2 eggs, beaten
Salt and pepper to taste
1 or 2 tablespoons Jack cheese, grated

Melt butter and sauté scallions, mushrooms, and crumbled smoked trout for 2 minutes. Add more margarine if necessary. Add beaten eggs, salt, and pepper and cook until eggs are set. Sprinkle with grated Jack cheese and serve or fold first and serve. Makes one serving.
Michael Jonckheere
Tehama County

SHRIMP CREOLE

3 pounds raw shrimp in shells
4 cups hot seasoned rice or polenta
1½ seeded green peppers, cut in ½-inch pieces
3 or 4 cloves garlic, minced
3 large onions, chopped (not too fine)
6 tablespoons oil
1 teaspoon salt
⅛ teaspoon pepper
½ teaspoon dried rosemary
½ teaspoon paprika
6 dashes of Tabasco
2 1-pound 13-ounce cans tomatoes (about 6 cups)
1 cup parsley, snipped

Early in day shell shrimp, cut out vein, drain and refrigerate. About 45 minutes before serving; cook rice or polenta according to directions on label, keep hot. Place all vegetables and oil in skillet and sauté until tender. Add salt, pepper, rosemary, paprika, Tabasco and tomatoes. Cook over medium heat for 15 minutes, stirring occasionally. Add shrimp and cook just until tender and shrimp turn pink. Garnish with parsley. Serve with hot rice or polenta. (Some of the parsley can be added to the cooked rice.) Makes 8 to 10 servings.
Sharon Vanni
Santa Clara County

CALIFORNIA FLAVORFUL FISHCAKES

1½ cups cooked, flaked, California farm raised catfish or trout
1 cup chopped celery
1 cup chopped onion
1 cup bread crumbs (whole wheat, if possible)
¼ cup scallions, chopped
½ cup parsley, chopped
½ teaspoon Lawry's garlic powder
1 teaspoon salt
¼ teaspoon pepper
¼ cup nonfat dry milk (in dry form)
2 eggs
2 teaspoons Worcestershire sauce
About ½ cup water
Oil for frying

Mix first ten ingredients. In another bowl combine eggs, Worcestershire sauce, and water. Pour into the first mixture and mix thoroughly. Form mixture into 2-inch diameter cakes about ½-inch thick. Fry in oil at medium burner setting or 360 degree setting in electric fry pan until golden on one side. Turn and fry until golden on other side. Drain on paper towels. Serve with tartar sauce. Makes about 14 cakes.
Note: Amounts of each ingredient can be easily varied to suit individual taste or accommodate what is available in the vegetable bin.
Linda Jonckheere
Tehama County

LETTUCE SALMON CASSEROLE

2 cups canned salmon
¼ cup oil
¼ teaspoon sage
Salt
¼ cup onion, chopped
3 tablespoons butter
3 tablespoons flour
1⅓ cups milk
¾ cup Jack cheese, cubed
2 teaspoons lemon juice
2½ cups shredded lettuce

Break salmon into bite-size pieces. Gently mix with oil, sage, ½ teaspoon salt and onion. Melt butter in saucepan. Blend in flour and ¼ teaspoon salt. Stir in milk. Heat and stir until mixture is thickened and comes to a boil. Stir in cheese until melted. Add lemon juice. Turn half of cheese sauce into a 1½-quart casserole. Top with shredded lettuce, salmon mixture, then remaining sauce. Broil until lightly browned. Serves four.
Christy Henning
Santa Barbara County

SALMON IN SOUR CREAM MASK

6 salmon filets
1 tablespoon onion, grated
Juice from ½ lemon
½ teaspoon salt
¼ teaspoon pepper
⅛ teaspoon paprika
⅛ teaspoon Tabasco sauce
½ cup sour cream

Preheat oven to 350 degrees. Place salmon filets in a shallow, buttered baking dish. Combine onion, lemon juice, salt, pepper, paprika and Tabasco sauce. Spread over fish. Spread sour cream over fish evenly. Bake for 30 minutes. Serves six.
Cheryl Crayne
Marin County

HAZEN SPRINGS BROILED BONELESS TROUT

2 8-10-ounce boneless California rainbow trout
2 tablespoons butter or margarine, melted
1 tablespoon Worcestershire sauce
Pinch of dill
Salt and pepper to taste

Preheat broiler and place rack close to heat source. Place trout, skin side down, in a shallow roasting pan. Combine Worcestershire and dill in melted butter and pour over trout. Broil 5 minutes or until meat flakes with a fork. Season with salt and pepper. Serve with California Golden Pearl Rice and garnish with fresh lemon slices.
Note: Lemon juice can be substituted for Worcestershire.
Michael Jonckheere
Tehama County

"ALWAYS ON SUNDAY" CHICKEN CASSEROLE

¼ pound bacon, diced
1 cup flour
1 teaspoon salt
¼ teaspoon pepper
10 to 12 pieces of chicken
2 cups chicken broth
1 cup light cream or half & half
1 bay leaf, broken
½ teaspoon thyme
1 teaspoon sage

Preheat oven to 350 degrees. Fry bacon until crisp, remove from pan. Combine flour, salt and pepper. Dredge chicken in flour mixture and brown in hot bacon fat. Remove chicken, add broth, cream, bay leaf, thyme and sage to drippings in pan and cook over medium heat until smooth. Place chicken in a casserole and pour sauce over chicken. Bake covered for 30-40 minutes. Sprinkle with crumbled bacon before serving.
Note: Serve this with buttered rice and a green salad—dinner's ready!
Bette Wegis
Kern County

CHICKEN ALA HAYFORK

3 chicken breasts
¼ cup flour
1 teaspoon salt
½ teaspoon pepper
½ cup evaporated milk
4 tablespoons cooking oil

Skin and debone chicken breasts and pound until flat. Mix flour, salt and pepper. Dip the chicken pieces in the evaporated milk and then the flour mixture. Fry in the cooking oil at 350 degrees for 8 to 10 minutes; turn and cook on the other side until golden brown, approximately 5 to 8 minutes. Delicious!
Olive Beamer
Trinity County

CRANBERRY CHICKEN

1 large can cranberry sauce (whole or jellied)
1 8-ounce bottle Russian dressing
6 chicken breasts
1 package dried onion soup

Mix cranberries with dressing and marinate the chicken parts for 24 hours. Lay chicken pieces flat. Sprinkle over 1 package of dried soup mix. Bake 1 to 1½ hours at 350 degrees.
Eloise Warren
San Luis Obispo County

"MY BEST CHICKEN"

¼ cup butter
2 large onions, finely chopped
1 cut up chicken
Salt and pepper to taste
1 cup half and half
1 tablespoon butter
3 level tablespoons flour
1 cup milk
1 tablespoon tomato paste
½ teaspoon curry powder
½ tablespoon paprika
2 teaspoons lemon juice
3 mushrooms, sliced

Melt butter in pan, add onions, and cook slowly until tender. Add more butter, brown chicken. Add salt, pepper and half and half. Cover and cook 30 minutes. Remove chicken, and keep it warm. Melt 1 tablespoon butter in small pan, stir in flour and add milk. Stir and bring to boil. Stir into onion mixture. Add tomato paste; then rub mixture through a strainer or ricer. Add curry powder and paprika, lemon juice and mushrooms that have been sautéed in butter. Bring slowly to boil. Replace the chicken and simmer for 10 minutes. Arrange chicken on deep platter, and pour sauce over chicken.
Betty Middlecamp
San Luis Obispo County

OMAR KHAYAM CHICKEN

½ cup butter
2 2-pound chickens (cut in ¼)
1 large onion, sliced thin
½ cup sherry
½ cup tomato juice
1 tablespoon paprika
1 tablespoon salt
Pepper to taste
1 cup water

Preheat oven to 400 degrees. Melt butter and fry chicken until light brown. Place in baking pan. Sauté onion in butter, add rest of the ingredients and one cup water. Pour over chicken. Bake uncovered. Turn chicken after one half hour. Continue baking for 20-30 minutes more.
Sandra Babich
Humboldt County

PHYLLIS' NUTSY CHICKEN

3 pounds chicken pieces
½ cup flour
Salt and pepper to taste
½ cup oil
3 cups rice
2 cans bouillon
1 cup celery, chopped
1 cup onion, chopped
1 cup walnuts or almonds, chopped

Preheat oven to 375 degrees. Dredge chicken in flour and seasonings. Brown in oil. Drain. In 9 x 13-inch pan, mix rice with bouillon and enough water to make 7½ cups liquid. Mix in celery, onion, and nut pieces. Allow to sit for a few minutes. Put chicken over rice mixture. Bake covered for 45 minutes. May be left uncovered for at least 10 minutes for crisper chicken.
Candy Jones
San Bernardino County

CHICKEN WINGS PIQUANT

⅓ cup soy sauce
⅓ cup brown sugar
12 ounces pineapple juice
Chicken wings (3 pounds approximately)
Garlic salt

Combine first three ingredients to make marinade. Marinate disjointed chicken wings for at least 3 hours. Turn once. Before baking, sprinkle with garlic salt. Bake at 350 degrees for 1 hour. Turn wings over half way through baking.
Susan Righetti
San Luis Obispo County

SANTA CRUZ SPICED CHICKEN

2 chickens, 2½ or 3 pound chickens, halved
1 large onion, sliced
3 cloves garlic
1-inch piece of fresh ginger, or ½ teaspoon ground ginger
1 teaspoon salt
½ teaspoon cloves
½ small hot chili pepper
3 tablespoons lime juice
¼ cup butter, melted

Preheat oven to 350 degrees. Put the 4 pieces of chicken in a shallow baking dish. Combine all other ingredients in a blender. Spread ⅓ of mixture on cut sides of chicken and arrange them, cut side down, in baking dish. Spread the rest of the mixture on top of the chicken. Bake, uncovered, one hour.
Hulda McLean
Santa Cruz County

ZEE'S SWEET & SOUR CHICKEN

1 can whole berry cranberry sauce
1 bottle Russian salad dressing
1 package of onion soup mix (Lipton's)
4 whole chicken breasts, cut in half

Preheat oven to 350 degrees. Combine first three ingredients. Place chicken breasts in pan and pour sauce over. Bake, covered, 30 minutes. Uncover and bake 30 minutes more.
Marilyn Britton
San Luis Obispo County

CHICKEN MARINADE

¼ cup soy sauce
3 tablespoons dry white wine
2 tablespoons lemon juice
1 clove garlic, minced
2 tablespoons salad oil
¾ teaspoon Italian seasoning
½ teaspoon ginger root, grated
¼ teaspoon onion powder
Chicken breasts, skinned, boned and cut into long, narrow strips

Combine soy sauce, wine, lemon juice, garlic, oil, Italian seasoning, ginger root and onion. Place strips of chicken in marinade for 3-12 hours. Chicken may be threaded on skewers for barbecueing or used in stir fry cooking. Note: Marinade will keep in refrigerator for up to a month and can be used again.
Cyndy Mickelson
Sacramento County

CALIFORNIA HOT CHICKEN SALAD

2 cups chicken, cooked, skinned and cut in small pieces
2 tablespoons onion, chopped
1½ cups rice, cooked
1 can cream of chicken soup
¼ cup water
¼ cup almonds, slivered
¼ teaspoon pepper
½ teaspoon salt
1 tablespoon lemon juice
1 cup celery, chopped
¾ cup mayonnaise
3 hard cooked eggs, chopped
1 cup potato chips, crushed

Preheat oven to 450 degrees. Mix all ingredients except chips and place in large casserole. Just before baking sprinkle generously with crushed potato chips. Bake for 15 minutes. The quick baking keeps the celery crisp.
Note: This recipe may be made the day before but do not put the chips on until just before baking.
Myra Eberspecher
Shasta County

CHICKEN & BROCCOLI CASSEROLE

2 packages frozen broccoli, prepare as directed and drain
4 chicken breasts, wrap in foil and bake, cut in 1-inch chunks
1 cup mayonnaise
½ teaspoon curry
2 cans cream of chicken soup
1 tablespoon lemon juice
1 cup sharp Cheddar cheese, grated
Buttered bread crumbs

Preheat oven to 350 degrees. In greased three-quart baking dish, lay broccoli flat, then add layer of chicken, layer of sauce made with mayonnaise, curry, soup, and lemon juice, layer of cheese, and sprinkle buttered bread crumbs on top. Bake for one half hour.
Lorraine Valine
Sacramento County

CHICKEN CREOLE

¼ cup butter or margarine
⅓ cup flour
1½ teaspoons salt
1 teaspoon paprika
¼ teaspoon pepper
¼ teaspoon poultry seasoning
2 to 3 pounds chicken, cut up
1 cup uncooked rice
½ cup green pepper, chopped
½ cup onion, chopped
1½ teaspoons salt
⅛ teaspoon pepper
3 cups hot chicken broth
2 large tomatoes, cut in wedges

Preheat oven to 400 degrees. Place butter or margarine in 13 x 9-inch baking dish. Place in oven until fat melts. Dredge chicken parts in mixture of flour, 1½ teaspoons salt, paprika, poultry seasoning, and ¼ teaspoon pepper. Place chicken in hot fat, skin side down. Bake, uncovered, for 25 minutes. Take chicken out of pan. Arrange rice, green pepper, and onion in the pan. Sprinkle rice with 1½ teaspoons salt and ⅛ teaspoon pepper. Return chicken to pan, skin side up. Pour hot chicken broth over all. Place tomatoes on top. Return to oven and bake, uncovered, for 45 minutes or until rice is tender. (If mixture becomes too dry, add a small amount of chicken broth or water.) Serves 6.
Edna M. Thompson
Sonoma County

CHICKEN PUFFS

1 basic recipe for cream puffs

Filling:

2 cups cooked chicken, chopped
1 cup celery, chopped
½ can pimiento, chopped
1 can mushrooms, chopped
½ cup almonds, sliced and browned in butter
1 cup cream of chicken soup
1 tablespoon lemon juice
¼ cup mayonnaise

Mix filling ingredients together. Heat. Fill warm cream puffs. Serves 4-6.

Geraldine Hillis
Shasta County

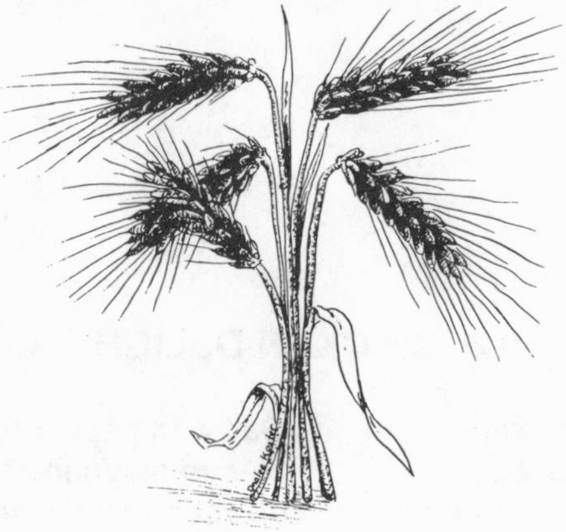

CHICKEN RICE CASSEROLE

2 cups chicken, cooked and diced
1 cup celery, cut very fine
1 medium onion, cut fine
1½ cups cooked rice, (½ cup raw)
1 can cream of chicken soup
¾ cup mayonnaise
¼ cup water
2 or 3 hard boiled eggs, sliced
Crushed potato chips

Preheat oven to 350 degrees. Mix chicken, celery, onion, rice and soup together. Mix mayonnaise with water, add to the rest of the ingredients. Gently stir in sliced eggs. Top with a few crushed potato chips. Bake for 45 minutes until bubbly.

Anne Wanner
Sacramento County

CHICKEN AND RICE DIVINE

1 whole breast of chicken, cooked and cut in pieces
6 green onions, sliced
1 tablespoon parsley, minced
Salt and pepper to taste
1 10¾-ounce can cream of mushroom or cream of celery soup
½ cup white or brown processed rice
1 small can of peas—if desired

Preheat oven to 350 degrees. Combine chicken, onions, parsley, salt and pepper, soup and rice and put in greased 9 by 9-inch pan. Bake for 30 minutes or until brown. Serves 4.
Hazel Patison
Calaveras County

HOT CHICKEN DELIGHT

3 cups cooked chicken
1½ cups celery, diced
3 teaspoons onion, grated
3 teaspoons lemon juice
1½ cups water chestnuts, drained and sliced
Salt and pepper to taste
¾ cup mayonnaise
1½ cups mild Cheddar cheese, grated
1½ cups potato chips, crushed

Preheat oven to 450 degrees. Combine chicken, celery, onion, lemon juice, water chestnuts, salt, pepper, and mayonnaise. Mix thoroughly. Spread evenly in a 9 x 13-inch baking dish. Sprinkle with grated cheese and potato chips. Bake for 10 minutes, or until cheese is melted. Serves 8-10.
Mary Louise Naugle
Yolo County

HOT COCKA-DOODLE-DOO

2 cups chicken (breasts), diced
2 cups celery, diced
½ cup nuts, chopped
2 tablespoons red pimiento
1 teaspoon salt
2 tablespoons lemon juice
1 can water chestnuts, sliced
1 can or 2 cups pineapple chunks
½ cup mayonnaise
½ can cream of chicken soup
1½ cups Cheddar cheese, grated
1 cup potato chips, crushed

Preheat oven to 350 degrees. Mix all ingredients except cheese and chips together and put in a greased 9 x 13-inch pan. Add Cheddar cheese and chips. Bake for 25 minutes.
Grace McChesney
San Luis Obispo County

MERLE'S CHICKEN CASSEROLE

2 cups cooked chicken
1 teaspoon onion, minced
1½ cups cooked rice
Salt and pepper to taste
1 can cream of chicken soup
1 cup celery, cut fine
1 7-ounce can water chestnuts, sliced
¾ cup mayonnaise
½ cup blanched almonds, sliced
2 cups potato chips, finely crushed

Preheat oven to 350 degrees. Mix all the above ingredients except chips together. Place in buttered casserole dish. Top with potato chips. Bake for 30 minutes.
Lorraine Valine
Sacramento County

SANTA CRUZ CHICKEN CASSEROLE

3 cups chicken, cooked, cut in small pieces
6 slices bread, no crusts, cubed
1½ cups milk
½ cup onions, diced
½ cup green pepper, chopped
½ cup mayonnaise
2 eggs, beat well add to milk
½ cup celery, sliced
½ teaspoon salt
1 can cream of mushroom soup
1 cup Cheddar cheese, grated
Crushed cornflakes or potato chips

Preheat oven to 325 degrees. Mix all ingredients except soup and cornflakes. Chill. Remove from refrigerator several hours before baking. Spread one can mushroom soup over top. Cover with Cheddar cheese and cornflakes or crushed potato chips. Bake one hour. Serves eight.
Lorraine Valine
Sacramento County

SWEET & SOUR TURKEY

3 pounds turkey breast
2 eggs
1 teaspoon salt
Flour
Oil
⅔ cup sugar
2 tablespoons cornstarch
1 tablespoon paprika
1 1-pound 4-ounce can pineapple chunks
¼ cup soy sauce
¼ cup vinegar
1 cup bell pepper, chopped (optional)
½ cup onion, chopped
2 medium tomatoes, chopped or
1 pint canned tomatoes

Cut turkey breast in 1-inch chunks. Dredge in beaten eggs then flour and salt. Brown in oiled skillet. Make sauce in crock pot of sugar, cornstarch, paprika, pineapple chunks and juice, soy sauce, vinegar, bell pepper, onion and tomatoes. Add turkey to crock pot. Cook until done, about 5 or 6 hours.
Carol Mitchell
Sacramento County

TURKEY SCALLOPINI

3 pounds turkey thighs
½ cup Parmesan cheese, grated
¼ cup flour
2 teaspoons salt
½ teaspoon pepper
½ teaspoon garlic salt
Butter
½ pound fresh mushrooms, sautéed
6 tablespoons onions, chopped
½ cup wine (optional)
Chicken bouillon
Parsley to taste

Cut thighs into 1-inch pieces and dredge in mixture of grated Parmesan cheese, flour, salt, pepper and garlic salt. Brown in butter and add to crock pot. Add mushrooms, onions, wine, bouillon and parsley to crock pot. Crock pot needs very little liquid. If cooking on stove add more liquid. Cook until done, about 5 or 6 hours.
Carol Mitchell
Sacramento County

POOR MAN'S ABALONE

3 pounds turkey breast, sliced ¼-inch thick
Clam juice or minced clams
Flour
2 eggs, beaten
2 tablespoons cold water
Butter

Marinate turkey overnight in clam juice or minced clams. Dredge each slice of turkey breast in flour, then in beaten eggs and water mixture, and back in flour. Cook until brown and done in buttered skillet.
Carol Mitchell
Sacramento County

FILET TURKEY BREAST

Turkey breasts
3 eggs, beaten
1 cup cracker crumbs
Seasoning to taste (salt, pepper, herbs)
Shortening

Bone turkey breasts and dip into beaten egg, then into cracker crumbs seasoned to your liking. Deep fry until golden brown and done.
Virginia Tenborg
Placer County

SWISS HAM QUICHE

5 tablespoons butter
5 tablespoons flour
¼ teaspoon nutmeg
3¾ cups milk
3 cups Swiss cheese, grated
8 eggs, slightly beaten
3 cups diced cooked ham

Preheat oven to 375 degrees. Melt butter in a saucepan, add flour, nutmeg and milk. Stir and cook until thick and bubbly, add cheese and stir till melted. Remove from heat to cool slightly, add some to beaten eggs and then return egg mixture to saucepan. Add ham and pour in buttered 9 x 13-inch casserole. Bake 30-35 minutes until set. Cool 5-10 minutes before slicing. Makes 12-15 servings.
Lorraine Valine
Sacramento County

NANA'S CHOCOLATE ROLL

5 large eggs
¾ cup sugar
1 6-ounce package semi-sweet chocolate chips
3 tablespoons water
Cocoa
½ pint whipping cream
¼ cup sugar
½ teaspoon vanilla

Preheat oven to 350 degrees. Separate eggs. Into yolks, add the ¾ cup sugar, beating until light and fluffy. Melt chocolate chips and water in saucepan over low flame, stirring until melted, then cool for 15 minutes. Beat the egg whites until they are stiff, then fold in to chocolate mixture. Pour batter into a jelly roll pan, oiled and lined with waxed paper. Bake at 350 degrees for ten minutes, then five minutes at 300 degrees. Cover with kitchen cloth, having been soaked then wrung out, and cool this way for one hour. Remove cloth, and sift cake heavily with cocoa. Flip cake over, onto a large piece of wax paper. Spread with beaten whipping cream, sugar and vanilla. Roll very carefully lengthwise (it will crack), using the wax paper to roll it. The cocoa will be on the outside. Chill thoroughly in wax paper for at least two hours. Slice to serve. Delicious!
Virginia Kupinski
Riverside County

EASY FRENCH COCONUT PIE

½ cup butter, melted
1½ cups sugar
3 eggs, beaten
1 teaspoon vinegar
1 teaspoon vanilla
1 cup coconut

Preheat oven to 350 degrees. To the melted butter, add the sugar, eggs, vinegar, vanilla and coconut. Mix well. Pour into greased pie pan. (Pie shell is not needed). Bake for 45 minutes. Easy and delicious.
Nell Hughes
San Luis Obispo County

PICKLED EGGS

1 16-ounce can sliced beets
12 eggs, hard boiled
¾ cup cider vinegar
½ cup sugar
2 tablespoons salt
½ teaspoon black pepper
⅛ teaspoon ground allspice
6 whole cloves

Day ahead or up to 3 days ahead:
Drain liquid from beets into a quart saucepan. Place beets and hard boiled eggs in 1½-quart jar or large bowl. Stir vinegar, sugar, salt, pepper, allspice and cloves into beet liquid. Heat to boiling over high heat. Pour hot mixture over eggs and beets. Cover and refrigerate at least 12 hours to allow flavor to penetrate eggs.
Note: To serve, drain eggs and beets. Eat for snack, light lunch or cut lengthwise, garnish and serve as an appetizer. Makes 12 pickled eggs.
Dolly Green
Sacramento County

CRESTON VALLEY CRUSTLESS QUICHE

½ cup melted butter
10 eggs
½ cup flour
1 teaspoon baking powder
1 pound Jack cheese, shredded
1 pint cottage cheese
Any of the following may be added:
1 7-ounce can green chilies, green onions, mushrooms, bacon bits, ham, broccoli, spinach (10 ounces, frozen or fresh)

Preheat oven to 400 degrees. Mix all the ingredients together. Put into a 9 x 13-inch greased pan. Bake for 15 minutes; reduce heat to 350 degrees and bake 40 minutes longer. Serves 10.
"E. J." Boulger
San Luis Obispo County

LAZY DAY BREAKFAST CASSEROLE

8 slices fresh bread
2 pounds small link sausages
4 eggs
1 can cream of mushroom soup
2¼ cups milk
¾ pound American cheese

Trim crust from bread and cube. Fry and drain sausage and cut into bite-sized pieces. Beat eggs and add soup and milk and blend together. Butter a 9 x 13-inch casserole dish and spread bread cubes evenly on bottom; spread sausage evenly on bread cubes. Grate the cheese and spread over sausage, then slowly pour egg mixture over entire bread, sausage, cheese mixture. Set in refrigerator for 12 hours or the night before. Bake at 325 degrees for 1½ hours. Let set 10 minutes before serving.
Note: This is an excellent holiday (Christmas) breakfast casserole since you make it the night before and just slip it in the oven the right time before serving.
Sarah Rosasco
Tuolumne County

QUICK CREAMY ONION QUICHE

One 9-inch pastry shell, unbaked
½ cup grated Swiss cheese
4 slices chopped ham, cubed
4 eggs
2 cups light cream or evaporated milk
1 package onion soup mix

Preheat oven to 350 degrees. Put grated cheese in bottom of unbaked pie shell. Then add the ham. Beat eggs, milk and soup mix. Pour over cheese and ham. Bake for 45 to 50 minutes or until lightly browned on top. Cool 5 minutes before serving.
Note: May use 4 slices bacon, fried, or 1 cup chopped broccoli or 6 ounces drained shrimp in place of ham.
N. Pierce
Marin County

CHICKEN LITTLE'S BROCCOLI-EGG CASSEROLE

4 eggs, beaten
1 cup mayonnaise
1 can Cheddar cheese soup
2 cups cheese, shredded
3 cups broccoli, cut up
Add any kind of seasonings you wish
1 cup bread crumbs, buttered

Preheat oven to 350 degrees. Mix all ingredients into baking dish and top with buttered crumbs. Bake for 50 minutes to 1 hour.
Jean Jaeger
Sonoma County

EASY BLENDER HOLLANDAISE SAUCE

2 egg yolks
1 tablespoon lemon juice
½ teaspoon dry mustard
⅛ teaspoon salt
½ cup butter or margarine, melted

Put egg yolks, lemon juice, mustard, and salt into container of electric blender. Turn blender to high speed and gradually add butter. Blend until creamy and thickened.
Note: This is especially good over fresh-cooked California vegetables such as asparagus or broccoli.
Lynnel Pollock
Yolo County

EVERLASTING PIE CRUST

6 cups flour
1 pound shortening
2 teaspoons salt
1 egg
2 tablespoons vinegar
Cold water

Mix flour, shortening and salt well. Break egg into 1 cup measuring cup, beat lightly with fork. Add vinegar and enough water to fill cup. Mix well. Add to flour mixture. Wrap dough in waxed paper; place in tight plastic bag and refrigerate. Break off dough and use as needed. Handling this dough does not toughen it.
Lea Moxon
Humboldt County

DANISH COOKIES

1 cup shortening
1 cup sugar
1 teaspoon vanilla
1 egg
2 cups flour
½ teaspoon soda
½ teaspoon cream of tartar

Preheat oven to 350 degrees. Mix all ingredients together at once. Drop teaspoonful of dough on greased cookie sheet. Dip glass in granulated sugar and press cookie on cookie sheet. (May use colored sugar at holiday time.) Bake for 12 to 15 minutes.
Nadine Pierce
Marin County

CALIFORNIA KISSES

2 egg whites
⅛ teaspoon salt
2 cups powdered sugar, sifted
1 teaspoon vinegar
1 teaspoon vanilla

Preheat oven to 300 degrees. In mixing bowl, beat egg whites with salt until soft peaks form. Gradually beat in sugar. Add vinegar and vanilla and continue beating until very stiff peaks form. Drop by teaspoonfuls on greased baking sheets. Bake for 15 to 20 minutes. Cookies should remain light colored. Cool on racks. Makes about 3½ dozen small cookies.
Note: These are best made one day ahead of use.
Audry Sepponen
Placer County

HUCKLEBUCK COOKIES

Cookie:

¾ cup shortening
2 eggs
¾ cup cocoa
1½ teaspoons vanilla
1½ cups sugar
1½ cups milk
3 cups flour
3 teaspoons baking powder
¾ teaspoon salt

Preheat oven to 400 degrees. Cream together shortening, eggs, cocoa, vanilla and sugar. Add milk alternately with sifted dry ingredients, mixing after each addition until smooth. Drop by teaspoonfuls onto ungreased baking sheets. Bake 7 to 8 minutes. Makes 24 soft cookies, each about 1¼-inch in diameter. When cool, place filling between flat sides of paired cookies and store in airtight container.

Filling:

¾ cup butter
⅛ teaspoon salt
1½ teaspoons vanilla
2 cups confectioners' sugar
1 cup marshmallow creme
1 tablespoon milk

Beat ingredients for filling together. Makes enough filling for 24 Hucklebucks.

Grace McChesney
San Luis Obispo County

FEATHERBED CAKE

4 eggs, separated
1 cup granulated sugar
4 tablespoons water
1½ cups sifted cake flour
1½ teaspoons vanilla
1 teaspoon almond extract
2 teaspoons baking powder

Preheat oven to 300 degrees. Set aside a 10-inch, 4-inch deep ungreased tube pan. In a large bowl beat the yolks of the separated eggs. Slowly add sugar while beating. Add the water, one tablespoon at a time, beating well after each addition. Add flour slowly, beating well. Continue beating while adding vanilla and almond extracts. In a separate bowl beat egg whites until frothy. When half beaten, add the baking powder and continue until meringue holds stiff peaks. Carefully fold the beaten whites into the yolk batter. Pour into tube pan. Bake one hour or until cake tests done. Invert and let hang until cool.

Note: This is an excellent cake for that saltless, milkless, shortening-free diet! It was my mother-in-law's favorite cake recipe that she gave me over 60 years ago.

Mrs. John C. Norton
Tuolumne County

GOLD AND WHITE ANGEL FOOD CAKE

1 cup sifted cake flour
⅞ cup sugar
1½ cups egg whites (turkey)
1½ teaspoons cream of tartar
¼ teaspoon salt
¾ cup sugar
4 egg yolks, beaten
1 teaspoon lemon extract
1 teaspoon vanilla extract

Preheat oven to 375 degrees. Sift flour and ⅞ cup sugar three times. Combine egg whites, cream of tartar and salt. Beat until foamy. Add ¾ cup sugar, 2 tablespoons at a time. Beat well. Continue beating until meringue holds stiff peaks. Sift flour mixture over meringue; fold gently until all is added. Divide batter in half. Fold lemon extract and egg yolks in half the batter, and fold vanilla in other half of batter. Drop by spoonful alternating batters into 10-inch tube pan. Cut through batter five or six times from center of pan to the outside with a knife. Bake for 35 minutes. Invert pan til cake is cool. Serve plain or with a lemon icing or cream cheese frosting.
Note: Approximately 10 turkey eggs are needed for the above. Chicken eggs can be substituted.
Jean Hart
Placer County

LEMON CAKE PUDDING

1 cup sugar
¼ cup sifted all-purpose flour
Dash of salt
3 egg yolks, beaten
1½ cups milk, scalded
2 tablespoons oil
5 tablespoons lemon juice
2 teaspoons grated lemon peel
3 egg whites, stiffly beaten

Preheat oven to 325 degrees. Sift sugar, flour and salt together. Combine beaten egg yolks, milk, oil, lemon juice and lemon peel; add to flour mixture. Fold in stiffly beaten egg whites. Pour into oiled custard cups. Set cups in pan of hot water. Bake for 45 minutes. Cool. Serves 8.
Carmel Humphrey
Tehama County

LEMON YOGURT CAKE

3 cups flour, sifted
1 teaspoon baking soda
¼ teaspoon salt
2 cups sugar
1 cup margarine, softened
6 eggs, separated
1 teaspoon lemon extract or lemon juice
1 cup plain yogurt
1 tablespoon lemon rind, grated

Preheat oven to 350 degrees. Sift flour, baking soda and salt together. Set aside. Beat together 1½ cups of sugar, margarine, egg yolks and lemon extract or lemon juice until thick. Add flour mixture alternately with yogurt. Mix well at low speed of mixer. Beat egg whites until foamy peaks form. Gradually add remaining ½ cup of sugar to egg whites until meringue forms soft peaks. Fold meringue into batter until no streaks of white show. Add lemon rind. Mix well. Pour into a greased 10-inch tube pan. Bake for 45 minutes or until top springs back. Cool 10 minutes on wire rack. Remove from pan and cool completely.
Dolly Green
Sacramento County

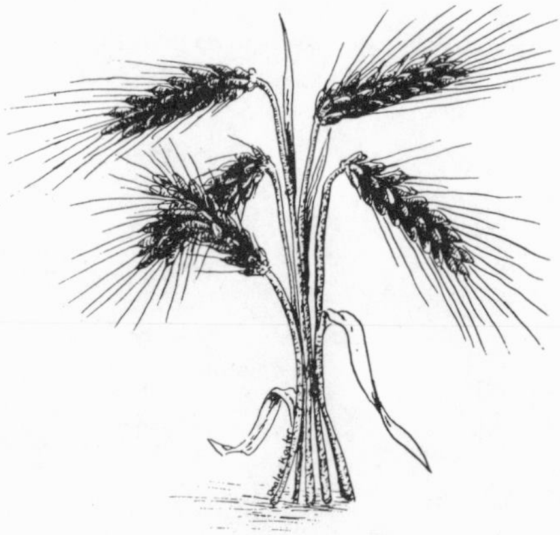

VEGETABLES

California produces over thirteen million tons of vegetables annually. There is an amazing range of products and varieties produced in the varying geographical areas of the state—everything from artichokes and asparagus to zucchini. California produces about one-third of the nation's vegetables. California's top vegetable crop is the processing tomato with a production record of well over 80% of the national output.

Vegetables

. . . from artichokes to zucchini

ARTICHOKE VELVET

2 9-ounce packages frozen artichoke hearts
1 pint fresh mushrooms, sliced (canned mushrooms may be used if fresh ones are not available)
2 tablespoons butter
1 package chicken gravy mix
1 cup water
4 ounces (1 cup) diced Swiss cheese
1 tablespoon dry white wine

Preheat oven to 350 degrees. Prepare frozen artichoke hearts according to package directions. Drain well. Sauté sliced mushrooms in butter. Combine cooked artichoke hearts and sautéed mushrooms in a 1-quart casserole. Using the one cup of water, prepare gravy according to package directions. Remove from heat and add herbs and Swiss cheese, stirring until cheese melts. Add the wine and pour the mixture over the vegetables. Bake for 30 minutes. Serves 6.
Note: This can be prepared ahead of time and then baked for 40 minutes at 350 degrees or the completely prepared dish can be heated in a microwave oven.
Robyn Payne
Sacramento County

GREEN GODDESS MOLD

1 14-ounce can cut asparagus, drained
1 3-ounce package lemon flavored gelatin
2 chicken bouillon cubes
½ cup cold water
½ cup green goddess salad dressing
1 tablespoon lemon juice
½ cup diced celery
2 tablespoons finely chopped green pepper

Measure fluid drained from asparagus, add enough water to measure one cup, heat to boiling. Dissolve gelatin and bouillon cubes in hot mixture. Add cold water, green goddess dressing and lemon juice. Beat with rotary beater until smooth. Chill until partially set. Fold in asparagus, celery, and green pepper. Turn into oiled mold. Chill until firm. Serves six.
Leatrice Moxon
Humboldt County

CALIFORNIA AVOCADO CAKE

1 medium avocado
1⅓ cups sugar
½ cup margarine
2 eggs
½ teaspoon cinnamon
½ teaspoon allspice
½ teaspoon nutmeg
½ teaspoon salt
1 rounded teaspoon soda
⅓ cup sour cream
½ cup chopped dates
¼ cup raisins
½ cup chopped nuts
1¼ cups flour

Preheat oven to 300 degrees. Blend together the avocado, sugar, margarine and eggs. Mix well. Add all other ingredients in order given making sure the batter is evenly mixed and blended. Batter will be quite stiff. Bake in a greased 9-inch square Pyrex pan for one hour or until cake tests done. Cool on wire rack.
Lillian Hinrichs
San Diego County

AVOCADO LOAF CAKE

¾ cup shortening, creamed
2 cups sugar
3 eggs
2 teaspoons vanilla
2 cups sifted all-purpose flour
3 teaspoons cinnamon
¾ teaspoon allspice
1½ teaspoons baking soda
1½ cups puréed California avocados (2 average)
¾ cup buttermilk
½ cup chopped walnuts
¾ cup raisins

Preheat oven to 350 degrees. Add sugar slowly to shortening until light and fluffy. Add eggs, one at a time, beating well after each one. Add vanilla. Sift dry ingredients together. Fold into egg-sugar mixture. Add puréed avocado and buttermilk. Add fruit and nuts. Grease and flour two 8½ x 4½ x 2⅝-inch loaf pans. Pour in batter. Bake for 60-65 minutes. (Cake freezes well.)
Judi Buchinger
Orange County

PACIFIC COAST AVOCADO DIP

1 tomato, chopped
4 ripe avocados
1 medium red onion
1 small can green chili salsa
Mayonnaise—enough to make the consistency of dip
Salt and pepper to taste

Mash avocados, chop onions, mix all ingredients together. This should be made just before eating as the avocados will turn brown. Squeeze lemon juice over the dip to keep it from turning brown.
Marlene Righetti
San Luis Obispo County

CHUCK WAGON SKILLET BEANS & FRANKS

2 tablespoons butter
1 cup diced fresh tomato
½ teaspoon crushed oregano
¼ teaspoon garlic powder
2 1-pound cans (4 cups) pork & beans
1 1-pound package franks

Melt butter in skillet. Add tomato, oregano and garlic powder; cook one minute to blend flavors. Add pork & beans and franks. Heat, stirring often, until mixture is piping hot. Serves 6.
Joan Scolari
Santa Barbara County

POT OF BEANS

8 cups beans (any dry bean—pink, pinto, kidney or lima bean)
2 onions, chopped
1 large smoked pork hock
1 tablespoon salt
1 quart tomatoes
1 8-ounce tomato sauce
2-3 large garlic cloves
2 tablespoons liquid smoke
1 teaspoon cumin (optional)
2 quarts water

Soak beans in water overnight. Drain off water from soaked beans. Put all the above ingredients in large pot and bring to boil. Cook over low heat for 2 to 3 hours until beans are tender.
Note: May mix variety of beans.
Onalee Koster
San Joaquin County

CALICO BEAN-BEEF CASSEROLE

¼ pound bacon
1 medium sized onion, chopped
½ pound mushrooms, sliced
1 medium sized bell pepper, cut in strips
1 pound hamburger, seasoned with salt and pepper
1 #2½ can pork and beans
1 #2 can green beans
1 #2 can yellow wax beans
½ cup brown sugar
2 tablespoons vinegar
1 #2 can garbanzo beans
1 #2 can baby lima beans
¼ cup mustard
½ cup catsup

Preheat oven to 300 degrees. Dice bacon. Fry and add mushrooms, onions, bell pepper and sauté with bacon. Add hamburger. Cook until pink color is gone. Drain liquid from all the beans except the pork and beans. Add to hamburger mixture. Add brown sugar, vinegar, catsup, and mustard. Combine and pour into large casserole. Bake for 1½ hours.
Note: This recipe makes a good electric fry pan dinner.
LaVonne Righetti
San Luis Obispo County

CALIFORNIA BAKED BEANS

1½ cups dry white beans, soaked
4 slices of bacon, diced
⅓ cup celery, diced
⅓ cup onion, diced
¼ cup green pepper, diced
¼ cup carrots, diced
2 tablespoons flour
2 tablespoons brown sugar
2 teaspoons salt
¼ cup light molasses or dark Karo syrup
1 pint tomato juice or pulp

Preheat oven to 300 degrees. Cook beans until done. Sauté bacon with vegetables, drain. Add rest of ingredients to bacon mixture. Put beans and sauce into ovenproof dish and bake at least 2 hours. Yield: 6-8 servings.
Emily Jorstad
Placer County

CRISP DILLED BEANS

2 pounds small tender beans
1 teaspoon red pepper
4 cloves garlic
4 large heads dill
2 cups water
¼ cup salt
1 pint vinegar

Steam green beans and pack in hot sterilized jars. To each pint, add ¼ teaspoon red pepper, 1 clove garlic and 1 head dill. Heat together water, salt and vinegar. Bring to boil and pour over beans. Seal at once and process in boiling water bath for five minutes. Chill thoroughly before serving.

Judy Sealock
Shasta County

FRENCH BEANS IN CREAM SAUCE

1 pound string beans, French cut
1 cup boiling water
Dash of salt
1 small onion
2 tablespoons butter
1½ tablespoons chopped fresh dill
1 tablespoon flour
1 tablespoon sugar
½ lemon
Salt and pepper to taste
¼ cup sour cream

String the beans, wash and French cut into 1-inch pieces. Put into the boiling water to which the salt has been added, cover and cook until tender. When done, remove beans and set liquid and beans aside. Chop onion and fry lightly in the butter with the chopped dill. Sprinkle the flour on the onion mixture and gradually add bean liquid with a little more water if needed to make a thick sauce. Add sugar, beans, lemon juice from the half lemon, and salt and pepper to taste. Just before serving stir in the sour cream. Heat but do not boil.

Note: This is a delicious recipe that came from Austria.

Nancy Rosasco
Tuolumne County

GREEN BEAN DELIGHT

4 17-ounce cans French style green beans
2 10½-ounce cans cream of mushroom soup
1 8-ounce can sliced mushrooms
1 jar of bacon and cheese flavored cheese spread
2 boxes frozen onion rings

Preheat oven to 350 degrees. Layer in a casserole: 2 cans green beans, 1 can undiluted soup, one-half of the mushrooms, one-half of the cheese spread, and 1 box of the onion rings. Repeat layering. Bake at 350 degrees for 30 minutes. Serves 12-16.
Cyndy Mickelsen
Sacramento County

BOONT SWEET PICKLED BEETS

24 small young beets
2 cups sugar
2 cups water
2 cups vinegar
2 tablespoons mixed pickling spice

Wash beets leaving 3-inches of top on and the roots. Cook until the skins slip easily (about 15 minutes). Put into cold water and remove skins, tops and roots. Pack beets into jars to within ½-inch of top. Mix sugar, water, vinegar and pickling spice in sauce pan and bring to a boil. Pour boiling syrup over beets to within ½-inch of top of jar. Process 30 minutes in hot water bath.
Evelyn Schoenahl
Mendocino County

EASY BROCCOLI CASSEROLE

3 packages frozen chopped broccoli
6 tablespoons margarine
4 tablespoons flour
1 tablespoon powdered chicken base
2 cups milk
⅔ cup water
4 tablespoons margarine
⅔ package (8-ounce size) herb stuffing mix (crumbled)
⅔ cup chopped walnuts

Heat oven to 400 degrees. Cook broccoli until barely tender, drain and place in buttered casserole dish. Melt 6 tablespoons margarine, remove from heat and blend in flour and chicken base. Gradually add milk and return to heat to cook, stirring constantly until it comes to a boil. Pour over broccoli. Heat together water and 4 tablespoons margarine. Add stuffing mix and walnuts. Pour on top of broccoli. Bake at 400 degrees for 20 to 30 minutes.
Lorraine Valine
Sacramento County

WALNUT BROCCOLI

3 heads broccoli, chopped
½ cup butter
4 tablespoons flour
1½ teaspoons powdered chicken stock base
2 cups milk
⅔ cup water
6 tablespoons butter
⅔ package seasoned stuffing
⅔ cup walnuts, chopped

Heat oven to 350 degrees. Cook broccoli just until tender. Drain and put in flat 2-quart casserole. Melt ½ cup butter, blend in flour and cook gently over low heat. Add chicken stock base. Gradually add milk, cooking until smooth and thick; pour over broccoli. Heat water and 6 tablespoons butter until melted. Pour over stuffing mix and toss; add nuts. Top broccoli with stuffing. Bake 30 minutes at 350 degrees. The amount of water used with stuffing mix may have to be adjusted to make a moist combination. Serves 12.
Sherry Leonhardt
Plumas County

BROCCOLI CASSEROLE

1 package frozen broccoli, cooked and chopped fine
½ cup mayonnaise
½ can cream of mushroom soup (undiluted)
1 egg, beaten
2 tablespoons butter
1 small onion, grated fine
Salt and pepper to taste
½ cup grated sharp cheese
1 cup Ritz cracker crumbs

Preheat oven to 350 degrees. Combine broccoli, mayonnaise soup, egg, butter, onion, salt, pepper and cheese in order given. Top with Ritz cracker crumbs. Put in greased casserole dish. Bake uncovered about 45 minutes.
Mary Rosa
Sacramento County

SANTA CRUZ BROCCOLI CASSEROLE

4 cups broccoli
2 cups Minute Rice (uncooked)
2 10¾-ounce cans cream of chicken soup
1 chopped onion
1 8-ounce jar cheese spread

Heat oven to 350 degrees. Break or chop broccoli into small pieces. Mix with rice, soup and onion. Put in a large flat casserole and dot with cheese. Cover with foil and bake at 350 degreea for 30 minutes. Remove foil and bake 10 minutes.
Hulda McLean
Santa Cruz County

COASTAL BRUSSEL SPROUTS PIQUANT

3 cups brussel sprouts
⅓ cup mayonnaise
¼ cup water
2 teaspoons horseradish
2 tablespoons grated onion
½ cup breadcrumbs

Preheat oven to 375 degrees. Cook sprouts in rapidly boiling water until barely tender. Drain and transfer to shallow casserole. Combine mayonnaise, water, horseradish and onion. Pour over sprouts. Top with breadcrumbs. Bake 20 minutes. Serves 4.
Marybeth Bontadelli
Santa Cruz County

NINE HOUR COLESLAW

2 pounds green cabbage
1 pound red cabbage
1 green pepper
1 medium onion, chopped
2 small jars pimientos
2 cups sugar
1 cup salad oil
1 cup vinegar
2 teaspoons celery seed
2 teaspoons sugar

Toss together vegetables and 2 cups sugar. Mix salad oil, vinegar, celery seed and 2 teaspoons sugar and bring to a boil. Cool. Add to cabbage and chill several hours. Toss before serving.
Ruby Jeskey
Plumas County

MARINATED CARROTS

1 large package sliced frozen carrots (baby carrots are nice too) or 10 to 12 raw carrots
1 teaspoon prepared mustard
1 cup sugar
¾ cup vinegar
½ cup oil
1 onion, sliced
4 green onions, chopped
1 teaspoon Worcestershire sauce
1 can tomato soup

Cook carrots until tender. Mix rest of the above ingredients and add to drained cooked carrots and refrigerate. Serve chilled. Serves 8.
Faren Olsen
Sonoma County

COOL CARROTS

2 pounds carrots
1 cup onion, chopped
½ cup salad oil
⅔ cup sugar
¾ cup vinegar
1 can tomato soup
1 small green pepper, thinly sliced
1 teaspoon dry mustard

Peel carrots and slice thin (¼-inch). Cook in boiling water with onion until just tender. Drain. In another pan mix oil, sugar and vinegar. Heat to dissolve sugar, then cool. Add soup. Add pepper and mustard. Pour over carrots and onions. Can be kept in the refrigerator up to six weeks.
Note: Serve chilled as a side dish or in place of a salad.
Bernice Herman
Sutter County

MARINATED CARROTS IMPERIAL

2 pounds fresh carrots
1 green pepper
1 onion, medium size
1 can tomato soup
½ cup vegetable oil
1 cup sugar
¾ cup wine vinegar
1 teaspoon prepared mustard
1 teaspoon Worcestershire sauce
1 teaspoon salt
1 teaspoon pepper

Slice carrots into rounds about ¼-inch thick and cook in boiling water until fork tender. Cool slightly. Slice green pepper and onion. Layer carrots, pepper and onion in a shallow dish. Combine remaining ingredients and pour over carrot mixture. Marinate overnight or longer.
Note: Makes an excellent relish or substitute for salad.
Frances Mitosinka
Imperial County

SWEET AND SOUR CARROTS

2 pounds carrots, sliced
2 green peppers, sliced thin
1 medium red onion, sliced thin
1 11-ounce can tomato soup
½ cup salad oil
¾ cup vinegar
1 cup sugar
1 teaspoon prepared mustard
1 teaspoon Worcestershire sauce
1 teaspoon salt
½ teaspoon pepper
½ teaspoon garlic salt

Slice carrots diagonally. Cook until barely tender. Cool. Layer carrots, green peppers and onions in a shallow dish. Mix remainder of ingredients together and pour over the vegetables. Chill for 8-10 hours. Serve chilled. This serves 8-10.
Libby Pankey
Orange County

CHEESEY BAKED CARROTS

1 small onion
½ cup butter
1 bunch carrots, cooked and mashed (6-8 carrots)
1 cup milk
½ cup Parmesan cheese
2 eggs, beaten
½ cup cracker crumbs
Salt and pepper to taste

Heat oven to 350 degrees. Fry onion in butter. Add to all other ingredients. Put into greased baking dish. Bake for ½ hour or until firm at 350 degrees. Note: Zucchini can be substituted for carrots. This is a great take along dish.
Freda Gregory
Humboldt County

CARROT CASSEROLE

3 cups carrots, cooked and mashed
¼ cup yellow onion, finely chopped
2 tablespoons butter, melted
½ teaspoon salt
⅛ teaspoon pepper
¾ cup Cheddar cheese, shredded
10 Ritz crackers, crushed (not pulverized)

Heat oven to 350 degrees. Boil carrots in salted water until done (approximately 5 minutes). Drain and reserve ⅔ cup liquid. Mash carrots and add reserved liquid. Sauté onions in butter until opaque in color. Add salt and pepper to carrots. Put carrot mixture into greased casserole dish. Press onions and cheese into mixture. Sprinkle the top with crackers. Bake, uncovered, at 350 degrees for approximately 40 minutes.
Rebecca Wiseman
Kern County

CARROTS IN SAVORY CHEESE SAUCE

2 pounds carrots, peeled and sliced
2 onions, minced
1 tablespoon butter
¼ cup flour
1 teaspoon salt
½ teaspoon dry mustard
¼ teaspoon pepper
¼ teaspoon celery salt
2 cups milk
8 ounces Cheddar cheese, grated
6 tablespoons buttered bread crumbs

Heat oven to 350 degrees. Simmer carrots until crispy tender. Sauté onions in butter; add flour, seasonings and milk. Stir and cook until smooth and thickened. Arrange layers of carrots and cheese in a 1½-quart casserole. Pour cream sauce over carrots and top with crumbs. Bake uncovered at 350 degrees for 25 minutes. Serves 8.
Libby Pankey
Orange County

CARROT CAKE SUPREME

2 cups flour
2 teaspoons baking powder
1½ teaspoons soda
2 teaspoons cinnamon
1 teaspoon salt
2 cups sugar
4 eggs
1¼ cups oil
1 pound can crushed pineapple, well drained
2 cups carrots, grated fine

Heat oven to 350 degrees. Sift all dry ingredients. Mix sugar, eggs and oil. Add dry ingredients, beat well. Add well drained pineapple and carrots. Mix well. Bake 40 minutes at 350 degrees in a 9 x 13-inch pan or two 9-inch layer pans (35 minutes). Be sure to test for complete baking.

Frosting:

1 box powdered sugar
½ cup butter
1 teaspoon vanilla
8 ounces cream cheese, softened

Mix well, add small amount of milk if necessary to spread.
Rachel Moore
Placer County

CALIFORNIA CARROT CAKE

2 cups brown sugar
4 eggs
2 teaspoons baking soda
2 teaspoons baking powder
2 teaspoons cinnamon
4 cups grated carrots
2 cups flour
½ cup nuts, chopped

Preheat oven to 350 degrees. Mix brown sugar, eggs, baking soda, baking powder, cinnamon, carrots, flour and nuts. Put in greased 9 x 13-inch pan. Bake for 35-40 minutes.

Frosting:

1 8-ounce package cream cheese
1 cup butter
1 teaspoon vanilla
1 pound sifted powdered sugar

Beat cream cheese, butter, vanilla and powdered sugar until velvety. Frost cake when cool.
Cyndy Mickelson
Sacramento County

NUTTIER CARROT CAKE

2 cups sugar
1½ cups oil
4 eggs
2 cups flour
2 teaspoons soda
1 teaspoon cinnamon
1 teaspoon salt
3 cups carrots, grated
1 cup walnuts or raisins, or both

Preheat oven to 350 degrees. Grease and flour a 9 x 13-inch pan. Beat sugar and oil together, add eggs one at a time. Beat well after each egg. Sift dry ingredients and add to egg mixture. Add grated carrots and nuts or raisins. Pour into prepared pan. Bake for 40 to 45 minutes.
Betty Hansen
El Dorado County

SOURDOUGH RAISIN-CARROT CAKE

1 cup all-purpose flour
1 teaspoon baking powder
½ teaspoon salt
½ teaspoon baking soda
½ teaspoon cinnamon
4 eggs, separated
½ cup light brown sugar, firmly packed
½ cup cooking oil
½ cup sourdough starter
1 cup coarsely grated raw carrots
½ cup seedless raisins
2 tablespoons grated lemon peel

Heat oven to 350 degrees. Combine flour, baking powder, salt, baking soda and cinnamon. Set aside. Beat egg whites in small mixing bowl until soft peaks form. Set aside. In a large bowl combine sugar, oil, egg yolks and sourdough starter. Mix in carrots, raisins and lemon peel. Blend in dry ingredients. Fold in beaten egg whites. Turn batter into a well-greased and lightly floured 2-quart ring mold. Bake at 350 degrees for 30 minutes or until done. Cool in pan on wire rack for 10 minutes. Turn out onto rack to finish cooling.
Pauline McConnell
Imperial County

COCKTAIL SQUARES

2 cans Ortega green chilies, drained and dried
1 pound sharp Cheddar cheese, shredded
6 eggs, beaten

Heat oven to 350 degrees. Scatter peppers evenly over well-greased 9-inch baking dish and cover with shredded cheese. Pour eggs over cheese. Bake about 30 minutes at 350 degrees until firm and let cool. To serve, cut in 1-inch squares and serve with food picks.
Ruth Taylor
Santa Barbara County

CORN CASSEROLE

½ pound sausage
1 large onion, chopped
½ cup celery, diced
1 can cream style corn
1 egg
½ cup milk
½ cup bread crumbs
Salt to taste

Preheat oven to 300 degrees. Fry sausage, then drain; save drippings and cook onions and celery in this. Mix corn and milk together; then add to sausage and add celery and onions. Put in casserole dish; spread ½ cup bread crumbs on top. Bake for 30-40 minutes.
Gertrude Duncan
Shasta County

UNCLE RICK'S FAVORITE PICKLES

7 cups sliced cucumbers
1 cup sliced onions
1 green pepper, diced
2 cups sugar
1 clove garlic, minced
1 tablespoon salt
2 tablespoons celery seed
1 cup white vinegar

Combine all ingredients in a large covered container. Refrigerate, shaking (or stirring vigorously) 3 times a day for 3 days. Pickles will keep in refrigerator for one year.
Cyndy Mickelsen
Sacramento County

EUROPEAN CUCUMBER PIE

4 medium-sized European cucumbers, unpeeled
10 saltine crackers
4 slices bacon
½ bell pepper, chopped
1 onion, chopped
1 tablespoon parsley, freshly snipped or dry crushed leaves
1 egg, slightly beaten
½ to 1 cup Cheddar cheese, grated

Preheat oven to 350 degrees. Boil cucumbers in salted water until tender. Drain, saving juice. Mash cucumbers. Crumble in the saltine crackers. Fry bacon slices, saving fat, and crumble into mixture. Sauté in bacon fat the bell pepper, onion and parsley. Add to cucumber mixture. Beat egg, add. Grate cheese. Add and stir mixture until blended. The mixture should be fairly juicy. If not, add some of the drained juice. Brush a 10-inch pie plate with olive oil. Spoon mixture into plate. Bake at 350 degrees for 30 minutes. Serve as a main dish or as a vegetable.
Helen Munyon
San Joaquin County

EGGPLANT AND TOMATO CASSEROLE

2 cups water
1 teaspoon salt
2 pounds eggplant, pared and cut into ¾-inch cubes
2 eggs, beaten
½ cup fine dry bread crumbs
1 teaspoon salt
2 tablespoons finely chopped onion
½ teaspoon dried basil leaves, crumbled
¼ teaspoon pepper
2 tablespoons butter or margarine
3 medium tomatoes, sliced
¼ teaspoon dried basil leaves, crumbled
¼ cup plus 2 tablespoons grated Parmesan cheese

Heat oven to 375 degrees. Heat water and 1 teaspoon salt to boiling. Add eggplant and cook until tender. Drain well and then mash eggplant slightly with fork or spoon. In a large bowl, mix eggs, bread crumbs, 1 teaspoon salt, onion, ½ teaspoon basil and ¼ teaspoon pepper. Add mashed eggplant and mix together. Spread mixture in greased shallow baking dish. Dot with 1 tablespoon butter. Arrange tomatoes in rows over eggplant. Sprinkle with ¼ teaspoon basil and a little salt and pepper. Dot with remaining butter; sprinkle with grated Parmesan cheese. Bake for 20 minutes in 375 degree oven.
Winifred Schut
San Diego County

MARY'S EGGPLANT PICKLES

2 pounds (8 cups) eggplant, cubed
1 cup celery, sliced thin
1 each red and green bell pepper, chopped
1 large onion, cut up
⅓ cup salt
Ice cubes
1¾ cups sugar
1¾ cups vinegar
1 tablespoon dill seed

Combine eggplant, celery, bell peppers and onion in large bowl. Sprinkle with salt and cover with ice cubes. Soak for 3 hours or overnight. Combine sugar, vinegar and dill seed and bring to a boil. Add drained vegetables and bring to a boil again. Put in hot jars and seal.
Mary Theiler
Calaveras County

EGGPLANT PARMIGIANA

1 eggplant, sliced into ¼-inch slices
2 eggs, slightly beaten
¼ teaspoon salt
½ cup flour
4 tablespoons vegetable oil (add more if needed) for frying
2 8-ounce cans marinara sauce
Parmesan cheese
Mozzarella cheese (optional)

Preheat oven to 350 degrees. Beat eggs with salt and set aside. Coat slices of eggplant in flour and dip each into beaten egg. Fry in medium-hot oil on both sides until golden brown, and drain on paper towels. Pour ½ cup marinara sauce in baking dish. Place layer of eggplant, sprinkle generously with grated Parmesan cheese and ½ cup sauce. Repeat layers ending with cheese and sauce. If desired, arrange slices of Mozzarella cheese between layers. Bake in 350 degree oven about 20 minutes.
Jo Bruno
San Bernardino County

EGGPLANT SOUFFLE

1 large or 2 small eggplant
2 tablespoons chopped onions
2 tablespoons chopped parsley
3 eggs, well beaten
1 tablespoon Worcestershire sauce
1 cup cracker crumbs
1 cup Tillamook cheese (shredded)
½ cup milk
1 2½-ounce can mushrooms (stems & pieces)
1 teaspoon salt
½ teaspoon pepper

Heat oven to 350 degrees. Peel and cube eggplant and boil 5 minutes only. Drain thoroughly and mash. Add all ingredients. Mix well. Put in greased baking dish. Bake for 1 hour at 350 degrees.
Lena Lanza
Solano County

HERB HONEY

1 8-ounce jar honey, clover or orange flavor
2 teaspoons freshly crushed herbs, such as lemon balm, mint, sage, thyme or rose petals

Warm the honey in a saucepan until thin. Put the two teaspoons of freshly crushed herbs into a container and pour the warm honey over the herbs. Let stand in a warm place for one week.
Note: Use fresh herbs, crushed fine, as they are more succulent.
Margaret Martin
Sonoma County

OVERNIGHT LETTUCE SALAD

1 head lettuce, chopped
1 head cauliflower, chopped, (use flowerets only)
2 cups mayonnaise or salad dressing
1 medium onion, chopped
1 pound bacon, fried crisp and crumbled
⅓ cup grated cheese
½ cup white sugar

Place in large bowl in order given. Cover lightly and chill overnight or for several hours in refrigerator. Toss just before serving. This recipe will serve sixteen. Use one fourth of the amounts for a family of four.
Ruby Jeskey
Plumas County

LOMPOC LETTUCE BREAD

1½ cups flour
2 teaspoons baking powder
½ teaspoon soda
½ teaspoon salt
⅛ teaspoon ground mace
⅓ teaspoon ground ginger
1 cup sugar
½ cup oil
1½ teaspoons grated lemon peel
1 cup finely chopped lettuce
2 eggs
½ cup chopped walnuts

Preheat oven to 375 degrees. Sift flour with baking powder, soda, salt, mace and ginger. Combine sugar, oil and lemon peel. Mix in flour mixture and chopped lettuce. Add eggs, one at a time, beating well after each addition. Stir in walnuts. Turn into greased and floured 9 x 5-inch loaf pan. Bake 55 minutes. Cool in pan, inverted on wire rack. Remove from pan and sprinkle with powdered sugar, if desired.
Christy Henning
Santa Barbara County

LAYERED SALAD

1 head of lettuce
1 cup celery, chopped
4 eggs, cooked and chopped
½ cup green pepper (optional)
8 slices cooked crisp bacon, chopped fine
2 cups mayonnaise with 2 tablespoons sugar
8 ounces grated cheese

Clean and dry lettuce. Then tear in small pieces. Layer in 9 x 13-inch pan. Then layer other ingredients on top. Spread mayonnaise on top of everything like frosting. Then top with 8 ounces grated cheese. Chill.
This can be made 24 hours ahead of time. It should set a few hours before serving. Also, you can grate a carrot through the salad if you like.
Geri Van Leeuwen
San Bernardino County

CREAMY PEA SALAD

1 20-ounce bag frozen peas, thawed or preferably 20 ounces fresh peas
5 to 6 strips of bacon, fried crisp and crumbled
¼ cup sour cream
¼ cup mayonnaise
1 teaspoon lemon juice
¼ teaspoon garlic powder
¼ teaspoon salt
¼ teaspoon pepper
¼ teaspoon flavor enhancer (Accent)
1¼ cups chopped cashew nuts

Mix all ingredients except nuts together, chill. Just before serving add 1¼ cups chopped cashew nuts. Makes 4 to 6 servings.
Christie Music
Kern County

SNOW PEA SALAD

2 2-pound bags of frozen peas
1 onion, chopped
1 bunch celery, chopped
1 pint sour cream
1 cup mayonnaise
¼ cup salad dressing
2 cans real bacon bits
2 1-pound cans cashew nuts

Rinse peas and thaw, but do not cook. Mix all ingredients together just before serving. Yield: 20 servings.
Note: Excellent for potlucks, school gatherings, and special parties.
Roselle Peters
Fresno County

EASY PEAS

2½ cups fresh early garden peas, blanched and chilled
4-6 slices bacon
1 cup sour cream
1 green onion, chopped
½ teaspoon salt
Pepper to taste

Prepare peas by blanching and chilling. Fry bacon till crisp and drain on absorbent toweling. When cool, crumble into small pieces. Place peas in medium-sized bowl and add the bacon, sour cream, chopped green onion, salt and pepper. Chill before serving. Serves 6.
Note: Frozen peas that are first thawed before adding to the other ingredients can be used in place of the fresh peas. Do not cook the peas. This can be served either as a cold vegetable or cold salad.
Jean Rosasco
Tuolumne County

"KOSHER" SAUSAGES—ISRAEL

¾ cup dried peas
¾ cup dried lima beans
1 bay leaf
1 egg
¾ cup bread crumbs
1 teaspoon salt
Dash pepper
½ teaspoon sage
1 tablespoon parsley, finely chopped
¼ cup Wesson oil
¾ cup cracker crumbs (about 18 soda crackers)
⅓ cup milk

In a large pan rinse and soak the dried peas and lima beans in enough cold water to cover. Add bay leaf and cook until done. Remove bay leaf and put through a blender or rub through a sieve until mixture forms a very thick purée. Measure out 2 cups of the purée into a medium-sized bowl and add the egg, bread crumbs, salt, pepper, sage, and parsley. Mix until well blended.

Heat the Wesson oil in a large skillet. Measure about 1 level tablespoon of the vegetable mixture and form in a ball, rolling first in the cracker crumbs, then the milk, and again in the crumbs. Fry in the heated oil until golden brown on each side. Makes about 18 3-inch "sausages."

Note: Serve with grilled tomatoes, either plain or with catsup. You can use any dried vegetable you wish, but the purée has to be thick—much like cold mashed potatoes! Fresh from Israel's Sabbath.

Pauline Bennett
Tuolumne County

CALIFORNIA WONDER PICKLED GREEN PEPPERS

3 pounds green peppers (7-9 large)
Boiling water
2½ cups apple cider flavored vinegar
2½ cups water
1¼ cups granulated sugar
8 cloves garlic, peeled
4 teaspoons salad oil
2 teaspoons salt

Wash peppers. Remove seed pods and white "seams". Cut lengthwise into ¾-inch strips. Place pepper strips in bowl; cover with boiling water. Let stand 5 minutes; drain. Combine vinegar, water and sugar in saucepan; simmer 5 minutes. Meanwhile, pack peppers in clean, hot jars. To each jar, add 2 cloves garlic, 1 teaspoon salad oil and ½ teaspoon salt. Pour hot liquid over peppers to within ½-inch of top making sure vinegar solution covers peppers. Cap each jar at once. Process 5 minutes in boiling-water bath. Makes 4 pints.

Beryl Nichols
Fresno County

SWEET PEPPER RELISH

¼ cup chili peppers, chopped
1½ cups sweet red or green bell peppers, chopped
6½ cups sugar
1½ cups cider vinegar
Few drops red or green food coloring depending on use of red or green bell peppers
1 bottle Certo pectin

Mix chopped chilies, chopped bell peppers, sugar, vinegar and food coloring in 4-quart pan. Bring to a brisk boil in high heat, stirring occasionally. Boil exactly three minutes. Pour in bottle of Certo quickly. Boil one minute more. Remove pan from heat. Let set for five minutes. Pour into hot jars and seal according to jelly jar directions or cover with melted paraffin. Yield: 8 8-ounce jars.
Note: This is a great accompaniment for meat such as beef roast or leg of lamb.
Cynthia Icardo
Kern County

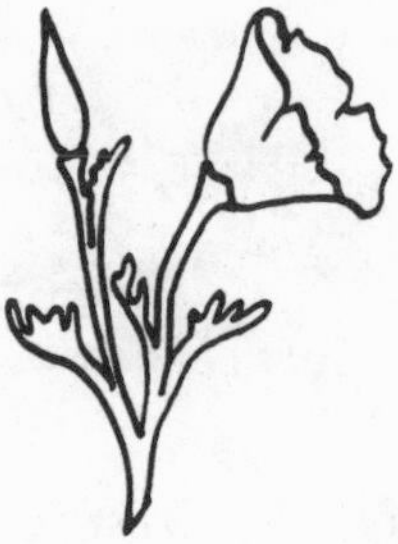

CROCK POT POTATO SOUP

6 potatoes, peeled and chopped
2 onions, chopped
1 carrot, grated
1 stalk celery, chopped
4 chicken bouillon cubes
1 tablespoon parsley flakes
5 cups water
Salt
Pepper
⅓ cup butter
1 13-ounce can evaporated milk

Put all ingredients except milk in crock pot and cook on low 10-12 hours (high, 3-4 hours). Approximately one hour before soup will be served, remove from crock pot and blend in blender. Put it back in the crock pot. Add 1 13-ounce can evaporated milk and heat til correct temperature.
Louise Correia
Fresno County

CHEESE POTATO CASSEROLE

½ cup butter, melted
1 can cream of chicken soup
1 8-ounce carton sour cream
1 teaspoon salt
¼ teaspoon pepper
½ cup onion, diced
1 2-pound package frozen Ore-Ida hash browns
8 ounces grated Cheddar cheese

Preheat oven to 350 degrees. Combine first six ingredients. Add these to the Ore-Ida hash browns. Sprinkle top with grated Cheddar cheese. (As an added extra you may top with 2 cups crushed corn flakes in ¼ cup melted butter, but it is not necessary.) Bake, uncovered, 45 minutes to 1 hour.

Geri Van Leeuwen
San Bernardino County

HOLIDAY POTATO BAKE

4 pounds potatoes, boiled with skins on
1 cup onion, chopped
½ cup butter
1 10½-ounce can cream of celery soup
1 pint dairy sour cream
1½ cups shredded Cheddar cheese
½ cup crushed corn flakes
3 tablespoons melted butter

Remove skins from potatoes and shred into a bowl. Sautée onions in ¼ cup of butter. Stir in soup and sour cream. Pour over potatoes and cheese and mix well. Turn in to greased 13 x 9 x 2-inch baking dish, cover and refrigerate overnight. Sprinkle with corn flakes and drizzle with 3 tablespoons of melted butter. Bake in 350 degree oven 1 hour. Garnish with pimiento and parsley if desired. This can be made without refrigerating overnight.

Rita Bradley
Sierra County

OLD FASHIONED POTATO CAKE

¾ cup butter
2 cups sugar
4 eggs, separated
4 squares Bakers chocolate, melted
1½ cups mashed potatoes
½ cup milk
2 cups flour
1 teaspoon nutmeg
1 teaspoon cinnamon
¼ teaspoon cloves
½ teaspoon salt
2½ teaspoons baking powder
1 cup chopped nuts
1 cup raisins

Preheat oven to 350 degrees, and place the rack in the middle of the oven. Cream butter and sugar; add egg yolks and beat well, then add melted chocolate. Add potatoes and milk. Sift the flour, spices, salt and baking powder. Add this to the other ingredients. If using a mixer, remove beaters at this point and stir in the nuts and raisins. Beat the egg whites until stiff and dry peaks form, then fold them into the cake batter. Bake in a 9 x 13 x 2-inch pan for 1 hour. Cool in pan for 10 minutes, then turn out on rack. Frost with your favorite frosting. Will keep in a cool place for a long time.
Erma Schluter
Modoc County

BLUE CHEESE POTATO SALAD

Five medium size potatoes
¾ cup crumbled blue cheese
1 cup chopped celery
2 tablespoons chopped chives or green onions
¾ cup sour cream
¾ cup mayonnaise
3 tablespoons vinegar
1 tablespoon sugar
1 teaspoon salt
½ teaspoon pepper

Cook potatoes, peel and dice. Combine potatoes, cheese, celery, chives, or onions; mix well. Combine sour cream and mayonnaise. Dissolve sugar in vinegar. Add to the sour cream and mayonnaise mixture and then add to the potatoes, celery and cheese. Season with salt and pepper. Mix well, chill. Yield: 4-5 servings.
Olive Beamer
Trinity County

PUMPKIN CAKE ROLL

⅔ cup pumpkin (or banana squash)
3 eggs
1 cup sugar
1 teaspoon lemon juice
¾ cup flour
1 teaspoon baking powder
2 teaspoons cinnamon
1 teaspoon ginger
½ teaspoon salt
½ teaspoon nutmeg
1 cup finely chopped walnuts
½ cup powdered sugar

Prepare pumpkin or banana squash by washing, peeling, cutting into small pieces, and boiling in enough water to cover until done. Drain off water and run through a ricer or blender until fine consistency, measuring ⅔ cup for the pumpkin cake. Set aside to cool. Any remainder can be frozen. Preheat oven to 375 degrees. Beat eggs on high speed for 5 minutes, gradually adding sugar the last 2 minutes. Stir in prepared pumpkin and lemon juice. Sift together flour, baking powder, cinnamon, ginger, salt and nutmeg and add to pumpkin mixture. Spread in a greased and floured 15 x 10 x ½-inch pan. Top with finely chopped walnuts and bake for 15 minutes. Turn out on a cloth sprinkled with the ½ cup powdered sugar. Roll towel and cake together and let cool.

Filling:

1 cup powdered sugar
2 3-ounce packages cream cheese
4 tablespoons butter or margarine
1 teaspoon vanilla

Combine the cup of powdered sugar, cream cheese, butter or margarine and vanilla and beat until creamy. Unroll cake and spread with filling and re-roll and chill. Slice like a jelly roll to serve. Serves 8-10.
Note: Can use canned pumpkin but it is not so tasty. Also, this can be frozen.

Myrtle Sinclair
Stanislaus County

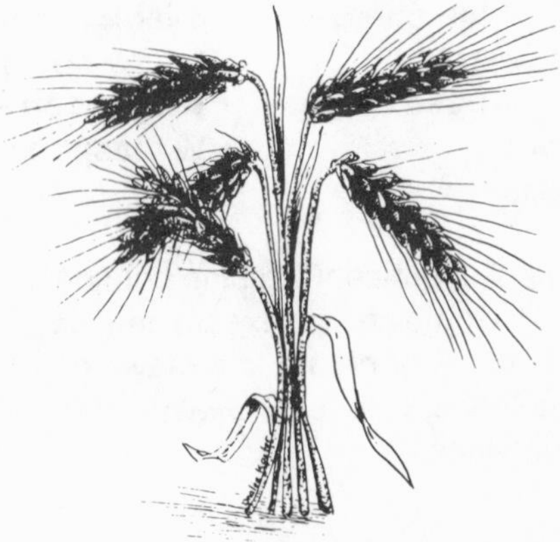

PUMPKIN BREAD

3½ cups flour
2 teaspoons soda
½ teaspoon salt
½ teaspoon baking powder
1 teaspoon cinnamon
1 teaspoon cloves
1 teaspoon nutmeg
3 cups sugar
4 eggs, beaten
1 16-ounce can pumpkin
1 cup salad oil
⅔ cup water
1 cup walnuts, chopped

Preheat oven to 325 degrees. Sift together flour, soda, salt, baking powder, cinnamon, cloves and nutmeg. Combine sugar, eggs, pumpkin, salad oil and water. Add to dry ingredients and mix well. Add nuts. Pour into two greased 8½ x 4½-inch loaf pans. Bake 1 hour.
Fleeta Hudson
San Bernardino County

FROZEN PUMPKIN PIE

1 one-pound can pumpkin
1½ cups sugar
½ teaspoon salt
1 teaspoon cinnamon
¼ teaspoon nutmeg
¼ teaspoon cloves
¼ teaspoon ginger
3 tablespoons rum
1½ cups whipping cream
1 baked 9-inch pastry shell

Blend pumpkin, sugar, salt, spices and rum. Whip cream until stiff. Fold two thirds of the whipped cream into the pumpkin mixture. Turn into pastry shell. Freeze until firm. Top with remaining whipped cream and return to freezer. Thaw slightly before serving.
Christine Van Steyn
Sacramento County

PUMPKIN CRUNCH COOKIES

½ cup butter
1¼ cups sugar
2 eggs
1½ cups pumpkin
2 cups flour
½ cup wheat germ
2 teaspoons baking powder
1 teaspoon baking soda
1 teaspoon cinnamon
½ teaspoon salt
1 cup raisins
½ cup chopped walnuts

Preheat oven to 400 degrees. Mix all ingredients well. Drop by spoonfuls on cookie sheet. Bake for 15 minutes. Makes about 50 cookies. Because these cookies are so moist, they have a very short storage life so freeze extra.

Candy Jones
San Bernardino County

OATMEAL PUMPKIN CAKE

1 large can pumpkin
1 13-ounce can evaporated milk
3 eggs, slightly beaten
⅔ cup sugar
1½ teaspoons cinnamon
½ teaspoon ginger
½ teaspoon nutmeg
½ teaspoon cloves
½ teaspoon salt
1 package yellow cake mix
1 cup quick cooking oats
1 cup nuts, chopped
¾ cup margarine, melted

Preheat oven to 350 degrees. Combine pumpkin, milk, eggs, and spices. Pour into greased 9 x 13-inch pan. Sprinkle 1 package yellow cake mix, which you have added 1 cup quick cooking oats and 1 cup chopped nuts to, over top of filling. Melt margarine and drizzle over top. Bake for 50 minutes or until set. Serve with whipped cream, if desired. Serves 15 to 20.

Betty Jo Sharrett
Shasta County

CREAMY SPINACH PIE

1 3-ounce package cream cheese
1 cup half and half
½ cup soft bread crumbs, lightly packed
¼ cup Parmesan cheese
2 eggs, slightly beaten
1 cup cooked spinach, finely chopped
4 tablespoons butter
1 large onion, finely chopped
½ pound mushrooms, sliced
1 teaspoon tarragon
¾ teaspoon salt
Unbaked pie shell, 9-10-inch

Preheat oven to 400 degrees. Mash cream cheese and gradually add half and half. Add bread crumbs, Parmesan cheese and eggs to cream mixture. Beat with rotary beater to break up bread pieces. Stir in spinach. Melt butter, cook onion and mushrooms until lightly browned, stirring frequently. Add tarragon when vegetables are soft. Blend hot vegetables with spinach mixture. Salt to taste. Pour into pastry shell. Bake on lowest rack of oven for 25 minutes, or until crust is well browned. Let stand 10 minutes. Serve hot or cold. Serves 6-8.
Dolores Cerro
Kern County

SESAME-SPINACH SALAD

2 tablespoons sesame seeds
⅓ cup vegetable oil
¼ cup lemon juice
2 tablespoons soy sauce
1 teaspoon salt
⅛ teaspoon Tabasco sauce
½ pound fresh mushrooms, thinly sliced
1 can (6 to 8½-ounce) water chestnuts, drained and sliced
1 package fresh spinach

Heat sesame seeds in large sauce pan over medium heat until toasted. Remove from heat. Add oil, lemon juice, soy sauce, salt and Tabasco. Stir in mushrooms and chestnuts. Cover. Chill. Rinse and drain spinach, tear into bite-size pieces. Toss with mixture just before serving.
Bill Pierce
Marin County

SPINACH SALAD EXTRAORDINAIRE

1 large bunch spinach
1 medium tart apple
4 slices crisp bacon
¼ cup salad oil
½ orange, juiced
½ teaspoon salt
Dash of pepper
¼ teaspoon dry mustard
⅛ teaspoon Tabasco sauce
1 teaspoon lemon juice (optional)

Wash spinach well, drain, and pat dry. Tear into bite-size pieces. Add finely-diced apples and crumbled bacon. Refrigerate until ready to serve. In small bowl, combine salad oil, orange juice, lemon juice, and seasonings. Beat with a fork or wire whip until frothy and mix with spinach, apple and bacon just before serving. Serves 4.
Elinor Heath Clow
Mendocino County

SPINACH SUPREME

2 10-ounce packages frozen chopped spinach
1 heaping teaspoon instant chicken bouillon crystals
1 heaping teaspoon instant onion
½ cup sour cream
½ cup white sauce (canned or make your own)
Grated Cheddar cheese (optional)

Preheat oven to 350 degrees. Cook spinach as directed on package. Drain very well. Combine spinach and all other ingredients except cheese and place in casserole. Sprinkle cheese over top and bake for 20 minutes. Note: Also excellent with broccoli in place of spinach.
Leatrice Moxon
Humboldt County

SUMMERTIME BAKED SQUASH

2 pounds summer squash—any kind
1 clove garlic, or more
⅓ to ½ cup yellow cheese, shredded
8 soda crackers, crushed
2 eggs
4 tablespoons cooking oil, divided
1 teaspoon parsley flakes
Salt to taste
Monosodium glutamate
Parmesan cheese

Preheat oven to 375 degrees. Cook squash and garlic together and mash. Add cheese and cracker crumbs to hot mixture. Beat in eggs. Add 2 tablespoons oil, parsley, salt and monosodium glutamate. Oil 9 x 13-inch pan with remaining 2 tablespoons of oil. Pour in squash mixture and spoon any oil that comes up in the corners or sides of the pan over squash. Sprinkle with Parmesan cheese. Bake 40 to 45 minutes or until browned.
Leora Tower
Calaveras County

CHEESE STUFFED SQUASH

6 summer squash (yellow crookneck or zucchini)
1 small onion, minced
2 tablespoons butter or margarine
½ teaspoon salt
¼ teaspoon pepper
1 cup fine bread crumbs
½ cup shredded Cheddar cheese
3 slices bacon, partially cooked

Preheat oven to 400 degrees. Cut off stem ends of squash. Cook squash in 1-inch of simmering salted water until barely tender, about 8 to 10 minutes. Cool. Cut squash in half lengthwise. Scoop out the pulp, leaving the shells about ¼-inch thick. Cook onion in butter until tender but not browned. Add squash pulp, salt, pepper and crumbs. Mix well and spoon into squash shells. Arrange in a shallow baking dish and top with the cheese. Cut bacon strips in halves and put a piece on top of each squash. Bake for 15 minutes or until browned. Makes 6 servings.
Elayne Doran
Imperial County

SUPER SQUASH

1 13-ounce can evaporated milk
3½ cups banana squash, steamed and mashed (or one can pumpkin)
4 eggs
½ cup white sugar
½ cup brown sugar
2 teaspoons pumpkin pie spice
Pinch of salt
1 box yellow cake mix
¾ cup butter
1 cup chopped walnuts

Preheat oven to 350 degrees. Pour canned milk into blender; add squash, eggs, sugar, spices and salt. Beat until smooth. Pour into buttered pan, 9 x 13 x 2-inch. Sprinkle dry cake mix over squash, cut butter into thin slices and distribute evenly over entire surface. Sprinkle walnuts evenly over all. Bake for 45-50 minutes. Cool and slice. Serve with whipped cream if desired.

Betty Middlecamp
San Luis Obispo County

TWO SQUASH PIES

2 cups banana squash, cooked and mashed
¾ cup sugar
2 eggs, well beaten
½ teaspoon cinnamon
½ teaspoon salt
½ teaspoon nutmeg
¼ teaspoon ginger
2 cups milk
2 9-inch unbaked pastry shells

Preheat oven to 450 degrees. Mix squash, sugar, eggs, cinnamon, salt, nutmeg, and ginger. Beat with an egg beater. Add the milk and beat until well mixed. Pour into two 9-inch shells. Bake at 450 degrees for ten minutes and then turn heat down to 325 degrees for 30 to 40 minutes. Bake until knife inserted in the middle comes out clean.

Helen Barlogio
San Luis Obispo County

PICKLED SUGAR BEETS

1 young sugar beet
4 cups sugar
1 cup white vinegar
1 cup water
1 teaspoon ground cloves
1 teaspoon ground allspice
1 teaspoon ground cinnamon

Peel sugar beet, cut into desired pieces (enough to make 2 quarts) and cook until tender. Drain. Put cloves, allspice and cinnamon in small bag, tie securely, and combine with sugar, vinegar and water. Bring to a boil and pour over beets. Let set overnight. Boil syrup and beets for 5 minutes and seal in hot, sterilized jars.

Leora Tower
Calaveras County

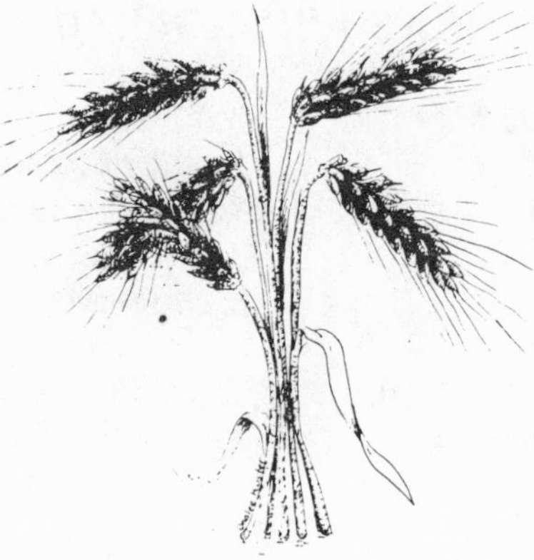

TOMATO-CHEESE DIP

1 pound Velveeta cheese
1 16-ounce can whole tomatoes, drained
1 4-ounce whole Ortega green chilies, drained

Melt cheese in double boiler or over very slow fire. Chop and seed the tomatoes. Chop half or all of the green chili peppers, according to taste. Add ingredients to cheese, cook slowly and stir until smooth. Pour into a bowl and return to room temperature. Use heavy corn chips for dipping. Refrigerate any leftover dip and use as sandwich spread.

Submitted by: California Tomato Research Institute, Inc.

GAZPACHO

4 large cucumbers, diced and drained well
¼ cup salt
1½ quarts tomatoes, diced
4 ounces pimientos, diced
6 large green onions, sliced
¼ cup vinegar
¼ cup olive oil
1 clove garlic
¾ tablespoon sugar
⅛ teaspoon cumin
Salt and pepper to taste
2 cans consomme
1 can water

Combine first five ingredients. In a bowl, mix the vinegar, oil, garlic, sugar, cumin, salt and pepper and let stand for a while. Add the consomme and water to the vegetables. Add the dressing and chill overnight. Stir before serving. You may like it thinned with more water. Garnish with chives.
Josie Steffanic
Plumas County

CRAB ASPIC SALAD

2 envelopes Knox gelatin
½ cup cold water
½ cup weak vinegar
1 tablespoon sugar
1 teaspoon salt
2 tablespoons lemon juice
1 pint of tomatoes, strained
1 6-ounce can crab meat, drained
2 cups celery, chopped

Combine first 7 ingredients in a saucepan. Bring to a boil; let cool. Add crab meat and celery. Pour into mold and chill in refrigerator.
Gladys Younger
Yolo County

HERBED TOMATO SALAD

6 firm ripe tomatoes
⅛ teaspoon instant minced garlic
½ teaspoon salt
½ teaspoon pepper
½ teaspoon oregano leaves
½ teaspoon basil leaves
2 tablespoons cider vinegar
2 tablespoons olive oil

Wash tomatoes; do *not* peel. Cut into 1-inch cubes. Mix with garlic, salt, pepper, oregano leaves, basil leaves, vinegar, and oil. Chill 30 minutes and serve as salad, with or without lettuce. Serves 6.
Sandy Harlan
Yolo County

MYSTERY SALAD

3 #303 cans stewed tomatoes
6 dashes Tabasco sauce
3 3-ounce packages wild raspberry jello
1½ cups boiling water
Sour cream
Salt
Horseradish (about 1 teaspoon)

Crush tomatoes in juice and add Tabasco sauce. Dissolve jello in boiling water. When cool, combine with tomato mixture. Refrigerate. When set, serve with sour cream seasoned with salt and horseradish.
Nell Hughes
San Luis Obispo County

SPICED GREEN TOMATO PICKLES

4 quarts green tomatoes (24-28)
2 cups onion, sliced
½ cup salt
2 green peppers, finely chopped
3 cups white or brown sugar
1 quart vinegar
2½ teaspoons mustard seed
2 tablespoons whole cloves
2 tablespoons allspice
3 sticks cinnamon

Wash all vegetables, cut tomatoes into slices or quarters, sprinkle alternate layers of tomatoes and onions with salt, cover and let set overnight. In morning drain real well, put into a kettle, add peppers, sugar and spices which have been tied in a bag. Add enough vinegar to cover mixture, bring to a boil, and simmer 15 minutes or until vegetables are tender. Pack into hot, sterilized jars. Cover with liquid. Seal. Process 5 minutes in boiling water bath.
Violet Rose
San Luis Obispo County

WINTER TOMATO SOUP

½ cup celery, chopped
2 tablespoons butter or bacon drippings
1 1-pound can stewed tomatoes
1 10½-ounce can chicken broth
½ cup dry white dinner wine
3 tablespoons green onions, chopped
1 tablespoon lemon juice
1 tablespoon cornstarch
½ cup water
¼ teaspoon curry powder

Sauté celery in butter or drippings, about five minutes. Add tomatoes, chicken broth, wine, onions and lemon juice. Simmer for 15 to 20 minutes. Add water to which the cornstarch and curry powder have been blended and cook for five minutes longer. Garnish with cheese croutons if desired. Serves four.

Olive Beamer
Trinity County

SPICED TOMATO-PINEAPPLE JAM

2 cups prepared tomatoes (about 1¾ pounds ripe tomatoes)
5½ cups sugar
1 box Sure-Jell fruit pectin
1 13½-ounce can crushed pineapple
½ teaspoon ground cinnamon
½ teaspoon ground allspice
¼ teaspoon ground cloves

Scald, peel, and chop about 1¾ pounds fully ripe tomatoes. Bring to a boil over high heat; then simmer ten minutes. Remove from heat. Measure two cups into a large saucepan. Measure sugar; set aside. Add Sure-Jell fruit pectin, pineapple and spices to the tomatoes; mix well. Place over high heat; stir until mixture comes to a hard boil. At once stir in sugar. Bring to a full rolling boil and boil hard for one minute, stirring constantly. Remove from heat. Skim off foam, then stir and skim for 5 minutes. Ladle into glasses. Seal. Makes about 8 medium glasses.

Charlotte Davis
Siskiyou County

THE CALIFORNIA TOMATO TOUCH

3 pounds chicken, cut in pieces
Salt and pepper
¼ cup olive oil
2 large yellow globe onions, sliced
1 large clove garlic, finely chopped
2 small bell peppers—one green, one red, cut in strips
Dash of Fines Herbs
1 cup ham, chopped
2 #303 (1-pound) cans whole tomatoes, drained and cut up
2 ounces Brandy
4 tablespoons red currant jelly

Preheat oven to 300 degrees. Pat chicken dry; salt and pepper. Brown chicken in olive oil in skillet, remove and set aside. Add onions, garlic, peppers, Fines Herbs and ham. Stir frequently for 10 minutes. Now, add tomatoes. Cook long enough to thicken to a heavy sauce. Then, put chicken, Brandy and red currant jelly into a casserole. Add thickened sauce, cover casserole tightly and heat in oven for 1 hour. Serve with rice.
California Tomato Research Institute, Inc.

HEAVENLY HAMBURGERS

¼ cup chopped onion
¼ cup chopped green pepper (optional)
¼ cup chopped celery
2 tablespoons oil
1 pound hamburger
6 slices American cheese
2 cups narrow egg noodles (crushed)
1 large can (28-ounce can) whole tomatoes
½ teaspoon salt
¼ cup water

In a large skillet sauté onion and green pepper in oil; add hamburger and brown, drain and leave in skillet. Layer over hamburger: celery, cheese slices overlapping, add noodles. Then pour can of whole tomatoes over all ingredients and sprinkle with salt. If needed add more water and on low heat cook slowly without stirring for 30 minutes or until noodles are done. Serves 6.
Fern Taylor
Kings County

JUDY'S "CLARA" (ELECTRIC SKILLET)

½ pound link sausage
½ pound lean ground beef
½ cup chopped celery
½ cup chopped onion
1 chopped green pepper
1 teaspoon salt
1 tablespoon sugar
1 tablespoon Worcestershire sauce
1 4-ounce can mushrooms, stems and pieces
1 28-ounce can California whole tomatoes
½ cup elbow spaghetti

Cut sausage in ½-inch pieces and cook until brown. Add ground beef and cook through. Pour off fat. Add vegetables and spices. Use blender to coarsely chop tomatoes in their juice, add to other ingredients and bring to a boil. Add spaghetti, reduce heat to simmer, cover and cook 15 minutes. Let stand, covered, 10 minutes before serving. Serves 4 to 6.
Note: Be sure to use *elbow spaghetti!* Results are disappointing if elbow macaroni is used. Also, flavor is enhanced if made early in the day and reheated. Fresh tomatoes can be used in the summertime in place of canned.
Kathie Merwin
Yolo County

TOMATO BUDGET BAKE

1 large globe onion
1 pound ground lean beef
6 slices bacon
1 10-ounce can tomato soup
1 10-ounce can cream of mushroom soup
¼ cup Marsala wine
½ cup water
3 cups cooked elbow macaroni
½ cup shredded Cheddar cheese

Preheat oven to 325 degrees. Slice and brown onions lightly. Remove from skillet. Brown lean ground beef, drain and remove. Fry and then chop bacon. Blend soups, water and wine. Add all previous ingredients to cooked macaroni and place in uncovered casserole. Sprinkle cheese on top. Bake about one hour or until bubbly and nicely browned on top. Serves 6.
California Tomato Research Institute, Inc.

CRUNCHY FRIED TOMATOES

4 firm ripe or green medium tomatoes
1 egg, beaten
1 cup dry bread crumbs
⅓ cup butter or margarine
Salt and pepper

Cut tomatoes into ¾-inch slices. Dip into egg and then into crumbs. Melt butter in large skillet. Add tomato slices and cook until golden brown on each side. Season to taste with salt and pepper. Serves 4.
Elaine Timothy
Yolo County

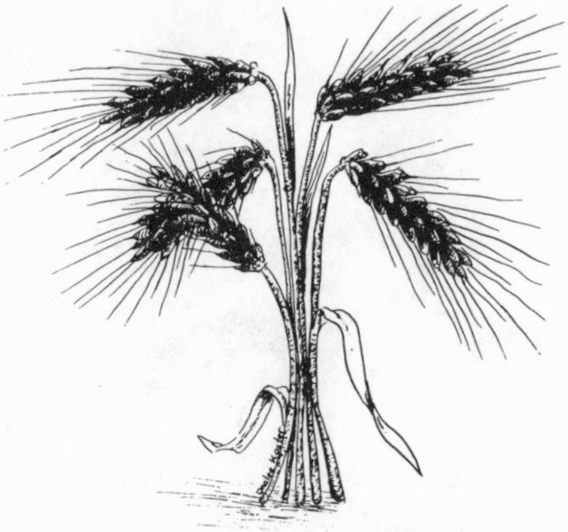

MARINARA SAUCE

1 medium onion, chopped fine
1 clove garlic, chopped fine
½ cup olive oil
1 tablespoon dried parsley
1 teaspoon dried basil
½ teaspoon dried oregano
Salt and pepper to taste
2 cans (#2½) tomatoes, chopped fine
1 can (#2½) tomato purée

Sauté onion in oil until clear. Add garlic and dry seasonings. Turn off heat and let stand at least 5 minutes or longer, so flavors will permeate oil. Turn on heat again, add tomatoes, purée, salt and pepper. When mixture comes to a boil, lower heat to simmer. Cover and allow to cook slowly for 2 hours, stirring occasionally. This is the basic sauce used in a variety of Italian recipes. A meat sauce can be made by sautéeing the meat of your choice and adding it to the sauce. This sauce freezes beautifully. After it cools, put it in containers with date on it.
Jo Bruno
San Bernardino County

ZUCCHINI HORS D'OEUVRES

3 cups unpeeled zucchini, shredded
1 cup Bisquick
½ cup Parmesan cheese
½ cup oil
4 eggs, beaten
½ teaspoon oregano
½ teaspoon parsley
½ teaspoon salt
¼ teaspoon pepper

Preheat oven to 350 degrees. Mix all ingredients together. Put in greased miniature muffin tins or 9 x 12-inch greased pan. Bake for 30 minutes. Cool and cut into squares or turn out of muffin tins when cooled.
Note: May be frozen and reheated to serve warm.
Margaret Vandegrift
San Luis Obispo County

EXOTIC ZUCCHINI SOUP

2 zucchini (large ones should be seeded), approximately 6-8 inches long
1 14½-ounce can chicken broth or equivalent home-made
1 onion, chopped
3 strips bacon (do not pre-cook), cut in 1-inch pieces
Basil, fresh or dried, to taste
Pepper and salt to taste

Cut zucchini in 2-inch pieces into saucepan. Add broth, onion, and 3 strips of bacon. Bring to a boil and cook until zucchini is tender. Cool. When cool enough to put in liquifier blender, blend until all is smooth and liquid. Reheat, adding basil, salt and pepper, if desired. Serves 4.
Frances Gentry
Sutter County

SUMMERTIME ZUCCHINI LASAGNA

½ pound mushrooms
1 pound Mozzarella cheese, fresh, grated medium
1 small container small curd cottage cheese
3 eggs, beaten
2 teaspoons parsley flakes
½ cup dry bread crumbs
½ cup grated Parmesan or Romano cheese
Dash of onion salt
6 cups unpeeled zucchini, sliced
2 small garlic cloves
Margarine
1½ pounds lean ground beef
1 16-ounce can herb-seasoned tomato sauce
1 10½-ounce can condensed tomato soup, undiluted
2 teaspoons salt
½ teaspoon oregano
½ teaspoon basil

Preheat oven to 350 degrees. Wash and slice mushrooms, set aside. Grate Mozzarella cheese, return to refrigerator. Blend together cottage cheese, eggs and parsley flakes. Return bowl to refrigerator. Mix together bread crumbs and dry Parmesan cheese. Add dash of onion salt. Set aside. Steam zucchini over boiling water about 5 minutes. Drain immediately. Cool. Slice garlic cloves very thin and brown in large skillet in small amount of margarine. Make sure to coat the entire surface of skillet with this mixture. Remove garlic, discard. Add ground beef and brown well. Skim off any excess grease. Remove from heat. Add tomato sauce, soup, salt, oregano and basil to meat mixture. ASSEMBLY: Use two 8-inch square baking dishes. Layer the mixtures as follows: First, make one layer of zucchini slices, slightly overlapped. Then sprinkle about ¼ of bread crumb mixture lightly over zucchini. (Use ¼ in second dish also.) Spoon in a layer of cottage cheese/egg mixture (about ½-inch thick). Use about ½ the mixture in each dish. Lay in fresh mushrooms to cover third layer. Do not overlap. Spoon in ¼ of beef and sauce mixture in each dish, completely covering the mushrooms. Lay in a second layer of zucchini, overlapping slightly. Sprinkle with another one fourth of bread crumb mix. Repeat a layer of beef and sauce mix. Liberally coat top of each baking dish with grated Mozzarella. Set baking dishes in oven on foil to catch possible boil-over. Bake 25-35 minutes. Serve immediately with salad, red wine and French bread. Makes 8-12 servings.

Liese Wiegand
Sonoma County

ZUCCHINI PICKLE CRISPS

4 quarts unpeeled zucchini, thinly sliced
6 medium white onions, sliced
2 green peppers, sliced
3 cloves garlic
½ cup pickling salt
Cracked ice
5 cups sugar
3 cups cider vinegar
2 tablespoons mustard seed
1½ teaspoons turmeric
1½ teaspoons celery seed

Combine zucchini, onions, green pepper, garlic and salt. Cover with cracked ice; mix well. Let stand for about 3 hours; drain well. Remove garlic. Combine remaining ingredients; pour over zucchini mixture. Bring to a boil. Pack zucchini and liquid into hot jars, leaving ½-inch headspace. Adjust lids. Process in boiling water bath 5 minutes. Makes 8 pints.
Jean L. Brady
Sonoma County

ZUCCHINI QUICHE

1½ pounds zucchini
1 teaspoon salt
8 slices bacon, quartered
1 9-inch unbaked pie shell
½ pound natural Swiss cheese, grated
4 eggs
1½ cups light cream
⅛ teaspoon nutmeg
⅛ teaspoon salt
Dash of pepper

Preheat oven to 375 degrees. Wash zucchini, trim ends, slice into rounds ¼-inch thick. In large skillet, bring 1 cup of water to boil. Add salt and zucchini. Cover and boil for three minutes. Drain well. Sauté bacon until crisp. Drain. Sprinkle bottom of pie shell with bacon and grated cheese. Arrange half of the zucchini over cheese. Beat together the eggs, cream, nutmeg, salt and pepper. Pour cream mixture over mixture in pie shell, then arrange remaining zucchini on top. Bake 40 minutes or until puffy and golden. Yield: 6 servings.
Susan Koon
Imperial County

CALIFORNIA GARDEN CASSEROLE

6-8 zucchini
¼ cup butter or margarine
1 cup sour cream
1 10¾-ounce can cream of chicken soup (undiluted)
1 cup carrots, shredded
½ cup butter or margarine
1 box stove top dressing, chicken flavor

Preheat oven to 325 degrees. Slice zucchini and sauté in ¼ cup butter about 15 minutes, turning gently. Take off burner and add sour cream, chicken soup and carrots. In another pan melt 1 cube butter and add stove top dressing. Mix well. Layer ½ dressing in bottom of casserole. Layer zucchini mixture over dressing and top with rest of dressing. Bake in oven for 25 to 30 minutes.
Onalee Koster
San Joaquin County

CALIFORNIA ZUCCHINI CASSEROLE

7-8 medium zucchini, cut ¼-inch thick
8 slices bacon, diced
1 large onion, chopped
1 large clove garlic, minced
4 slices bread, cubed
2 cups shredded Cheddar cheese
1 teaspoon salt
1 teaspoon Italian seasoning
1 8-ounce can tomato sauce
¼ cup grated Parmesan cheese

Preheat oven to 350 degrees. Cook zucchini in water until crisp tender. Drain. Cook bacon until crisp. Add onion and garlic and cook until tender. Drain grease. Mix in remaining ingredients except Parmesan. Add cooked zucchini and place in 13 x 9-inch casserole. Bake for 25 minutes. Makes 10 to 12 servings.
Sonja Medearis
Imperial County

EASY ZUCCHINI CASSEROLE

3 medium zucchini, sliced
2 cups whole kernel corn
2 cups celery, chopped
½ cup oil
1 cup onion, chopped
2 large cloves garlic, chopped
½ cup parsley
3 eggs, beaten
⅛ teaspoon oregano
3 cups grated cheese
½ cup bread crumbs

Preheat oven to 350 degrees. Mix ingredients in order given and pour into greased 9 x 13-inch casserole. Grated cheese and crumbs may be reserved and sprinkle over top if desired. Bake about 30 minutes or until set. Makes 10 to 12 servings.
Madeleine Robinson
Fresno County

GOLD AND GREEN ZUCCHINI CASSEROLE

2 pounds zucchini
½ teaspoon salt
½ cup water
2 eggs, beaten
¼ teaspoon salt
⅛ teaspoon pepper
1 small onion, grated
1 can whole kernel corn, drained
½ pound mild Cheddar cheese, grated

Preheat oven to 350 degrees. Wash zucchini, slice into ¼-inch slices. Boil in salted water 10 minutes. Drain well, mash. Mix eggs, salt, pepper and onion. Combine zucchini with egg mixture, corn and ½ of the cheese. Pour into oiled 2-quart casserole dish. Top with remaining cheese. Bake for 35 minutes or until set.
Lorraine Valine
Sacramento County

HARVEST CASSEROLE

2 tablespoons cornstarch
1½ cups milk
¼ cup margarine
1 teaspoon salt
¼ teaspoon pepper
6 carrots
3 small zucchini
1 10-ounce package frozen peas & carrots
Basil
1 cup croutons

Preheat oven to 350 degrees. Prepare sauce using cornstarch, milk, margarine, salt and pepper. Cook carrots, cut in strips, in salted water five minutes. Drain. In a one-quart shallow baking dish, mix carrots, 3 small zucchini, sliced, and one package frozen peas & carrots. Pour sauce over. Sprinkle with 1 teaspoon dried basil. Bake 25 minutes. Top with 1 cup croutons. Serves 4-6.
Judy Sealock
Shasta County

SAN LUIS OBISPO ZUCCHINI

2½ pounds zucchini (6 medium or 3 large), diced or chopped
1 egg, beaten
¼ cup half and half
Salt and pepper
Few drops Tabasco sauce (optional)
5 soda crackers, crushed
⅓ pound Cheddar cheese (1 cup grated coarsely)
¼ pound bacon, cooked crisp and crumbled

Preheat oven to 300 degrees. Steam chopped zucchini for 5 minutes until barely tender. Drain, pressing out as much water as possible. Mix beaten eggs, half & half, salt, pepper, and Tabasco sauce to taste in a bowl. Add crackers and cheese; mix well. Add this egg mixture to zucchini and put into a greased casserole. Bake for 25 minutes. Sprinkle crumbled bacon over casserole the last 10 minutes. Serves 6.
Inez Gianolini
San Luis Obispo County

ZIGGY ZUCCHINI

2 pounds zucchini, diced
1 medium onion, chopped
1 medium green pepper, chopped
½ pound fresh mushrooms, or 1 medium can
2 tablespoons butter
½ pound grated Cheddar cheese
1½ cups bread crumbs
2 tablespoons butter

Preheat oven to 350 degrees. Sauté onion, pepper and mushrooms in first 2 tablespoons butter. Butter a medium casserole, arrange a layer of diced zucchini, follow with a layer of onion-pepper-mushroom mix, then layer with half of the grated cheese. Repeat. Top with bread crumbs, browned in second two tablespoons of butter. Bake for 45 minutes.
Betty Middlecamp
San Luis Obispo County

ZUCCHINI STUFFING CASSEROLE

6 medium-sized zucchini, sliced ½-inch thick
1 cup carrots, shredded
½ cup onions, chopped
6 tablespoons margarine
1 can cream of chicken soup
½ cup sour cream
2½ cups herbed stuffing cubes

Preheat oven to 350 degrees. Cook zucchini in boiling, salted water until tender and drain. Cook carrots and onions in margarine until tender. Stir in soup, sour cream, and stuffing cubes. Gently stir in zucchini. Bake in 1½-quart casserole for 40 minutes. Serves 6 to 8.
Irene Gruenberg
Imperial County

ITALIAN SQUASH CAKE

3 cups unpeeled zucchini, shredded
3 cups sugar
1½ cups vegetable oil
4 eggs, beaten
1 cup walnuts, chopped
3 cups flour
2 teaspoons baking powder
1 teaspoon soda
½ teaspoon salt
1½ teaspoons cinnamon

Preheat oven to 325 degrees. Mix zucchini, sugar, oil and eggs until well blended. Combine remaining ingredients with squash mixture. Pour batter into 2 greased and floured 9-inch square glass pans or a 13 x 9 x 2-inch pan. Bake at 325 degrees for glass pans, or 350 degrees for metal pans. Bake for 30 to 40 minutes or until cake tests done. Cool slightly. Frost with cream cheese frosting. Recipe follows.

Frosting:

3 ounces cream cheese
¼ cup butter
1 teaspoon vanilla
2 cups powdered sugar

Cream cheese and butter well; add vanilla and powdered sugar. Mix.
Edith Glud
Imperial County

ZUCCHINI PIE

1 egg
1 cup sugar
1 tablespoon flour
½ teaspoon salt
½ teaspoon cinnamon
½ teaspoon nutmeg
¼ teaspoon cloves
½ teaspoon ginger
1½ cups zucchini, grated
1½ cups canned milk
1 9-inch pastry shell, unbaked

Preheat oven to 450 degrees. Beat egg slightly; add sugar mixed with flour, salt and spices. Add zucchini and milk, and stir until blended. Pour into a pie shell and bake ten minutes. Reduce heat to 325 degrees and bake 30 minutes longer or until firm.
Rita Bradley
Sierra County

ZUCCHINI MINI BARS

¼ cup margarine
¼ cup brown sugar
1 teaspoon vanilla
1¾ cups flour
½ teaspoon salt
1½ teaspoons baking powder
½ cup coconut (flakes)
½ cup raisins
2 cups unpeeled zucchini, grated

Preheat oven to 350 degrees. Beat margarine and sugar. Add vanilla. Blend flour, salt and baking powder. Then add dry ingredients to sugar mixture. Stir in coconut, raisins and zucchini. Spread on greased 11 x 15-inch cookie sheet. Bake 25 minutes. Cool and frost.

Frosting:

1 tablespoon margarine, melted
1 tablespoon milk
1 teaspoon vanilla
1 teaspoon cinnamon
1 cup powdered sugar
1 cup walnuts, chopped

Blend ingredients well; frost. Then sprinkle walnuts over.
Violet Rose
San Luis Obispo County

ZUCCHINI MILK

1 large zucchini

Peel large zucchini. Get rid of all the green on the outside, then place inside part of zucchini in blender and liquefy. Zucchini milk can be frozen for a later date, and can be used in same amounts as regular milk in any recipe.
Ruth Haines
Mendocino County

LOGGER'S ZUCCHINI BREAD PUDDING

2 cups zucchini milk
1½ cups bread cubes (3 bread crusts)
2 tablespoons butter
¼ cup honey
¼ teaspoon salt
2 eggs, slightly beaten
1 teaspoon vanilla
½ teaspoon cinnamon
½ cup raisins

Preheat oven to 350 degrees. Bring zucchini milk to boiling point, pour over bread cubes, add butter. Combine honey, salt, and beaten eggs. Add to bread and milk mixture. Add vanilla, cinnamon and raisins. Pour into greased casserole dish. Set dish in shallow pan of hot water. Bake for about 1 hour. Cinnamon and raisins can be omitted if desired.
Ruth Haines
Mendocino County

ZUCCHINI LEMON PIE

1 8-inch pie shell, baked
1 cup zucchini milk
1 cup water
1 tablespoon butter
6 tablespoons honey
4 tablespoons cornstarch
1/16 teaspoon salt
1 lemon rind, grated
¼ cup lemon juice
2 egg yolks
2 egg whites
1 tablespoon honey

Preheat oven to 400 degrees. Heat zucchini milk, water, butter and honey together. While this mixture heats; combine cornstarch, salt, lemon rind, and juice; then add to zucchini mixture. Cook, stirring constantly, until thick. Beat egg yolks and add a little of the hot zucchini mixture to them, stirring well. Then put yolks into hot zucchini mixture and cook about 1 minute. Remove from heat. Pour into baked pie shell and top with meringue made by beating egg whites until stiff, then adding 1 tablespoon warmed honey slowly while continuing to beat. Bake until golden brown (about five minutes). Cool and serve.
Ruth Haines
Mendocino County

PICK-OF-THE-GARDEN SOUP

5 to 6 pounds beef soup bones
6 quarts water
1 cup diced potatoes
1 cup diced celery
1 cup diced carrots
1 cup diced yellow and green squash, combined
1 cup diced onion
1 cup diced tomatoes
1 cup string beans, cut in 1-inch pieces
1 cup cabbage, sliced thin
½ cup dried pink beans
½ cup dried lima beans (large)
½ cup dried lima beans (small)
1 tablespoon basil, chopped fine
2 cloves garlic, mashed or chopped
½ cup parsley, chopped fine
Salt and pepper to taste
1½ cups dried noodles

Bring beef to a boil in water and skim surface. Add potatoes, celery, carrots, squash, onion, tomatoes, string beans, cabbage, dried pink and large and small lima beans, basil, garlic, parsley, and salt and pepper. Cook until dried pink and dried lima beans are done.
When the soup is almost done, add dried noodles. If part of the soup is to be frozen, only add the noodles to the portion to be used. The soup is better if the noodles are not frozen.
Marge Kiriluk
Tuolumne County

FRENCH VEGETABLE CASSEROLE

1 cup canned peas, drained
1 cup canned tomatoes, mashed
1½ cups medium white sauce
10 strips bacon, cooked and crumbled
½ cup Cheddar cheese, grated
1 cup sliced canned mushrooms
1 cup buttered bread crumbs or Kelloggs croutons

Preheat oven to 350 degrees. In a greased 1½-quart baking dish, layer ½ peas, tomatoes, white sauce, bacon, cheese and mushrooms. Repeat layering. Cover with buttered bread crumbs or croutons. Bake for 30 minutes. Yield: 6 servings.
Jeanne Good
Sonoma County

Onalee Koster

FRUITS

California farmers produce more than 40% of the nation's fruit supply. California ranks first in the nation in the production of the following major fruits: apricots, avocados, dates, figs, grapes, lemons, nectarines, olives, peaches, pears, plums, pomegranates, prunes, and strawberries. Some of the other major fruits produced are apples, cherries, grapefruit, oranges, and tangerines.

From the magnificent display of blossoms in the springtime, to the cool shade of the dense trees in the summer, followed by the bountiful harvest, the orchards of California are a sight to behold, in addition to the delicious fruits they provide for us. There is nothing more tempting than a bowl of fresh fruits waiting on the table for your family.

Fruits of the Golden State

PARTY SALAD

1 21-ounce can cherry pie filling
1 20-ounce can chunk pineapple, drained
1 cup miniature marshmallows
2 or 3 bananas

Mix pie filling, pineapple and marshmallows together. Chill. When ready to serve, slice bananas and mix with chilled ingredients. Serve.
Note: Other pie fillings may be used, such as apple. The pie filling sauce is all the dressing that is needed.
Susan Righetti
San Luis Obispo County

APRICOT JELLO

1 package (3-ounce) apricot Jello
1 cup boiling water
1 pint orange or pineapple sherbet
1 cup Dream Whip

Dissolve Jello in boiling water. Add the sherbet, stirring until melted. Add Dream Whip, beat until frothy. Put in 1-quart mold. Refrigerate until Jello has set.
Note: Apricot nectar may be used in place of water.
Dede Mariani
Santa Clara County

FREDDIE'S EDNA VALLEY SALAD

3 packages of orange gelatin
1 (No. 2½) can of cling peaches
miniature marshmallows
1 ripe cantaloupe

Drain peaches and reserve juice. Dissolve gelatin in 3 cups boiling water. Measure juice and add enough water (cold) to make 3 cups and add to orange gelatin. Then add in peaches and cantaloupe (in balls) to gelatin, cover with miniature marshmallows and set in refrigerator to congeal. Use 9 x 13-inch glass dish.
LaVonne Righetti
San Luis Obispo County

EL DORADO SWEET CHERRY FRUIT PLATTER

1 pound sweet cherries
2 Kiwi fruit
1 small pineapple
1 small cantaloupe
Lime mayonnaise (recipe follows)

Wash and stem cherries; pit if desired. Peel and slice kiwi fruit. Peel pineapple and cut into chunks. Peel cantaloupe and slice into wedges. Arrange fruits on platter. Serve with Lime mayonnaise. Makes 6 servings.
Elsa Dean
El Dorado County

LIME MAYONNAISE

1 egg
¼ cup frozen limeade concentrate, thawed
2 teaspoons sugar
½ teaspoon dry mustard
½ teaspoon salt
½ teaspoon grated lime peel
1 cup oil, divided
Green food coloring (optional)

Combine egg, limeade concentrate, sugar, mustard, salt, lime peel and ¼ cup of the oil in blender container. Blend 5 seconds. With motor running, slowly add remaining oil in a steady stream. Blend until all oil is absorbed and mayonnaise is thick. Blend in coloring if desired. Chill. Makes about 1½ cups dressing.
Elsa Dean
El Dorado County

CRANBERRY SALAD

1 package fresh cranberries
2 cups sugar
1 20-ounce can pineapple (drained)
1 small package raspberry or cherry Jello
½ cup chopped celery
¼ cup chopped nuts

Combine cranberries, sugar and pineapple. Use ½ of the mixture, freeze the other half for future use. Make Jello, partially set. Mix in cranberry mixture, celery and nuts. Chill till firm.
Dorothy McGrew
Placer County

LEMON JELLO SALAD

1 6-ounce package lemon Jello
1 10½-ounce package miniature marshmallows
3 bananas, sliced
1 8-ounce can crushed pineapple (drained), save juice
1 cup pineapple juice (add water)
½ cup sugar
3 tablespoons cornstarch
Juice of 2 lemons
8 ounces of Cool Whip
Grated cheddar cheese and nuts (optional)

Prepare lemon Jello as directed on box.Add marshmallows, bananas and drained crushed pineapple. Save juice. Refrigerate. Cook topping over medium heat until thick. Topping consists of pineapple juice, sugar, cornstarch and lemon juice. Cool. Fold in Cool Whip. Put topping on Jello. Garnish with grated cheese and nuts.
Sally Donati
Placer County

SANTA CINNAMON SALAD

¼ cup red cinnamon candies
2 tablespoons sugar
1 cup boiling water
1 3-ounce package cherry gelatin
1 cup cold water
1 cup diced apple (leave skin on)
½ cup diced orange
¼ cup walnuts, chopped
Red food coloring, optional

Dissolve candies and sugar in hot water. Heat just to boiling. Pour over gelatin, stir to dissolve and add cold water. May add red food coloring at this time. Chill until partially set and stir in remaining ingredients. Pour into prepared mold. Chill until set. Serve on lettuce bed.
Candy Jones
San Bernardino County

SIMPLE ORANGE SALAD

1 head romaine lettuce, broken into pieces
1 11-ounce can mandarin oranges, drained
1 4-ounce package salted peanuts

Combine lettuce, oranges and peanuts. Toss with the poppy seed dressing and served chilled.

Poppy seed dressing:

¾ cup sugar
1 cup vegetable oil
1 teaspoon dry mustard
1 teaspoon salt
⅓ cup vinegar
1½ tablespoons onion, minced
2 tablespoons poppy seeds

To make the dressing: combine all ingredients and mix in a blender.
Chris Pankey
San Diego County

ZESTY NECTARINE SALAD

2 medium or large fresh nectarines
½ pound mushrooms, quartered
1 cup cherry tomatoes, halved
½ cup pitted ripe olives
½ cup green onion, cut into 1 inch lengths
½ jar (6 ounces) marinated artichoke hearts
¼ cup vegetable oil
¼ cup lemon juice
¼ teaspoon salt
¼ teaspoon pepper
1 teaspoon sugar
1 teaspoon tarragon, crumbled
½ teaspoon thyme, crumbled

Cut nectarines into thick slices then cut each slice in half. Combine nectarines with mushrooms, tomatoes, olives, and onion in large salad bowl. Drain and save marinade from artichokes. Add artichokes to salad. Combine reserved marinade with oil, lemon juice, salt, pepper, sugar, tarragon and thyme in jar. Shake well and pour over salad. Cover salad and chill for at least 2 hours, tossing once or twice. Makes 6 (1 cup) servings.
Patrice Bussell
Kern County

PICKLED CRAB APPLES

4 quarts crab apples
2 cups vinegar
5 cups brown sugar
1 tablespoon whole cloves
2 sticks cinnamon
1 tablespoon whole allspice

Wash crab apples and remove blossom end. Do not pare. Combine vinegar, brown sugar, cloves, cinnamon and allspice in saucepan and simmer 20 minutes. Add apples a few at a time and simmer until tender. Pack apples in hot sterilized jars adding syrup to cover apples. Seal. Makes 6 pints.
Emily Gowan
Mendocino County

NORTHERN CALIFORNIA APPLE CHUTNEY

12 medium sized tart cooking apples, peeled and diced
6 green tomatoes
4 small white onions
3 large green peppers
1 cup seedless raisins
2 tablespoons mustard seed
2 cups sugar
1 quart vinegar
2 teaspoons salt

Dice the apples. Chop green tomatoes, onions and green peppers. Combine all ingredients. Cook slowly, about 30 minutes or until desired consistency. Pack into hot sterilized jars and seal. Process in boiling water bath 10 minutes. Makes about 8 half pints. This recipe makes a delicious chutney.
Gerry Hillis
Shasta County

GRANDMA'S MINCEMEAT

3 pounds lean meat
6 pounds sour apples
2 pounds seedless raisins
2 pounds brown sugar
1 cup apple cider
1 cup apple cider vinegar
1 cup meat stock
1 teaspoon nutmeg
1 teaspoon cloves
1 teaspoon cinnamon
1 teaspoon mace
1 tablespoon salt

Cut meat in cubes, cover with water and simmer until tender. Cool. Grind meat in food chopper and the pared and cored apples should be put through the chopper also. Add remaining ingredients and simmer 1 hour, stirring frequently. This may be put into freezer containers and frozen or put into sterilized jars, sealed and kept in a cool place.
Josephine Gowan
Mendocino County

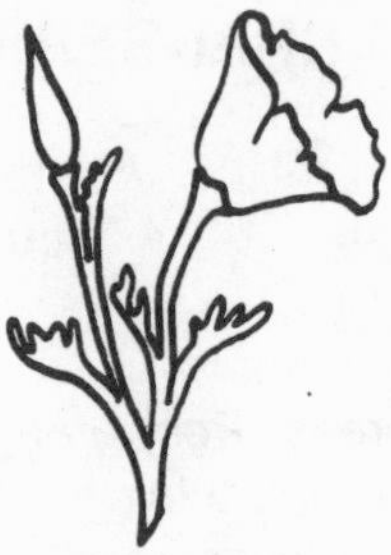

SPICED APRICOT PICKLES

2 cups dried apricots
Water
2 cups sugar
6 tablespoons cider vinegar
24 whole cloves
1½ teaspoons mustard seed
2 sticks cinnamon

Wash apricots well. Barely cover with water; boil gently for about 5 minutes. Add sugar, vinegar, cloves, mustard seed and cinnamon sticks. Simmer gently until apricots are tender—about 15 minutes. Cover and refrigerate in the syrup. If you plan to give them as a gift, seal them while they are still hot. Makes about three (3) 8-ounce jars. They will keep a couple of weeks without sealing. Delicious with ham, pork or lamb.
Geraldine Hillis
Shasta County

COLACE BROTHERS CANTALOUPE RELISH

4 medium firm ripe cantaloupes
3 cups white vinegar
⅔ cup lemon or lime juice
7 cups sugar
4 teaspoons salt
2 lemons or limes, thinly sliced
2 cups chopped onions
4 cups California raisins
4 cups chopped nuts
4 cinnamon sticks
3 teaspoons whole cloves
2 teaspoons whole allspice
4 tablespoons pickling spices

Peel cantaloupes, discarding seeds. Cut into small chunks. Combine spices and secure tightly in a cheesecloth bag. Combine all ingredients in large kettle. Simmer for 2½ hours. Ladle into hot sterilized pint jars and seal. Makes 6 pints.
Frances Colace
Imperial County

BAKED CRANBERRY RELISH

1 orange
1 pound fresh cranberries
2 cups sugar
⅛ teaspoon salt (optional)
1 cup coarsely chopped nuts

Preheat oven to 325 degrees. Peel orange and cut into 1-inch pieces. Using half the peel, cut into very thin slivers; set aside. Wash cranberries. Place cranberries in 2-quart casserole, sprinkle on sugar and salt. Add orange and slivers of peel. Stir to mix. Cover tightly and bake for 1 hour and 15 minutes. Stir in nut meats. Allow to chill in refrigerator overnight before serving. If using for gifts, spoon hot mixture into sterilized jars. Seal and store in cool dry place.
Mary Theiler
Calaveras County

AUNT NORA'S FIG JAM

3 cups figs, chopped
3 cups white sugar
1 (6-ounce) package strawberry Jello

Mix figs, sugar and Jello in a large saucepan. Boil until thick as desired. Pour into sterilized jars and seal.
Louise Correia
Fresno County

GREEN-RIPE OLIVES - IN A PICKLE

1 cup "Merry War" lye to 6 gallons of water, or 2 ounces of lye to each gallon of water
4 ounces of salt to each gallon of water
2-3 gallons of olives

Pick olives before completely black, if possible, to avoid bruising. Using a crock or wooden barrel or gallon jars, place olives to within 2 or 3 inches from top. Mix lye solution and cover olives. Let stand 3 days. stirring occasionally. When several olives show full penetration of the lye, the bitterness will be gone. Pour lye solution down the drain. Cover with fresh water. Change fairly often, soaking for a week. You may safely taste for clean olive taste after the water stays clear. The olives will darken. To cure in brine, store the olives in a brine of 4 ounces of salt to a gallon of water. Hold for 3 days in this brine. If brine darkens, change to fresh. Put olives in jars with fresh boiling brine made of 4 ounces of salt to the gallon. Process at 10 pounds pressure in a pressure cooker for 10 minutes.
Gloria Hildreth
Shasta County

PEACH CHUTNEY

1½ pints cider vinegar
8 cups sugar
3½ pounds diced Alberta peaches
6 medium Gravenstein apples, diced
2 cups chopped white onions
3 large chopped bell peppers
1 cup currants
1 cup raisins
½ bottle Certo
½ teaspoon cloves
2 teaspoons cinnamon
1 teaspoon ginger
1 teaspoon allspice
1 teaspoon salt
¼ teaspoon cayenne pepper

In a large pan, boil the cider vinegar and sugar for 10 minutes and skim. Add the peaches and apples and cook until soft. Add onions, bell peppers and cook 45 minutes. Add currants, raisins and Certo and cook for 10 minutes. Add the cloves, cinnamon, ginger, allspice, salt, and cayenne pepper and cook 2-3 minutes. Pour into hot sterilized ½ pint jars and seal at once.
Note: Delicious served with ham, turkey, etc. Makes 6 pints.
Lois Armstrong
Stanislaus County

SHASTA PURPLE PLUM MINCEMEAT

4 pounds northwest purple prunes (plums)
2 pounds Bartlett pears
1 pound seedless raisins
1 tablespoon grated lemon rind
¼ cup lemon juice
2½ tablespoons grated orange rind
½ cup orange juice
1½ pounds light brown sugar
½ cup cider vinegar
1 teaspoon salt
1 tablespoon ground cinnamon
2 teaspoons ground cloves
1 teaspoon ground nutmeg
½ teaspoon ground allspice

Quarter and pit purple prune plums. Core and dice unpeeled pears. Combine fruits with remaining ingredients in a large kettle. Bring to boil. Reduce heat and simmer 30 minutes covered. Remove cover and simmer 1 hour until slightly thickened, stirring from time to time. Ladle hot mixture to within ⅛ inch of top of sterilized jars; wipe off tops with clean damp cloth. Put sterilized lids on jars; screw sterilized bands tight. Stand each filled jar on a rack in a canner full of hot, not boiling, water. Water should cover jars 1-2 inches. Put cover on canner, bring water to boil. Process jars in boiling water bath 25 minutes. Remove jars from canner and let cool about 12 hours. Remove bands and test for seal. Store in a cool, dark, dry place. Mincemeat may be used in pies, cakes, cookies, or in other ways.
Sylvia Clair
Shasta County

PENNY'S PIONEER PICKLED PRUNES

3 cups water
1 cup cider vinegar
2 cups brown sugar
2 cups dried prunes
1 teaspoon whole cloves
1½ sticks cinnamon

Place in heavy pan: water, cider vinegar, brown sugar, dried prunes, cloves, and cinnamon. Simmer 1 hour until prunes are plump. Place prunes in jar and cover with strained liquid. Refrigerate.
Mary Jenkins
Sutter County

LIVE OAK CANNERY PICKLED PRUNES

1 field box prunes (approximately 35-40 pounds)
1 gallon apple cider vinegar
4 packages whole cloves
3 packages stick cinnamon
25 pounds sugar

In a large kettle boil vinegar, cloves, and cinnamon for 5 minutes, then slowly add sugar, stirring until dissolved. When comes to boil add prunes, slowly so boiling does not stop. Using a slotted spoon, place prunes in hot, sterilized jars, add enough liquid to within ½ inch of top, seal.
Note: Prunes will burst and become soft, if left in boiling liquid too long. If there is too much juice left over, use as basting for ham, or one can pickle peaches in balance of liquid.
Blythe Gentry
Sutter County

APPLESAUCE CAKE

4 cups flour
2 tablespoons cornstarch
4 tablespoons ground chocolate
4 teaspoons soda
2 cups sugar
½ teaspoon cinnamon
½ teaspoon nutmeg
½ teaspoon allspice
½ teaspoon cloves
2 cups chopped nuts
2 cups raisins
½ teaspoon salt
3 cups cool applesauce
1 cup oil

Preheat oven to 350 degrees. Sift together all the dry ingredients in a large bowl. Stir in the nuts and raisins, then add the cooled applesauce and oil. Mix well. Bake for 1 hour. This can be baked in a bundt pan or in loaf pans.
Marjorie Clarke
Plumas County

APPLE CAKE

¾ cup flour
1 teaspoon baking soda
½ teaspoon salt
1 teaspoon cinnamon
¼ cup salad oil
1 cup sugar
1 egg, slightly beaten
2 cups coarsely chopped apples
1 cup chopped walnuts

Preheat oven to 350 degrees. Sift flour, baking soda, salt and cinnamon together. Mix all other ingredients together and combine with flour mixture. Pour into a greased 8 x 8-inch square pan. Bake for 45 minutes.
Alice Barnes
San Diego County

CALAVERAS GUM DROP CAKE

4 cups sifted flour
1 pound raisins
1 pound gum drops (cut up)
1 cup nuts, chopped
1 teaspoon cinnamon
¼ teaspoon nutmeg
¼ teaspoon cloves
¼ teaspoon salt
1 teaspoon soda
2 cups sugar
1 cup shortening
2 eggs
2 cups applesauce
1 teaspoon vanilla

Preheat oven to 300 degrees. Mix raisins, nuts and gum drops with a little of the flour. Cream sugar and shortening. Add beaten eggs, applesauce, flour and spices. Then add nuts, raisins, and gum drops. Mix well. Use greased and floured angel food cake pan or bundt pan. Bake 2 hours.
Nadine More
Calaveras County

FRESH APPLE CAKE

1 cup sugar
¼ cup butter
1 egg
3 cups finely chopped, unpeeled apples
1 cup sifted flour
1 teaspoon baking soda
⅛ teaspoon salt
1 teaspoon cinnamon
½ teaspoon nutmeg

Preheat oven to 350 degrees. Cream sugar and butter in large mixing bowl. Beat egg and add to creamed mixture. Add chopped apples. Sift together flour, soda, salt, cinnamon and nutmeg. Add walnuts to dry ingredients and stir into apple mixture. Spread batter into greased 9 x 9 x 2-inch baking pan. Bake for 30 to 40 minutes. Serve with Hot Lemon Sauce.

Hot Lemon Sauce:

½ cup sugar
2 teaspoons cornstarch
⅛ teaspoon nutmeg
1 cup boiling water
2 tablespoons butter
1½ tablespoons lemon juice

Mix sugar, cornstarch, and nutmeg in saucepan. Gradually add boiling water. Cook over low heat until thick and clear. Add butter and lemon juice, and blend thoroughly.
Evelyn Sonka
Tuolumne County

GAZELLE GOODIE FRESH APPLE CAKE SNACK

4 cups grated apple
2 cups sugar
2 eggs
½ cup oil
1 teaspoon vanilla
2 cups flour
1½ teaspoons soda
1 teaspoon salt
2 teaspoons cinnamon
1½ cups chopped nuts

Preheat oven to 375 degrees. Peel 5 apples. (Golden Delicious are fine.) Grate raw apples until there are four cups. Pour two cups of sugar over the apples. Add well-beaten eggs, oil, and vanilla. Sift together flour, cinnamon, salt, and soda. Stir into the apple mixture. Add chopped nuts. Pour into a greased pan 9½ x 13½-inch. Bake for 35 to 40 minutes. Serves 15 people.
Ruth Robertson
Sutter County

PIPPIN CAKE

2 eggs
2 cups sugar
2 cups flour
2 teaspoons baking soda
¼ teaspoon salt
2 cups Newtown Pippin applesauce
1 teaspoon vanilla
½ cup chopped or ground nuts

Preheat oven to 350 degrees. Grease 10½ x 15½-inch jelly roll or similar size pan and sprinkle with flour or sugar. Sift together or mix the flour, baking soda, and salt. Beat the eggs well and gradually beat in the sugar. Fold in about half the flour mixture, then the applesauce and vanilla, the rest of the flour, and the nuts. Spread in pan and bake 30 to 35 minutes or until toothpick comes out clean.
Note: Other applesauce may be used by Newtowns are best. Set cake on rake to cool.

Frosting:

1 8-ounce package cream cheese, warmed to room temperature
¼ cup margarine
1¾ cups powdered sugar
1 teaspoon vanilla
½ cup chopped or ground nuts

Cream together the margarine and cream cheese. Add powdered sugar and vanilla and beat until smooth. Spread on the cake while hot and sprinkle with nuts. Serves 24 and freezes well.
Virginia Rider
Santa Cruz County

MENDOCINO NOBBY NUBBINS APPLE CAKE

3 tablespoons butter or margarine
1 cup sugar
1 egg, beaten
½ teaspoon cinnamon
½ teaspoon nutmeg
½ teaspoon salt
1 teaspoon baking soda
1 cup sifted flour
3 cups diced apples
¼ cup chopped walnuts
1 teaspoon vanilla

Preheat oven to 350 degrees. Cream butter and sugar. Add eggs, mix well. Sift flour, cinnamon, nutmeg, salt, and baking soda together. Add to creamed mixture. Stir in diced apples, walnuts, and vanilla. Pour into greased 8 x 8 x 2-inch baking pan. Bake 40 to 45 minutes. Serve hot or cold with whipped cream or ice cream.
Evelyn Schoenahl
Mendocino County

SEE CANYON APPLE CAKE

4 cups diced peeled apples
2 cups sugar
1 cup oil
2 eggs, beaten
1 cup chopped walnuts
2 teaspoons cinnamon
1 teaspoon vanilla
2½ cups flour
2 teaspoons soda
1 teaspoon salt

Heat oven to 350 degrees. Soak together, at least four hours, the apples, sugar, oil, eggs, walnuts, cinnamon and vanilla. Sift together the flour, soda, and salt and add this to apple mixture. Mix well. Pour into 13 x 9 x 2-inch pan or 10 cup bundt pan or 10-inch tube pan. Bake one hour or until it tests done.
Margaret Hager
San Luis Obispo County

CALAVERAS JUMPING FROG APPLE CAKE

6 tablespoons margarine
2 cups sugar
2 eggs, beaten
1 teaspoon cinnamon
½ teaspoon nutmeg
½ teaspoon salt
2 teaspoons soda
2 cups sifted flour
6 cups diced apples
1 cup chopped nuts
½ cup raisins if desired
2 teaspoons vanilla

Preheat oven to 350 degrees. Cream margarine and sugar. Add eggs and mix well. Sift dry ingredients together. Add to creamed mixture. Stir in apples, nuts, raisins and vanilla. Spread in greased 13 x 9 x 2-inch pan. Bake for 50 to 60 minutes. Serve with topping hot or cold or it may be frosted. Yields 12 to 14 servings.
Leora Tower
Calaveras County

CALIFORNIA RAW APPLE CAKE

2 cups flour
1½ cups sugar
½ teaspoon salt
2 teaspoons baking soda
1 teaspoon cinnamon
½ teaspoon nutmeg
½ cup Wesson oil
2 eggs
4 cups diced raw apples
½ cup chopped walnuts
½ cup raisins

Preheat oven to 350 degrees. Sift all dry ingredients together. Add apples, nuts, raisins, oil and eggs. Mix well until all are moistened. Batter will be thick. Pour into greased floured 13 x 9 x 2-inch pan. Smooth out dough. Bake about one hour. Can be served with ice cream or whipped cream. Serves about 15 generously.
Emma Benevenga
Marin County

DEWY FRESH SUNSHINE APPLE CAKE

2 cups white sugar
1 cup shortening
2 eggs
3 cups flour
2 teaspoons baking soda
1½ teaspoons cinnamon
¼ teaspoon salt
6 cups peeled, diced apples
¾ cup chopped nuts (optional)

Preheat oven to 325 degrees. Cream sugar, shortening and eggs. Sift flour, soda, cinnamon and salt. Mix into creamed mixture. Work in apples and nuts-dough is thick. Spread into 9 x 13-inch greased glass pan. Bake for 50 to 60 minutes.

Topping:

½ pint half and half
1 cup brown sugar
2 tablespoons cornstarch
dash salt
2 tablespoons butter
1 tablespoon vanilla

Combine half and half, brown sugar, cornstarch, salt and butter. Boil until thick and add vanilla. Spread on cake as soon as it is taken from the oven.
Candy Jones
San Bernardino County

"KEEP THE DR. AWAY" APPLE CAKE

2 cups sugar
1 cup oil
2 eggs
2 cups flour
1 teaspoon soda
¾ teaspoon salt
1 can apples (slightly drained)
1 cup nuts (chopped)
1 teaspoon vanilla

Preheat oven to 350 degrees. Mix in order given. Bake for 45 minutes in 9 x 13-inch pan. Serve plain or with whipped cream or vanilla ice cream.
Dorothy McGrew
Placer County

BERRY CAKE

4 eggs
1 package white cake mix
10 ounces berries
1 package Jello (match flavor to type of berries used)
⅓ cup oil
2 tablespoons flour

Preheat oven to 350 degrees. Beat eggs. Add cake mix, berries, Jello, oil and flour. Bake in greased tube or bundt pan for 55-60 minutes. Let cake cool for 20 minutes before removing from pan.
Cyndy Mickelsen
Sacramento County

CALIFORNIA KIWIFRUIT SHORTCAKE

1 quart peeled, sliced kiwifruit
⅓ cup sugar, or to taste
¼ cup sugar
1¾ cups all-purpose flour
½ cup shortening
⅓ cup milk
1 egg
1 tablespoon baking powder
1 teaspoon grated lemon peel
¾ teaspoon salt
Butter or margarine
1 cup whipping cream
½ teaspoon vanilla

Preheat oven to 450 degrees. Combine kiwifruit with ⅓ cup sugar, or to taste. Toss together and set aside. Combine¼ cup sugar with flour, shortening, milk, egg, baking powder, lemon peel, and salt. Beat with electric mixer at medium speed to form a soft dough. Grease a 9-inch round pan, and pat dough evenly in place. Bake for 15 minutes or until golden. While shortcake bakes, whip cream with vanilla. Set aside. Turn out hot shortcake onto platter and split horizontally while still hot, using a long, sharp knife. Butter split halves and spoon half the kiwifruit onto the bottom half. Cover with the top half. Then put all the rest of the kiwifruit on top. Frost with whipped cream. Garnish with more kiwifruit slices if desired. Serves 8.
Note: Strawberries or freestone peaches may be substituted for part or all of the kiwifruit.
Miriam Zachary
Sutter County

SUNSHINE LEMON CAKE

1 package Lemon Cake mix
1 package (small) lemon Jello
¾ cup oil
¾ cup water
1 teaspoon lemon extract or lemon rind (grated)
4 eggs

Glaze:

2 cups powdered sugar
¼ cup plus 2 tablespoons lemon juice

Preheat oven to 350 degrees. Mix together first 6 ingredients and beat 4 minutes. Pour into ungreased 9 x 12-inch cake pan. Bake 40 minutes. While baking cake, mix together glaze ingredients. Take cake out of oven—poke holes all over top of cake with fork. Pour glaze over top. Let cool before serving.
Betty Levera
San Luis Obispo County

ORANGE GLAZED CHEESECAKE

1½ cups zweiback crumbs (about 18 zweiback pieces)
2 tablespoons sugar
¼ teaspoon cinnamon
⅓ cup butter or margarine, melted
2 8-ounce packages cream cheese, room temperature
1 cup sugar
¼ unsweetened cocoa powder
¼ teaspoon almond extract
2 eggs
1 cup dairy sour cream
⅓ cup sugar
2 tablespoons cornstarch
¾ cup orange juice
¼ cup orange-flavored liqueur
2 oranges, peeled and sectioned

In a small bowl, combine zweiback crumbs, 2 tablespoons sugar, cinnamon and melted butter or margarine. Press on bottom and 1½ inches up side of an 8-inch springform pan; refrigerate. Preheat oven to 350 degrees. In a large bowl cream the cheese, 1 cup sugar and the cocoa. Add almond extract and eggs, beating until smooth. Stir in sour cream. Pour into prepared crust. Bake 45 to 50 minutes. Cool in pan several hours. In a small saucepan, combine ⅓ cup sugar and cornstarch. Stir in orange juice. Bring to boil over medium heat, stirring constantly. Simmer 1 minute longer. Remove glaze from heat. Add liqueur. Cool to lukewarm. Spoon half of glaze over cooled cheesecake. Arrange orange sections on top of glaze. Spoon remaining glaze over orange sections. Chill until firm. Remove from pan. Makes 8 to 10 servings.
Vicki Lacouague
Orange County

FRESH PEACH MOUSSE CAKE

1 cup whipping cream
¼ cup sugar
½ teaspoon vanilla
¼ teaspoon almond extract
4 egg whites
1 pound fresh peaches (sliced)
1 Angel food cake
Powdered sugar

Whip cream until stiff. Gradually beat in ½ of the sugar (⅛ cup). Fold in flavorings. Now set aside. Beat egg whites until stiff and add remaining sugar. Fold beaten egg whites and ½ peaches into cream mixture and chill. Cut Angel food cake in 4 layers and spread filling between layers and on top. Garnish with remaining peaches and chill until ready to serve.
Janis German
Solano County

FRESH PEAR CAKE

2 cups mashed fresh pears
1 cup seedless raisins (plumped)
1 cup margarine
1½ cups sugar
2 eggs
2 cups flour
2 teaspoons cinnamon
1 teaspoon cloves, (optional)
2 teaspoons soda
1 teaspoon salt

Topping:

½ cup brown sugar
1 cup chopped walnuts

Preheat oven to 350 degrees. Cream shortening and sugar. Add eggs. Beat until fluffy. Add dry ingredients; mix well. Add pear pulp and raisins. Blend well. Pour into greased 9 x 13-inch pan. Sprinkle topping over unbaked cake and bake for 30-40 minutes.
Judy Culbertson
Sacramento County

LULU PERSIMMON CAKE

2 cups persimmon pulp
2 cups sugar
1 cup sweet milk
2 teaspoons baking powder
¼ teaspoon salt
2 cups raisins
2 cups walnuts
3½ cups sifted flour
2 teaspoons baking soda
½ teaspoon cinnamon
3 tablespoons butter or margarine

Preheat oven to 325 degrees. Mix persimmon pulp, milk and sugar. Add flour, soda, baking powder, spices. Beat well after each addition. Add butter, raisins, nuts and mix well. Bake in two greased loaf pans for 1½ hours.
Violet Jensen
Fresno County

GOLDEN GATE PERSIMMON CAKE

½ cup margarine
1¼ cups sugar
2 eggs
1¾ cups flour
1½ teaspoons baking powder
¼ teaspoon salt
½ teaspoon soda
1 cup sieved persimmon pulp
¼ cup sour or buttermilk (1 teaspoon vinegar or lemon juice added to sweet milk)
1 cup ground nuts

Preheat oven to 350 degrees. Cream sugar and margarine. Add eggs and beat smooth. Combine dry ingredients and add. Dissolve soda in persimmon pulp, and add with milk to other mixture. Add nuts. Divide batter between 2 bread loaf pans, and bake for 45 to 50 minutes or until toothpick comes out clean. When cool, slice and dust with powdered sugar. Serves 20 to 24.
Maria Clark
Sutter County

PRUNE SOUR CREAM COFFEE CAKE

1½ cups Sunsweet prunes
1 teaspoon grated lemon rind
2 cups sifted flour
1 teaspoon baking powder
1 teaspoon baking soda
½ teaspoon salt
1 cup soft butter
1 cup granulated sugar
2 eggs
1 cup sour cream
1 teaspoon vanilla extract
½ cup light brown sugar, firmly packed
1 tablespoon cinnamon
¾ cup chopped walnuts

Preheat oven to 350 degrees. Pour boiling water over prunes. Let stand 15 minutes. Drain, pit and dice prunes. Add lemon rind and set aside. Grease and flour 9-inch tube pan. Sift together flour, baking powder, baking soda, and salt. Remove ¼ cup and toss with prunes. Cream butter and sugar until fluffy. Beat in eggs one at a time slowly. Beat in flour mixture alternatley with sour cream and vanilla, beginning and ending with flour. Fold in prunes. (Combine brown sugar, cinnamon and nuts; turn ⅓ batter into pan.) Sprinkle with ⅓ mixture of brown sugar; repeat; layer twice. Bake 55 minutes or until done. Cool in pan in rack 10 minutes. Remove from pan.
Virginia Marfia
Santa Clara County

PRUNE APPLE CAKE

2 cups sugar
1½ cups vegetable oil
3 eggs
3 cups flour
2 teaspoons baking soda
1 teaspoon *each* salt & cinnamon
½ teaspoon cloves
2 cups pitted prunes, coarsely chopped
2 cups coarsely shredded apples
1 cup chopped nuts
Powdered sugar

Preheat oven to 325 degrees. In a large bowl beat sugar, oil and eggs 2 minutes with electric mixer at medium speed. In another bowl combine dry ingredients; gradually mix into egg mixture. Mix in prunes, apples and nuts at low speed to blend thoroughly. Spoon into buttered and floured 10-inch tube pan; smooth top. Bake in oven about 1 hour and 30 minutes, until springy to the touch and pick inserted in center comes out clean. Cool in pan 15 minutes. Invert onto rack to cool completely. Place on serving plate and dust with powdered sugar.
Virginia Marfia
Santa Clara County

GOLDEN STATE HARVEST CAKE

1 cup cut-up, pitted, uncooked prunes
1 cup boiling water
2 cups sifted all-purpose flour
1½ cups sugar
1 teaspoon salt
1¼ teaspoons soda
½ cup cooking oil
1 teaspoon *each*, cinnamon, nutmeg, cloves
3 eggs
1 cup chopped nuts (walnuts, almonds, etc.)

Pour boiling water over prunes, and let stand two hours. Preheat oven to 350 degrees. Sift dry ingredients together. Add prune mixture and rest of ingredients. Blend thoroughly (1 minute). Beat 2 minutes at medium mixer speed, or 300 strokes by hand. Add nuts. Pour into greased and floured 9 x 13-inch pan. Bake 35 minutes or until toothpick comes out clean.

Icing:

2 cups confectioner's sugar
⅓ cup margarine
¼ cup lemon juice
1 teaspoon grated lemon rind

Frost with lemon icing, made by combining last four ingredients and beating until creamy. Serves 15 to 18.
Alice Dewey
Sutter County

LESTER'S PRUNE CAKE

¼ cup butter or oleo
1½ cups sugar
2 eggs
½ teaspoon salt
1 cup prunes (cooked, pitted)
2 cups flour (sifted)
1 teaspoon baking soda
½ teaspoon each of allspice, cinnamon, nutmeg, cloves
1 teaspoon vanilla
1 cup prune juice
1 cup chopped walnuts

Preheat oven to 325 degrees. Cream butter and sugar. Add eggs and pitted prunes (may chop prunes, if preferred). Beat. Measure dry ingredients together. Add to batter alternating with liquids. Mix thoroughly and add nuts. Bake in loaf pan or tube pan (9½ x 5¼ x 3-inch) 1¼ hours in preheated oven. Grease pan before adding batter. (One double recipe makes 3 loaf pans. Good for camping or moist fruit bread dessert. This recipe is an heirloom from the descedents of the Lester Family. I make this loaf each year for Christmas presents and the family has in past years taken the cake on camping outings. If used as presents, I have enough pans to make the recipe as fast as it will bake. I have made as many as 12 in an afternoon. If for camping, I would bake in a tube pan.)
Hazel Lester
Santa Clara County

PRUNE SPICE CAKE

1½ cups dried prunes
2 cups sifted enriched flour
1½ cups sugar
1¼ teaspoons soda
1 teaspoon salt
3 eggs
½ cup salad oil
1 teaspoon nutmeg
¼ teaspoon cloves
1 teaspoon cinnamon
½ cup broken walnuts
½ cup sugar
2 tablespoons flour
2 tablespoons butter

Preheat oven to 350 degrees. Cover prunes with water. Simmer 20 minutes or until tender. Drain and reserve ⅔ cup liquid, add more water if necessary. Pit and chop prunes. Sift together dry ingredients, add reserved prune liquid and salad oil. Mix to blend. Beat vigorously 2 minutes. Add eggs and beat 1 minute longer. Stir in prunes. Pour into a 13 x 9 x 2-inch baking dish. Mix ½ cup sugar, 2 tablespoons flour and 2 tablespoons butter until crumbly for crumb top. Sprinkle cake with crumb top, then walnuts. Bake 35 minutes or until done. Serve warm. Makes 12 to 14 servings.
Luda Myers
Shasta County

PRUNE CAKE

1 cup salad oil
2 cups sugar
2 cups all-purpose flour
1 teaspoon salt
1 teaspoon baking soda
1 teaspoon nutmeg
1 teaspoon cinnamon
1 teaspoon allspice
1 cup buttermilk
1 cup chopped nuts
1 cup pitted prunes, chopped

Preheat oven to 350 degrees. Beat oil, sugar, eggs, and vanilla until smooth. Mix flour, salt and spices together. Stir the flour mixture into the oil mixture and pour in buttermilk, a little at a time. Add the nuts and chopped prunes and stir well. Pour into greased and floured 9 x 13-inch pan. Bake for 40 to 50 minutes. When cake is cool, puncture top with a fork and drizzle topping over.

Topping:

1 cup sugar
½ cup buttermilk
½ teaspoon baking soda
1 tablespoon light corn syrup
½ teaspoon vanilla
½ cup butter

Combine all ingredients in saucepan. Bring to boil and boil until mixture reaches the soft ball stage (234-240 degrees) on a candy thermometer. It takes 20 minutes. Mixture will be a reddish brown color. Pour hot topping over cake.

Winona Bassett
Kings County

OUR GANG'S PRUNE CAKE

3 eggs
½ cup salad oil
1½ cups sugar
3 tablespoons cocoa
½ teaspoon cloves
1 teaspoon cinnamon
2 cups sifted flour
1 teaspoon baking soda
½ teaspoon salt
1 heaping cup chopped stewed prunes
½ cup prune juice
1 teaspoon vanilla
1 cup chopped nuts

Preheat oven to 350 degrees. Beat eggs. Add salad oil and beat well. Add sugar, cocoa and spices, mix well. Sift flour, soda and salt and add to above, alternating with prune juice. Add chopped prunes, walnuts, and vanilla, and mix well. Bake in 7 x 11-inch pan lined with wax paper for 50 to 55 minutes.

Phyllis Patane
Sutter County

PACIFIC PRUNE CAKE

1 cup buttermilk
2 cups plus 1 tablespoon flour
1 teaspoon salt
1 teaspoon baking powder
1 teaspoon soda
1 teaspoon nutmeg
½ teaspoon allspice
1 teaspoon cloves
1 teaspoon cinnamon
1 teaspoon vanilla
1 cup nuts, chopped
1 cup prunes, chopped
1 cup oil
3 eggs
2 cups sugar

Preheat oven to 325 degrees. Mix all dry ingredients including spices together, set aside. Blend oil, eggs, sugar, and buttermilk together and mix well. Combine dry ingredients with buttermilk mixture until thoroughly mixed. Pour into a large cake pan and bake for 1½ hours.

Ethel German
Mendocino County

PACIFIC PRUNE CAKE FROSTING

½ cup butter
1 cup brown sugar
¼ cup milk
1¾ cups powdered sugar
1 teaspoon vanilla

Melt butter, stir in brown sugar and cook for two minutes. Stir in milk, cook for two more minutes. Cool and add powdered sugar and vanilla. Mix well and frost prune cake with icing.

Ethel German
Mendocino County

OLD TIME FRUIT CAKE

Brandy
1½ cups prunes
1 cup dried apricots
2 cups seedless raisins
1½ cups seeded raisins
1½ cups currants
1½ cups dates, pitted and sliced
2½ cups preserved diced citron
1½ cups preserved diced pineapple
1½ cups candied cherries, halved
1 cup diced preserved orange peel
1 cup diced preserved lemon peel
1½ cups blanched almonds
1 cup pecan halves
3 cups sifted all-purpose flour
2 teaspoons allspice
2 teaspoons cinnamon
1½ teaspoons nutmeg
1 teaspoon mace
½ teaspoon ginger
½ teaspoon ground cloves
½ teaspoon baking soda
1½ teaspoons salt
1 cup soft butter
1½ cups brown sugar
6 eggs, beaten
½ cup molasses
⅔ cup strawberry jam

Soak fruit in brandy to cover, overnight. Preheat oven to 275 degrees. Grease pans. Put a piece of greased brown paper in bottom of each greased pan; then line pan completely with wax paper and grease again. Rinse prunes, apricots; cover with water; boil five minutes; drain; cool. Cut prunes from pits into pieces; slice apricots. Rinse and drain raisins, currants; then add to prunes and apricots. Add dates, citron, pineapple, cherries, orange peel and lemon peel. Sliver almonds; chop pecans coarsely, add both to fruits. Sprinkle one cup flour over all. Mix well. Sift remaining 2 cups flour, spices, baking soda and salt, together. With electric mixer at "cream," thoroughly beat butter with sugar until very light and fluffy; then add eggs one at a time, until very creamy- 8 minutes in all. Then at low speed or "blend" beat in alternately in fourths, flour mixture, molasses and jam, just until smooth. Pour over fruit and nut mixture; mix well with spoon. Pack lightly into pans. Put nuts and cherries on top of cakes; cover with brown paper and tie. Bake with a small shallow pan of hot water on floor of oven 3-3½ hours, or until done. Remove from oven; brush with leftover brandy to soak fruits, and then with hot corn syrup while loaves are still hot. *Cool completely* in pans on wire racks. Remove from pans; pull off paper. Makes four bread loaf pans plus one small loaf (about 14 pounds of cake).

Millie Pedrazzini
Humboldt County

QUICK CHOCOLATE RAISIN CAKE

1 cup sugar
½ cup shortening
2 eggs
1½ cups cocoa
2 cups flour
1½ cups applesauce
2 teaspoons soda
1 teaspoon each of cloves, nutmeg and cinnamon
1 cup raisins
1 cup walnuts

Preheat oven to 350 degrees. Cream sugar and shortening, add eggs. Stir in cocoa and flour. Add the soda and spice to the applesauce before adding to the mix. Beat well before adding the raisins and walnuts.

Optional Topping:

1 6-ounce package chocolate chips
½ cup chopped walnuts
2 tablespoons sugar

Mix the three topping ingredients and sprinkle on top of cake. Use pan 7½ x 11½-inch. Bake for 40 minutes.
Arline Cederquist
Fresno County

FRESNO RAISIN CAKE

1 package seedless raisins
2 cups water
1 cup sugar
1 cup shortening
1 teaspoon cloves
1 teaspoon cinnamon
1 teaspoon salt
3 cups flour
1 teaspoon soda

Preheat oven to 350 degrees. Boil raisins, water, sugar, and shortening 5 minutes. Cool. Add spices, soda, flour and mix well. Put into 2 greased and floured loaf pans. Bake about 1 hour. Needs no icing. Can be kept a long time.
Louise Correia
Fresno County

APPLE PIZZA PIE

1¼ cups flour
1 teaspoon salt
½ cup shortening
1 cup shredded cheese
¼ cup ice water
½ cup powdered non-dairy creamer
½ cup brown sugar
½ cup white sugar
½ cup flour
¼ teaspoon salt
1 teaspoon cinnamon
6 apples

Preheat oven to 400 degrees. Mix flour, salt, shortening, cheese, and ice water. Roll, shape and crimp edges in pizza pan. Mix non-dairy creamer, brown sugar, white sugar, flour, salt and cinnamon and sprinkle one-half mix on pizza pie dough. Cut, slice, peel apples and cover sprinkle mixture. Mix other one-half powder mixture with ¼ cup margarine and sprinkle over apples. Bake 35-45 minutes until apples are done.
Margaret Huston
El Dorado County

SIERRA BEAUTY APPLE PIE

⅓ cup shortening
1 cup flour
⅓ teaspoon salt
¼ cup water
6 medium Sierra Beauty apples
¾ cup sugar
3 tablespoons flour
½ teaspoon cinnamon
1 teaspoon cream
1 teaspoon sugar

Preheat oven to 350 degrees. Put shortening in bowl. Sift flour and salt together into bowl with shortening. Blend with blender until flakes are about pea size. Add water and mix. Take ½ mixture and roll out on pastry board. Put in 9-inch pie pan. Roll out remaining dough for top of pie. Peel apples. Slice into pie pan with crust. Mix sugar and flour and sprinkle into apples. Sprinkle top of apples with cinnamon and slice butter on top spreading around. Cover with remaining crust, spread cream over top of crust, sprinkle with sugar. Bake for 1 hour.
Josephine Gowan
Mendocino County

SUNSHINE LEMON PIE

1 pie crust, already baked
1 cup sugar
3 tablespoons cornstarch
¼ teaspoon salt
1 grated lemon rind
5 tablespoons lemon juice
4 egg yolks
1½ cups boiling water
3 tablespoons butter
4 egg whites, stiffly beaten
½ cup sugar
1 teaspoon vanilla

Place in cooking pan: 1 cup sugar, 3 tablespoons cornstarch, and ¼ teaspoon salt. Blend. Add grated rind of 1 lemon, lemon juice, egg yolks and boiling water, butter and cook over medium heat. Stir constantly until boiling. Cook four minutes longer. Let mixture cool slightly. Beat egg whites until stiff and add approximately 1 egg white to pie filling. Stir well. Pour into pie shell. Beat into remaining 3 egg whites, ½ cup sugar, and 1 teaspoon vanilla. Spread on pie and bake meringue until brown in a 325 degree oven.

Florence VanAlstyne
Sutter County

LEMON MERINGUE PIE

3 tablespoons cornstarch
1 cup plus 2 tablespoons sugar
grated rind of one lemon
4 tablespoons lemon juice
1 tablespoon butter
3 egg yolks (beaten)
1½ cups boiling water
Pastry for 8-inch pie

Preheat oven to 300 degrees. Combine cornstarch, with sugar in saucepan. Add lemon rind, lemon juice, butter and egg yolks (well beaten). Mix well. Add water very slowly. Cook over slow heat until thick and clear. Place in baked pastry shell. Prepare meringue.

Meringue:

3 egg whites
6 tablespoons sugar

Beat egg whites until almost stiff, add sugar while continuing to beat until stiff. Arrange on pie. Bake for 30 minutes.

Venita Pitkin
Tehama County

GLAZED BOYSENBERRY PIE

3 cups berries
1½ cups boiling water
1½ cups sugar
⅓ heaping cup flour
¼ teaspoon salt
1 teaspoon lemon juice
2 tablespoons butter
One 9-inch baked pie shell

Cover fresh berries with boiling water, let stand five minutes. Combine sugar, flour and salt. Stir in warm water drained from berries. Cook until clear, about eight minutes. Remove from heat, stir in lemon juice and butter, fold in drained berries; spoon into baked pie shell, and chill. Serve with whipped cream. Serves 6 to 8.
Marjorie Conrad
Fresno County

GLACÉ RASPBERRY PIE

1 quart raspberries
3-ounce package cream cheese, softened
1 9-inch pie shell
½ cup water
1 cup sugar
3 tablespoons cornstarch
1 cup cream, whipped

Wash and drain the berries. Spread the softened cream cheese over the bottom of the cooled pie shell. Cover with half the berries. To the remainiing berries add ½ cup water and mash these berries. Bring this to a boil then press through a fine sieve to extract all the juice. Bring the juice to a boil and add the mixture of sugar and cornstarch. Cook over low heat, stirring constantly, until boiling. Boil 1 minute. Cool. Pour over berries in the pie-shell. Chill at least 2 hours. Just before serving, decorate with whipped cream.
Marjorie Clarke
Plumas County

BLUEBERRY PIE

6 cups blueberries (raw)
3 tablespoons flour
4½ teaspoons butter
⅜ teaspoon salt
4½ tablespoons lemon juice
¾ cup granulated sugar
¾ cup light brown sugar
1 10-inch baked pie shell or 8 baked tart shells

Mix 3 cups blueberries, flour, butter, salt, lemon juice, sugar, and light brown sugar in a saucepan. Bring to a boil over low heat and continue cooking until mixture thickens, approximately five minutes. Cool. Add the remaining 3 cups raw blueberries, mix thoroughly and pour into baked pie shell or tart shells. Serve with whipped cream if desired.
C. Geotz
Sonoma County

EASY STRAWBERRY PIE

3 ounce package cream cheese
1 baked 9-inch pie shell
1 quart strawberries
⅔ cup water
1 cup sugar
3 tablespoons cornstarch
⅓ cup water
3 cups whipped cream, Cool Whip or other substitute

Spread cream cheese evenly in bottom of baked pie shell. Simmer together:½ cup of sliced strawberries and ⅔ cup water for 2 minutes. Blend together sugar, cornstarch, ⅓ cup water. Add to simmered strawberries and boil 1 minute. Let cool. Put uncooked remaining strawberries on top of cream cheese. Cover with cooked mixture. Refrigerate. Cover with whipped cream before serving.
Peg Johnson
San Diego County

ANGEL PINK CLOUD RASPBERRY PIE

1½ envelopes unflavored gelatin
¼ cup cold water
4 eggs, separated
1 tablespoon lemon juice
¾ cup sugar
2 pints fresh raspberries (frozen raspberries may be used)
⅛ teaspoon salt
¾ cup heavy cream, whipped
1 baked 9-inch pie shell

Soften gelatin in the cold water. Combine egg yolks, lemon juice and ½ cup of sugar in small saucepan. Heat slowly, stirring constantly, until mixture coats the back of a metal spoon. Remove from heat and add softened gelatin to hot mixture. Stir to dissolve. Put 1½ pints raspberries thru sieve to make 1 cup puree. Stir into gelatin mixture. Cool until it mounds slightly when dropped from a spoon. Do not let it get too firm. Beat egg whites with salt until frothy. Gradually beat in remaining ¼ cup sugar and continue beating until meringue is stiff and shiny but not dry. Fold into raspberry mixture along with whipped cream, reserving about ⅓ cup of whipped cream. Pour into pie shell and chill a few hours. Decorate with remaining whipped cream and berries. Frozen Raspberry Pie: Substitute 1 package (10-ounce) frozen raspberries for fresh raspberries.
Geraldine Hillis
Shasta County

CALIFORNIA ORANGE NUT PIE

1 cup white corn syrup
4 tablespoons melted butter
4 tablespoons sugar
½ teaspoon salt
1 tablespoon orange juice
1 tablespoon grated orange rind
3 eggs, lightly beaten
1 cup nut meats, broken
1 unbaked 9-inch pie shell

Preheat oven to 350 degrees. Combine syrup, melted butter, sugar, salt, orange juice, orange rind and beaten eggs. Stir in nut meats. Pour into unbaked pie shell. Bake until well browned.
Elsa Dean
El Dorado County

PEAR PIE

1 9-inch crust, filled three fourths with pears, sliced thin
⅓ cup butter, melted
1 egg
¾ cup sugar
4 tablespoons flour
¼ teaspoon salt
¼ teaspoon cinnamon
¼ teaspoon nutmeg
1 teaspoon vanilla

Preheat oven to 450 degrees. Pour ingredients over top of sliced pears in pie crust. Bake 10 minutes at 450 degrees, reduce to 350 degrees and continue baking 35 to 45 minutes or until brown.
Lorraine Valine
Sacramento County

GOLDEN PEAR CRUMBLE

7-8 Bartlett pears
3 tablespoons lemon juice
½ cup sugar
3 tablespoons flour
½ cup brown sugar
½ cup flour
½ cup butter
½ teaspoon cinnamon
½ teaspoon ginger
10-inch unbaked pastry shell

Preheat oven to 400 degrees. Into large bowl, slice pared and cored pears. Sprinkle with lemon juice. Mix together ½ cup granulated sugar and flour in smaller bowl, then toss lightly with pears. Spoon pear mixture into unbaked pastry shell, arranging slices as evenly as possible. Mix together brown sugar, flour, butter, cinnamon and ginger; sprinkle on top of pears. Bake for 45-50 minutes or until pears are done. Serves 8.
Emily Gowan
Mendocino County

SAN JOAQUIN NECTARINE PIE

2 cups sifted unbleached flour
1 teaspoon salt
⅓ cup shortening
⅓ cup unsalted butter
5 to 7 tablespoons cold water
2 tablespoons butter
¾ to 1 cup sugar
3 tablespoons unbleached flour
¼ teaspoon ground cinnamon
dash of salt
5 cups sliced ripe fresh nectarines

Preheat oven to 400 degrees. Sift flour and salt together; cut in shortening and unsalted butter with pastry blender till pieces are the size of small peas. Sprinkle 1 tablespoon water over mixture and gently toss with fork. Repeat process adding 1 tablespoon at a time until mixture is a workable dough. Divide dough in half. Flatten one half on lightly floured surface. Roll to ⅛-inch thick. Line a 9-inch pie pan with dough. Add nectarine filling: FILLING: (Combine ¾ to 1 cup sugar, 3 tablespoons flour, ¼ teaspoon cinnamon, dash salt and nectarines.) Dot with 2 tablespoons butter. Top with remaining dough. Flute edges. Bake at 400 degrees for 45 to 50 minutes.
Note: To avoid burning edges of crust, cover edges with a 1½-inch strip of aluminum foil.
Davida Delis
Kern County

CALIFORNIA PEACH PIE

Pastry for a 2-crust pie
¾ cup sugar
3 teaspoons flour (all-purpose)
½ teaspoon cinnamon
Dash nutmeg
¼ teaspoon salt
5 cups fresh peaches (sliced)
2 tablespoons butter
1 egg white

Preheat oven to 400 degrees. Prepare pastry for a 2-crust pie. Line the bottom of a 9-inch pie plate with pastry. Combine: sugar, flour, cinnamon, nutmeg, and salt. Mix in the fresh peaches. Fill pastry shell. Dot with butter. Adjust top crust, cutting a circle on top for the steam to escape. Beat egg white and coat the top crust. Bake 40-45 minutes. Serves 6-8.
Helen Richardson
Kern County

FRESH PEACH PIE

4 cups sliced fresh peaches
1 unbaked 9-inch pie shell
1 egg
1 cup sugar
1 teaspoon salt
2 tablespoons flour
1 teaspoon nutmeg

Preheat oven to 450 degrees. Slice fresh peaches into the unbaked pie shell. Beat together egg, sugar and salt and pour over peaches. Sprinkle flour and nutmeg over mixture and bake at 450 degrees for 10 minutes. Reduce heat and finish pie at 325 degrees for 30 minutes or as long as it takes to bake peaches. Serve cold either plain or with a whipped topping or ice cream.
Maun Baker
Tuolumne County

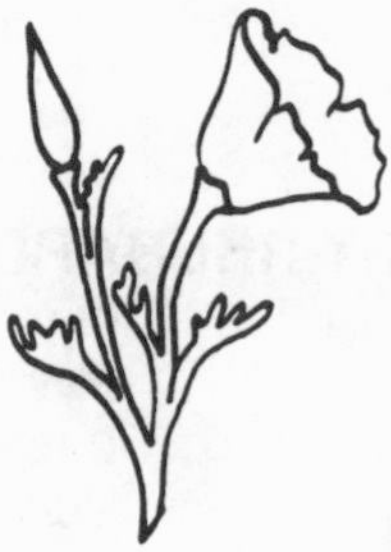

CRISP PERSIMMON PIE

1½ tablespoons tapioca
½ cup sugar
1 teaspoon grated lemon or orange peel
¼ teaspoon cinnamon
2 tablespoons lemon juice
4 cups peeled and sliced crisp persimmons (Fuyn or Maru)
Pastry for a 2-crust 9-inch pie

Preheat oven to 375 degrees. Combine tapioca with sugar, stir in lemon peel, cinnamon, and lemon juice and persimmons mixing gently until blended. Let stand 15 minutes, stirring once or twice. Place filling in pastry lined pie pan. Cover with top crust, seal and flute edge. Make vents in top crust. Bake on lowest rack of oven at 375 degrees for 50-55 minutes or until filling is bubbling and pastry is brown.
Lorrene H. Rosa
Sacramento County

RHUBARB SURPRISE PIE

1 9-inch unbaked pie crust
3 cups rhubarb, diced
1 3-ounce package Strawberry Jello
½ cup flour
1 cup sugar
¼ teaspoon cinnamon
¼ cup melted butter

Preheat oven to 350 degrees. Arrange the diced rhubarb in the pie crust. Sprinkle over the rhubarb the Strawberry Jello. Mix together the flour, sugar and cinnamon. Add the melted butter to the dry ingredients. Sprinkle this mixture over the pie filling and bake for fifty minutes or until the rhubarb is tender. Let cool to set the jello. This can be served plain or topped with whipping cream.
Lila Jury
Tuolumne County

STRAWBERRY-RHUBARB PIE SUPREME

3 cups rhubarb
2 cups hulled strawberries
1¾ cups granulated sugar
½ teaspoon salt
4 tablespoons bread flour
3 whole eggs
Pastry for a 2-crust pie
2 tablespoons soft butter
Yolk of 1 egg beaten and combined with 1 tablespoon milk

Preheat oven to 450 degrees. Prepare rhubarb by cutting crosswise into 1-inch long and ¼-inch wide strips. Hull and wash strawberries. Mix sugar, salt, flour and eggs and add to rhubarb-strawberry mixture. Put into pie shell (two crust) and dot with butter. Then top with lattice strips, brushed with egg yolk-milk combination. Bake in a 450 degree oven for 20 minutes, then reduce heat to 350 degrees and bake about 35-40 minutes longer. May be served with whipping cream. Serves 8.
Gloria Hildreth
Shasta County

PINEAPPLE PIE

1 No. 2 can crushed pineapple, drained
6 level tablespoons flour
1 cup sugar
2 eggs, separated
¼ cup butter
2 tablespoons sugar

Preheat oven to 375 degrees. Mix pineapple juice, flour, sugar and beaten yolks. Boil in a double boiler until thick, then add butter, crushed pineapple. A little lemon juice may be added if desired. When mixture is cool, put in a baked pie shell. Beat egg whites and add 2 tablespoons sugar. Mix well to form meringue mixture. Put meringue on pie and brown in oven, 10-12 minutes.
Lela Hughes
Fresno County

AMAZING RAISIN PIE

¾ cup seedless raisins
1 cup water
½ cup sugar
2 tablespoons butter or margarine
2 tablespoons flour
3 egg yolks
1 tablespoon grated lemon rind
4 tablespoons lemon juice
¼ teaspoon cloves
½ teaspoon cinnamon
½ cup nuts, chopped
1 9-inch baked pie shell

Preheat oven to 325 degrees. Simmer raisins, water and sugar over low heat for about 10 minutes or until raisins are tender. Mix a little raisin mixture into flour and return to low heat, stirring constantly until thickened (about 10 minutes). Remove from heat. Beat egg yolks slightly; add remaining ingredients to raisins. Return to heat and simmer until well blended. Place in baked 9-inch pie shell.

Meringue:

3 egg whites
¼ cup sugar

When filling is cool, top with meringue made by beating egg whites with sugar until stiff enough to hold peaks. Place in oven and brown in slow oven about 15 minutes at 325 degrees.
Violet Jensen
Fresno County

APPLE CIDER COOKIES

½ cup butter or margarine
1⅓ cups brown sugar, firmly packed
1 egg
2 cups unsifted all-purpose flour
1 teaspoon soda
½ teaspoon salt
1 teaspoon cinnamon
½ teaspoon ground cloves
½ teaspoon nutmeg
¼ cup apple cider
1 cup finely chopped peeled apples
1 cup raisins

Preheat oven to 400 degrees. Cream butter and sugar together until fluffy; beat in egg. Sift flour with soda, salt, cinnamon, cloves and nutmeg. Add to creamed mixture alternately with apple cider. Fold in chopped apple and raisins. Drop by level tablespoonsful on a well greased cookie sheet. Bake for about 10 minutes, or until lightly browned. Remove from cookie sheet and spread with apple glaze while still slightly warm. Makes about 4½ dozen cookies.

Apple Glaze:

2 tablespoons soft butter or margarine
1½ cups sifted powdered sugar
¼ teaspoon vanilla
dash salt
2½ tablespoons apple cider

Cream together soft butter or margarine and powdered sugar. Beat in the vanilla, dash of salt, and apple cider to make a good consistency for spreading.
Evelyn Sonka
Tuolumne County

APPLE SPICE BARS

½ cup shortening
1 cup sugar
1 egg
1 teaspoon vanilla
2 cups flour
1 teaspoon salt
1 teaspoon nutmeg
2 teaspoons baking powder
1 teaspoon cinnamon
2 teaspoons cocoa
½ teaspoon soda
⅔ cup milk
1½ cups raw apples, chopped

Preheat oven to 350 degrees. Cream shortening and sugar until fluffy. Add egg and vanilla and beat well. Sift flour, measure and sift again with salt, nutmeg, baking powder, cinnamon, and cocoa. Dissolve soda in milk. Add flour mixture to the creamed shortening and sugar alternately with the milk. Mix thoroughly. Add diced apples and mix well. Pour batter in two 8-inch square pans or 1 10 x 12-inch pan. Bake for 25 minutes. When cool, cut into 3 x 1 bars and roll in powdered sugar. This is also good baked as cupcakes. Cream cheese frosting makes a good topping.
Eleanor Clow
Mendocino County

BITE-SIZE FRUIT CAKE COOKIES

¼ pound each, red and green candied cherries, quartered
6 slices candied pineapple, cut into pieces
4 ounces coconut
2 cups pecans or walnuts, chopped
¼ teaspoon salt (optional)
½ teaspoon vanilla
1 can Eagle Brand sweetened condensed milk
½ cup flour

Preheat oven to 325 degrees. Mix all the ingredients together in large bowl. Dampen hands and press into balls or drop by ½ teaspoon onto greased cookie sheet. Bake for 10 to 15 minutes or until golden.
Mary Theiler
Calaveras County

BRYAN'S RAISIN COOKIES

1 cup margarine or shortening
1 cup sugar
1 cup brown sugar
2 eggs
1½ cups sifted flour
1 teaspoon soda
1 teaspoon salt
3 cups rolled oats
1 cup chopped walnuts
1 cup chocolate coated raisins
1 teaspoon vanilla

Preheat oven to 350 degrees. Cream shortening or margarine, add both sugars and eggs and beat well. Add dry ingredients, then oats, nuts, raisins, and vanilla. Shape into long roll. Chill several hours or overnight. Cut into slices with sharp knife about 1-inch thick. Place on ungreased pan and bake about 8 to 10 minutes. Makes about 5 dozen.
Debbie Jensen
Fresno County

CINNAMON RAISIN BARS

½ cup butter or margarine
1 cup brown sugar
1½ cups flour
½ teaspoon soda
½ teaspoon salt
1½ cups quick rolled oats

Preheat oven to 350 degrees. Cream the butter and sugar. Sift together dry ingredients and stir into creamed mixture. Add oatmeal and 1 tablespoon water. Mix until crumbly. Firmly pat half the mixture into greased 9 x 13-inch pan. Spread with raisin filling. Mix remaining crumbs and 1 tablespoon water. Spoon over filling and pat smooth. Bake for 35 minutes. Cool. Then drizzle with cinnamon icing. Makes 2½ dozen.

Raisin Filling:

¼ cup granulated sugar
1 tablespoon cornstarch
1 cup water
2 cups raisins

Cook over medium heat till thick and bubbly. Cool.

Cinnamon Icing:

1 cup confectioners sugar
¼ teaspoon cinnamon

Mix and stir in about 1 tablespoon of milk.
Marjorie Conrad
Fresno County

MARGARET'S APRICOT BARS

1½ cups sifted flour
1 teaspoon baking powder
1 cup brown sugar
1½ cups quick cooking rolled oats
¾ cup butter
1½ cups apricot jam
½ teaspoon cinnamon
2 tablespoons sugar

Preheat oven to 350 degrees. Mix flour, baking powder, brown sugar and rolled oats. Cut in butter until crumbly. Pat ⅔ of this mixture into a 13 x 9 x 2-inch baking pan. Spread with jam. Cover with remaining crumb mixture. Sprinkle cinnamon and sugar on it. Bake 35 minutes. Cool. Cut into bars. Makes 24 bars.
Margaret Gates
Riverside County

PEARL'S PRUNE COOKIES

2 cups brown sugar
⅔ cup Crisco
2 eggs
3½ cups flour
½ cup sweet milk
1 teaspoon soda
1 teaspoon cinnamon
½ teaspoon salt
1 teaspoon vanilla
1½ cups cooked chopped prunes
1 cup nut meats

Preheat oven to 350 degrees. Cream butter and sugar. Add eggs, beating thoroughly. Add milk and stir. Add flour, soda, salt and cinnamon. Add chopped prunes and nuts together, mix well. Drop by teaspoonfuls on cookie sheet and bake 15 to 18 minutes.
Pearl Eckels
Sutter County

PERSIMMON OATMEAL DROP COOKIES

¾ cup margarine
1½ cups sugar
2 eggs
1 cup persimmon pulp
1 teaspoon soda
1 teaspoon vanilla
1½ cups flour
2 teaspoons baking powder
½ teaspoon salt
½ teaspoon nutmeg
½ teaspoon cloves
1 teaspoon cinnamon
1½ cups quick rolled oats
½ cup coconut
½ cup chopped nuts

Preheat oven to 375 degrees. Cream together margarine and sugar. Beat in eggs. Stir soda into persimmon pulp and add to creamed mixture. Add vanilla and sifted dry ingredients, mix well. Stir in rolled oats, coconut and nuts. Drop by teaspoonfuls onto greased baking sheet. Bake for about 12 minutes. Makes 5 dozen cookies.
Vera Hutchinson
Placer County

PERSIMMON BAR COOKIES

½ cup margarine
¾ cup brown sugar
2 eggs
1½ cups persimmon pulp
1¾ cups wheat flour
½ teaspoon cinnamon
1 teaspoon soda
1 teaspoon baking powder
¼ teaspoon salt
½ cup coconut
1 cup chopped walnuts or almonds
1 cup raisins
Sesame seeds (optional)

Preheat oven to 350 degrees. Mix ingredients thoroughly and spread in greased and floured 13 x 8-inch pan. To decorate, add sesame seeds on top.
Madeleine Robinson
Fresno County

PLACERVILLE PERSIMMON COOKIES

1 teaspoon soda
1 cup persimmon pulp
2 cups sifted flour
½ teaspoon cinnamon
½ teaspoon cloves
½ teaspoon nutmeg
½ teaspoon salt
½ cup shortening
1 cup sugar
1 egg, beaten
1 cup chopped nut meats
1 cup raisins

Preheat oven to 350 degrees. Dissolve soda in persimmon pulp and set aside. Sift together flour, spices, and salt, and set aside. Cream shortening and sugar until fluffy, then beat in eggs. Stir in dry ingredients and persimmon mixture. Stir in nuts and raisins. Drop by teaspoonsful on well greased cookie sheet. Bake 10 to 12 minutes. Makes about 6 dozen.
Elsa Dean
El Dorado County

PRUNE WHEEL COOKIES

½ cup butter or margarine
½ cup sugar
½ cup brown sugar
1 egg
½ teaspoon vanilla
1¾ cup flour
½ teaspoon baking soda
1⅓ cups pitted prunes
½ cup water
½ cup sugar
¼ cup walnuts, finely chopped
½ teaspoon vanilla

Preheat oven to 350 degrees. Cream butter and sugars. Add egg and vanilla. Sift flour and baking soda together and add to creamed mixture. Chill. Cook prunes, water and sugar 5 minutes. Pureé in blender until smooth. Add nuts and vanilla. Divide the chilled dough in half. Between two sheets of plastic wrap roll half the dough into a rectangular shape ¼-inch thick. Spread with half or prune mixture. Roll up like a long jelly roll (without plastic wrap). Chill. Repeat with other half of dough and prune mixture. Slice about ¼-inch thick. Bake in preheated 350 degree oven for 8 to 12 minutes.
Note: Both dough and prune mixture can be mixed in a food processor.
Gerda Faye
Yolo County

VALLEY PERSIMMON COOKIES

2½ cups sugar
1 cup butter or shortening
2 cups walnuts, chopped
1 cup raisins
4 cups flour
1 teaspoon nutmeg
1 teaspoon cinnamon
2 eggs, beaten
1 teaspoon salt
2 cups persimmon pulp
2 teaspoons baking soda, sprinkled on pulp

Preheat oven to 350 degrees. Mix the flour, salt, nutmeg and cinnamon together, add nuts and raisins. Beat eggs together, add persimmon pulp in which the baking soda has been dissolved. Cream butter and sugar, add the eggs and persimmon mixture, mix well. Add the flour, salt, nutmeg and cinnamon, stir well. Drop by teaspoonful onto greased cookie sheet. Bake for 15 minutes. Makes 4 to 5 dozen cookies.
Dorothy Sani
Fresno County

CALIFORNIA GOLDEN APPLES

8 large Golden Delicious apples
2 cups sugar
3 teaspoons cinnamon candy
⅓ cup butter
⅓ cup water
8 teaspoons golden raisins

Core apples and place in 2-quart casserole dish. Mix sugar, cinnamon candy, butter and water. Heat mixture until butter melts. Add mixture to center of apples. Add 1 teaspoon of raisins to each apple. Bake at 350 degrees for 1 hour or until tender. Serve warm with whipped cream or ice cream on each apple. Serves 8.
Joan Scolari
Santa Barbara County

APPLE CRUMB PUDDING

4 cups peeled diced apples
¾ cup brown sugar
½ cup butter
¾ cup flour
¾ cup oatmeal
¾ cup brown sugar
1 teaspoon baking soda
1 teaspoon baking powder

Preheat oven to 350 degrees. Grease a 9 x 9-inch pan. Put in diced apples and sprinkle the brown sugar on top. Melt the butter in a small pan. Mix the flour, oatmeal, brown sugar, baking soda and baking powder together and add to the butter. Mix well and spread evenly over the apples. Bake for 45 minutes or until the apples are done. Can top with whipped cream or serve plain. This is a quick and very tasty dish.
Lila Jury
Tuolumne County

NORTHERN CALIFORNIA APPLE DUMPLINGS

Pastry:

Enough to cover 6 whole apples—7-inch squares

Filling:
6 medium apples
½ cup sugar
1½ teaspoons cinnamon
1 tablespoon butter

Syrup:

1 cup sugar
¼ teaspoon cinnamon
4 tablespoons butter
2 cups water

Preheat oven to 500 degrees. Peel and core apples. Place an apple on each square. Fill the cavity of each with the sugar and cinnamon mixture. Dot with butter. Moisten each corner of pastry square and fold up around apple. Place 2 inches apart in an 8 x 12-inch baking dish. Chill thoroughly. To make syrup: Mix syrup ingredients in a saucepan and boil 3 minutes. Pour hot syrup over chilled dumplings and bake 3-5 minutes - until crust shows slight coloring - in *very hot oven* (500 degrees). Reduce temperature to 350 degrees and bake about 30 to 35 minutes. Serve warm with hot syrup or whipped cream.
Initz Schneck
Shasta County

CALIFORNIA APPLE TORTE

⅔ cup flour
3 teaspoons baking powder
½ teaspoon salt
2 eggs, beaten
1½ cups sugar
1 teaspoon vanilla
2 cups peeled diced apples
1 cup chopped walnuts

Preheat oven to 350 degrees. Mix first three ingredients together. Add eggs and sugar. Then add vanilla and dry ingredients. Stir in apples and walnuts and pour in a greased and floured 8 x 13-inch pan. Bake for 40 minutes. Serve with whipped cream or ice cream.
Gerry Hillis
Shasta County

CALIFORNIA'S BEST APPLE CRISP

½ cup brown sugar
½ cup white sugar
¼ cup butter or margarine
¾ cup flour
4 cups apples
2 tablespoons lemon juice
¼ cup water
½ teaspoon cinnamon
¼ teaspoon nutmeg

Preheat oven to 350 degrees. Work sugars, flour and butter or margarine together until crumbly. Spread coarsely sliced apples in greased shallow 1½ quart baking dish. Pour mixture of water and lemon juice over apples. Sprinkle with cinnamon and nutmeg. Spread crumbled mixture over apples. Bake uncovered in 350 degree oven until apples are tender and crust crispy browned. Serve warm with cream.
Edna Whittenburg
San Luis Obispo County

APPLE TORTE

1 cup sugar
4 tablespoons margarine or butter
1 egg
1 cup flour
1 teaspoon cinnamon
1 teaspoon soda
2 cups finely chopped apples
1 cup finely chopped nuts
1 teaspoon vanilla

Preheat oven to 350 degrees. Cream sugar and butter or margarine. Add egg. Beat well. Sift dry ingredients, and add to creamed mixture, mixing well. Add apples, nuts, and vanilla, mixing until well coated. Butter large pie plate; add batter, spreading evenly. Bake 35 to 40 minutes. Serve warm or cold with any kind of good topping. Serves 10.
Marie A. Krull
Sutter County

CALIFORNIA WALNUT SUMMER SURPRISE

2 eggs
1 cup sugar
1 teaspoon vanilla
⅓ cup all-purpose flour
1 tablespoon baking powder
⅛ teaspoon salt
2 cups chopped peeled apples
½ cup chopped walnuts
Whipped cream

Preheat oven to 325 degrees. In a large mixer bowl beat together the eggs, sugar, and vanilla until light and fluffy. Stir together the flour, baking powder and salt. Blend into creamed mixture. Fold in apples and walnuts. Turn into greased and floured 9 x 9 x 2-inch baking pan. Bake for 30 to 35 minutes. Serve warm with whipped cream. Serves 6 to 8.
Jane R. Henning
Santa Barbara County

BLUEBERRY MUFFINS

2 cups all-purpose flour
3 teaspoons double action baking powder
½ teaspoon salt
4 tablespoons sugar
1 egg
1 cup milk
3 tablespoons butter
⅔ cup blueberries (fresh or frozen)

Preheat oven to 425 degrees. Sift the flour, baking powder, salt and sugar 3 times. Beat egg and add milk and melted butter. Pour liquid ingredients, all at once, into dry ingredients. Stir quickly until flour is just dampened, then give 5 or 6 more quick stirs. Batter should *not* be smooth, but a little lumpy. Add ⅔ cup blueberries. Spray your muffin tins with PAM or grease well. Spoon batter into pans, filling about ⅔ full. Bake approximately 20 minutes, or until golden brown.
Carol Goetz
Sonoma County

BERRY ROLY-POLY

5 cups fresh or frozen (unsweetened) boysenberries, olallieberries, blackberries or raspberries
1 cup plus 6 tablespoons sugar
1¾ cups hot water
2 cups all-purpose flour
3 teaspoons baking powder
1 teaspoon salt
6 tablespoons solid shortening
⅔ cup milk
¼ cup melted butter
¼ teaspoon ground cinnamon
May be served with ice cream on top. Preferably have the roly-poly warm.

Bake in 450 degree oven for 25 minutes. If using frozen berries, let stand at room temperature for 30 minutes. Combine 1 cup of the sugar with water in a small pan and simmer over low heat for 5 minutes; pour into bottom of a buttered 9 x 13-inch baking dish; cool to room temperature. Meanwhile, combine flour, 2 tablespoons of the sugar; baking powder and salt in a large bowl; cut in the shortening until crumbs are as fine as cornmeal. Stir in the milk and melted butter to make a soft dough. Gather the dough into a ball and knead 10 times on a floured board, then roll out into an 8 x 12-inch rectangle. Distribute 2 cups of the berries over dough; sprinkle with the remaining 4 tablespoons sugar and the cinnamon. Roll up dough, starting from the short end; pinch seam securely to seal in filling. Cut the berry cylinder into 8 1-inch wide slices and arrange slices cut side down in the baking dish with syrup. Surround slices with the remaining 3 cups berries, pushing them down into the syrup. It is also good made with sliced apples or peaches. Recipe has been used for fifty years.
Gerry Hillis
Shasta County

MOUNT SHASTA BERRY PUDDING

1 quart boysenberries
¾ cup sugar
1 egg
8 tablespoons sugar
3 tablespoons cream or evaporated milk
¾ cup flour
1 teaspoon baking powder

Preheat oven to 350 degrees. Mix berries and sugar together, put into a 9 x 9-inch deep baking dish. Make a batter by beating egg, 8 tablespoons of sugar and cream together. Add flour and baking powder together, which has been sifted twice. Pour batter over berries and bake in oven for 35 minutes. Serve warm as is with whipped cream or ice cream. Serves about 8 or 9 people.
Sylvia Clair
Shasta County

RED RASPBERRY DELIGHT

1 small angel food cake
1 6-ounce package red raspberry Jello
10 ounces of red raspberries either fresh or frozen

Use a 9 x 9-inch pyrex pan. Make Jello using a little less than the 4 cups of water (to compensate for the juicyness of the berries). Pour a little Jello in the bottom of the dish. Cut the angel food cake into 1½-inch cubes (removing all the brown crust). When the Jello has congealed some in the dish put in the cubes, fill all the cracks with raspberries, pour on part of the remaining Jello, push the cake down so the Jello is absorbed by the cake. Place the raspberries over the top of the cake (reserve a few for the garnish). Pour on the rest of the Jello and put in refrigerator to set. Top with whipped cream or Cool Whip and garnish with remaining raspberries. It is a pretty dessert served on a glass plate when cut into squares.
Geraldine Hillis
Shasta County

FRESH BERRY FOAM FROSTING

1 egg white
1 cup sugar
1 cup fresh strawberries, or blackerries

Beat with electric beater the egg white and sugar about 5 minutes. Then add 1 cup of strawberries, or blackberries. Beat 15 minutes until very thick and stands in peaks.
Note: You can also substitute 1 cup Hersheys cocoa for the berries in the off seasons.
Ethel Bess
Humboldt County

CHRISTMAS DATE TORTE

2 tablespoons flour
1 teaspoon baking powder
2 eggs, beaten
¾ cup granulated sugar
1 cup chopped walnuts
1 cup chopped dates

Preheat oven to 300 degrees. Mix together and spread in two 10-inch pie pans (greased). Bake for 30-40 minutes. Cool. Break up and mix with whipped cream.
Note: Can be made ahead of time—broken up and stored in a plastic bag in refrigerator until needed and then mixed with cream several hours ahead of use.
Teresa Spring
Sonoma County

SUNNY LEMON DESSERT

1 package lemon Jello
1 cup boiling water
⅔ cup sugar
Juice of 2 lemons
Grated rind of 1 lemon
1 can evaporated milk (13 ounce)
14 graham crackers
¼ cup sugar
½ cup butter

Chill milk overnight in refrigerator. Dissolve Jello in boiling water. When this mixture begins to congeal add lemon juice and grated lemon rind. Whip chilled milk to stiff peaks and add to above mixture. Roll graham crackers, mix with ¼ cup sugar and ½ cube butter. Pat this into shallow 6 x 10-inch pan and pour lemon-milk into pan. Chill until firm.
Edna Whittenburg
San Luis Obispo County

FABULOUS FRUIT FREEZE

2 to 3 cups nectarine or peach pulp
1½ cups lime sherbert
1 teaspoon almond flavoring if desired
6 to 8 ice cubes
¼ to ½ cup sugar

Mix fruit pulp and lime sherbert in blender. Add ice and flavoring to blender. Add sugar to taste. You may add more ice or flavoring or sugar to get the thickness you would like and the flavor.
Note: This is wonderful for those hot, hot days of summer.
Janie Salonen
Fresno County

PEACH CRISP

4 large peaches, peeled and sliced
⅓ cup flour
⅔ cup brown sugar
¾ teaspoon cinnamon
¾ cup quick oats
½ cup melted butter

Preheat oven to 350 degrees. Place sliced peaches in an 8 x 8-inch pan. Combine all other ingredients until crumbly. Sprinkle over peaches. Bake 30 to 35 minutes. Serve warm with whipped cream.
Rosalie Richardson
Kern County

PEACHY CHIFFON DELIGHT

4½-5 cups 1-inch Angel cake cubes
1 3-ounce package instant vanilla pudding mix
1 cup cold milk
1 pint peach ice cream (soft enough to blend)
1 3-ounce package peach Jello
1½ cups boiling water
2 cups cold thinly sliced fresh peaches (cling or freestone)

Place cake cubes in 9 x 9 x 1½-inch pan. In mixing bowl combine instant pudding and milk. Add ice cream. Beat at low speed until blended. Pour over cake cubes and set aside. Dissolve Jello in boiling water. Add cold peaches and stir. Pour Jello mixture over pudding. *Do not stir*. Chill until set. Cut into 3-inch squares. Serves 8-9.
Jan Schmidl
Sutter County

CALIFORNIA PEACH BOWL COBBLER

3 cups fresh cling peaches, sliced
¼ cup sugar
½ cup brown sugar
2 teaspoons cinnamon
3 tablespoons flour
1 cup flour
1 teaspoon baking powder
¼ teaspoon mace
½ teaspoon salt
½ cup melted butter
1 egg, beaten

Preheat oven to 350 degrees. Cook cling peaches and ¼ cup sugar in saucepan for about 15 minutes. Pour into small 8 x 8 x 2-inch pan. Sprinkle brown sugar, cinnamon and 3 tablespoons of flour over peaches. In a bowl combine flour, sugar, baking powder, mace, salt, butter and egg. Mix well. Spread over peaches. Bake for 45 minutes or more until topping is completely cooked.
Debby Heenan
Sutter County

"GERMAN'S" OLD FASHIONED GERMAN FRUIT KUCHEN

1¼ cups flour
1 teaspoon baking powder
1 tablespoon sugar
½ cup butter
1 egg, slightly beaten
1 tablespoon milk

Filling:

4 to 6 peaches, peeled and halved
1 egg, slightly beaten
1 cup sour cream
1½ tablespoons flour
¾ cup sugar

Streusel:

¾ cup sugar
2 tablespoons butter
½ teaspoon cinnamon
2 tablespoons flour

Preheat oven to 350 degrees. Mix first 3 ingredients together, then add butter and mix or cut as for piecrust. Mix together egg and milk and add to above. Press in sides and bottom of 9 x 13-inch pan. Place peaches on crust, cut side up. Mix egg, sour cream, flour and sugar. Pour over fruit. Cream sugar and butter, cut in flour and cinnamon. Mix well and use to cover fruit. Bake at 350 degree for 45 minutes, or until fruit is baked and streusel is a delicate brown.
Note: Use 1½ cups cherry or blueberry pie filling instead of peaches if desired. Pitted plums or peeled quartered apples are also good.
Betty German
Solano County

PEAR BREAD

1 cup margarine
1½ cups sugar
1 cup buttermilk
2 eggs
1 cup brown sugar
2½ cups flour
½ teaspoon salt
2 cups raw pears, mashed
1 teaspoon baking powder
1 teaspoon soda
1 teaspoon vanilla
2½ teaspoons cinnamon

Preheat oven to 350 degrees. Cream butter, add eggs and sugar and blend. Add dry ingredients alternately with milk. Add vanilla, fold in pears. Bake at 350 degrees for 45 to 60 minutes.
Vicki Norgard
Mendocino County

SUTTER ISLAND PEAR CRISP

Topping:

1 cup flour
½ cup oatmeal
1 cup ground walnuts
1 cup brown sugar, packed
½ cup melted butter

Filling:

4 cups sliced pears
½ cup sugar
½ cup flour
½ teaspoon cinnamon

Preheat oven to 350 degrees. Combine flour, oatmeal and brown sugar. Mix well with a fork. Stir in melted butter to make a crumbly mixture. Make filling in a lightly greased pan 8 x 8 x 2-inch. Combine all ingredients and add ½ cup water. Mix well. Sprinkle topping evenly over filling. Bake uncovered for 35 minutes.
Cynthia Salman
Sacto County

POMEGRANATE TAPIOCA PUDDING

¼ cup tapioca
1¼ cups pomegranate juice
½ cup sugar
1¼ cup water
Dash of salt

Mix tapioca, pomegranate juice, water, sugar and salt. Let stand 5 minutes. Bring to boil over medium heat, stir often. Cool 20 minutes or more. Stir well. Serve warm or cold. Makes six servings. Top with whipping cream or sour cream. Great for Christmas with cookies.
Margaret M. Schlegel
Fresno County

FLOATING ISLAND PRUNE WHIP

½ cup water
1 12-ounce bag pitted prunes
½ teaspoon grated lemon rind
1 tablespoon lemon juice
¼ teaspoon cloves
¼ teaspoon cinnamon
3 tablespoons sugar
3 egg yolks
¼ cup sugar
⅛ teaspoon salt
2 cups milk
1 teaspoon vanilla
1 teaspoon sherry
3 egg whites
¼ teaspoon cream of tartar
6 tablespoons sugar

Place in blender: water, prunes, lemon rind and juice, cloves, cinnamon, 3 tablespoons sugar. Blend to form a purée. Set aside. In top of double boiler, beat 3 egg yolks with ¼ cup sugar, salt. Scald milk. Add milk slowly to egg mixture, stir. Cook and stir over hot water in double boiler until custard coats a spoon. Add vanilla and sherry. Cool. Place in medium or large bowl: 3 egg whites, cream of tartar. Beat until foamy. Continue beating and add 6 tablespoons sugar gradually. Beat to form a stiff meringue. Fold in half of the prune purée. Place servings of the prune whip in sherbert dishes, pour custard over each. Makes six servings.
Note: Proportion of prune purée to meringue may be varied to taste. Purée keeps well in refrigerator, may be used as pastry filling also.
Dorothy Lindauer
Tehama County

PRUNE DELIGHT

1 package orange Jello
¼ cup sugar
¼ cup orange juice
Juice of ½ lemon
1 large can of evaporated milk (chilled)
1 cup cooked, pitted prunes
½ cup graham cracker crumbs

Add one cup boiling water to Jello, sugar, orange juice and juice of ½ lemon. Stir well and chill until partially thickened then beat until fluffy. Beat evaporated milk until stiff. Add Jello mixture, beat until well mixed. Add 1 cup cooked, pitted prunes. Place ¼ cup graham cracker crumbs on bottom of dish, pour mixture in and sprinkle with remainder of crumbs. Refrigerate.
Josephine Blasi
Sonoma County

PRU-NUT SNACKS

½ cup margarine
½ cup granulated sugar
2½ cups cut up dried prunes
1 egg
1 tablespoon milk
½ teaspoon salt
1 teaspoon vanilla
1 cup chopped walnuts
2 cups crispy cereal such as Rice Krispies, Wheaties, Corn Flakes. (Rice Krispies work best. You can crush other kinds with your hands before adding).
Coconut and chopped walnuts

Mix margarine, sugar and prunes in a large pot. Cook on medium until margarine is melted. Remove from heat. Add egg, milk, salt and vanilla. *Stir* and cook over *low* heat. It takes about 5 minutes for prunes to get soft. When soft and blended, remove from heat and cool in pan. When *cool*, add cereal and walnuts and stir to mix well. Form into 2-inch balls. Roll half the balls in coconut and the other half in chopped walnuts. The color contrast makes an attractive arrangement.
Note: The author made this recipe up and plans to enter the recipe at Tehama Fair.
Alcy Thorne
Tehama County

STRAWBERRY DELIGHT

1 cup flour
½ cup butter or margarine
½ cup nuts (chopped)
¼ cup brown sugar (packed)
2 egg whites
1 cup sugar
2 teaspoons lemon juice
1 10-ounce package frozen strawberries
1 package instant whipped topping (whipped according to package directions)

Preheat oven to 350 degrees. Mix until crumbly the first four ingredients and press into an 8 x 8-inch pan. Bake for 20-25 minutes. Cool and break into crumbs - set aside. Next combine the egg whites, lemon juice, sugar, strawberries and beat at medium speed for 5-10 minutes. Fold Strawberry mixture into whipped instant topping. Put ½ of crumb mixture into bottom of 9 x 9-inch *greased* (lightly) pan. Spread strawberry mixture over crumbs, and top with the remaining crumbs. Freeze.
Jan Cox
Shasta County

RHUBARB PUDDING

1 pound rhubarb, chopped
1 egg, well beaten
½ cup sugar
2 tablespoons cooking oil
¼ cup milk
1 cup flour
1 teaspoon baking powder
¼ teaspoon salt
1 teaspoon vanilla

Preheat oven to 350 degrees. Place chopped raw rhubarb in greased baking dish. Mix batter. Beat egg well, add sugar, cooking oil. and milk and mix well. Sift together flour, baking powder, and salt. Pour into egg mixture and mix thoroughly. Add vanilla and stir in well. Pour this mixture over the rhubarb. Bake for 45 to 50 minutes. Should serve with whipped cream. Serves 6 to 8.
Barbara Humphrey
Tehama County

QUICK FRUIT COBBLER

½ cup margarine
1 cup flour
1 cup sugar
¾ cup milk
1 teaspoon baking powder
1 quart peaches or cherries and juice

Preheat oven to 350 degrees. Melt 1 cube margarine in bottom of 9 x 12-inch pan. Mix together flour, sugar, milk and baking powder. Pour batter over margarine. Add fruit and juice. Bake until golden brown. May be served with whipped cream or ice cream.
Rose Kinslow
Shasta County

CALIFORNIA DRIED FRUIT COMPOTE

2 cups raisins (seedless)
½ cup dried prunes
½ cup dried apricots
½ cup dried peaches
Small lemon, sliced (optional)

Bring 4 cups water to boil, add raisins and prunes. Cook well, then add peaches and apricots. Cook until apricots and peaches are soft. Slice lemon very thin and float on top of compote. Cool and serve as a dessert.
Mary Mirigian
Fresno County

BRANDIED RAISIN CIDER SAUCE

⅓ cup brown sugar
3 tablespoons cornstarch
¼ teaspoon salt
2 cups cider
½ cup chopped raisins
8 whole cloves
1 stick cinnamon
2 tablespoons butter
2 tablespoons brandy

Combine sugar, cornstarch and salt in saucepan. Stir in cider, raisins, cloves and cinnamon. Cook and stir 10 minutes over medium heat. Remove spices, add butter and brandy. Serve warm over French vanilla ice cream. Also over fruitcake or persimmon pudding. Can also be used over ham slices.
Bonnie Trask
Fresno County

GRANNA'S WATERMELON ICE

6 cups watermelon cubes (1 inch cubes)
3 tablespoons confectioners sugar
1 tablespoon lemon juice
¼ teaspoon salt

In a blender, mix 1 cup melon with the rest of ingredients till smooth. Add 1 more cup of melon cubes and mix till smooth. Continue this process adding 1 cup at a time until all melon has been used. Pour into 9 x 9-inch baking pan and freeze until partially frozen (approximately 2 hours). Spoon mixture into large chilled bowl and beat with electric mixer until fluffy. Return to cold pan and freeze. Let stand at room temperature about ten minutes before serving.
Note: Make at least 1 day to a week in advance.
Lorraine McIntosh
Orange County

Chalee Koster

NUTS AND GRAINS

In recent years, tree nuts have been one of the fastest growing segments of a more than two billion dollar California tree fruit industry. The production of the two biggest tree nut crops, almonds and walnuts has more than doubled in the last ten years. Almond production has jumped from 150 million pounds to almost 400 million pounds while walnut production has grown from 100,000 tons to 200,000 tons. Walnuts are grown in the Sacramento Valley, San Joaquin Valley and many coastal areas of California. The majority of almond production is in the southern San Joaquin Valley with over 79% of U.S. production coming from California. Walnuts and almonds play an important role, as do all agricultural products, in offsetting U.S. trade deficits. Over 60% of almond crops and 30% walnut crops are exported to other countries. Nevertheless, probably the brightest rising star in the California nut business is the pistachio nut industry. In five years the California pistachio nut industry has grown from producing almost no significant tonnage to being able to fulfill the U.S. domestic requirements. Like almonds, pistachios are grown primarily in the southern San Joaquin Valley.

Last year, California farmers harvested over 2.3 million acres of grain with approximately half of that acreage planted in wheat. In addition, 550,000 acres of rice were harvested, bringing total value of grain and rice production to $1.1 billion. Much of the market for the food grains produced, wheat and rice, has been from foreign buyers due to the varieties and quality of the grain which yields best under California conditions.

Wheat produced in California generally contains lower protein and gluten content than wheat produced in the Midwestern regions of this country. This characteristic makes this wheat less desirable for commercial baking purposes because the gluten gives dough its sticky quality and seals escaping air allowing it to rise. With handling and kneading, this wheat will produce good bread but for mechanized baking it will not hold up as a bread wheat. It can be used to make all-purpose flour and in cookies and pastries. Because of its characteristics, however, 60-80% of the wheat grown in California is sold for export.

Nuts and Grains

. . . country goodness

ALMOND STUFFED MUSHROOMS

36 mushrooms
¼ onion
⅔ cup unblanched whole almonds
2 tablespoons butter
2 tablespoons cooking oil
¼ teaspoon sweet basil
¼ teaspoon salt
¼ teaspoon pepper
6 slices Swiss Gruyere cheese, each slice cut in 6 squares

Preheat oven to 300 degrees. Wash and dry mushrooms and carefully remove stems. Put mushrooms aside. Chop mushroom stems, onion, and almonds in food processor until fine (or mince very fine with sharp knife). Sauté mixture in the butter and oil in a non-stick skillet. Add sweet basil, salt, and pepper. Fill each mushroom and top with one square of the cheese. Bake for 18 minutes.
Note: This is an exceptionally good recipe - different and with a rich nut flavor accented by the cheese and hidden spice. A must to try!
J. Carl Ferguson
Stanislaus County

LINDEN NIBBLES

1 cup walnuts, chopped
2 tablespoons whole wheat flour
4 tablespoons bran cereal
1 cup mild honey
1 cup peanut butter
½ cup raisins, dates or prunes
½ cup oatmeal
2 teaspoons vanilla
¼ cup sesame seeds or flax seeds

Combine all ingredients. Mix well. Form into 1-inch balls. Cover and refrigerate, or use as a spread on crackers.
Joan Mifsud
San Joaquin County

SPICE TOASTED WALNUTS

1 egg white
1 tablespoon water
2 cups walnuts
½ cup sugar
¾ teaspoon salt
1 teaspoon cinnamon
¼ teaspoon cloves
¼ teaspoon nutmeg

Preheat oven to 300 degrees. Beat egg white and water slightly with fork. Combine sugar, salt, cinnamon, cloves and nutmeg; mix well. Mix with egg white and sprinkle over walnuts, stirring till well coated. Bake 30 minutes in 300 degree oven, stir 2 or 3 times during baking time.
Diane Foster
San Joaquin County

SWEDISH NUTS

1½ cups blanched almonds
2 cups walnut halves
1 cup sugar
Dash of salt
2 egg whites
½ cup butter or margarine

Preheat oven to 325 degrees. Toast nuts in slow oven, 325 degrees till light brown. Fold sugar and salt into egg whites. Beat till stiff peaks form. Fold nuts into meringue. Melt butter in a 15½ x 10½-inch pan. Spread nut mixture over butter. Bake in slow oven 325 degrees about 30 minutes, stirring every 10 minutes or till nuts are coated with a brown covering and no butter remains in the pan. Makes about 4 cups.
Diane Foster
San Joaquin County

SWEDISH WALNUT NIBBLERS

3 cups walnut halves
1 cup sugar
Dash salt
2 egg whites
½ cup butter or margarine

Toast nuts in a slow oven (325 degrees) until they are light brown - about 25 minutes. Beat egg whites until stiff. Gradually add sugar and salt, beating to form very stiff peaks. Fold in nuts. Melt butter in jelly roll pan. Spread nut mix over butter. Bake in slow oven (325 degrees), stirring every 10 minutes, for 30-40 minutes or until nuts are coated with brown covering and no butter remains in pan. Cool. Serve. Enjoy!
Pat Repanich
Tehama County

SAN JOAQUIN ALFALFA SPROUTS

2 tablespoons alfalfa seed (untreated)
Water

Soak 2 tablespoons alfalfa seed overnight in a quart wide-mouth jar filled ⅓ with warm water. Cover top of jar with cheese cloth and secure with a rubber band. Drain well and place jar on its side. Cover with paper towel to exclude light, leaving end open. Rinse seed with fresh water twice daily. Drain well each time. On the third or fourth day expose jar to light to develop chlorophyll. Sprouts are ready for use at the end of the fourth or fifth day. Refrigerate in a plastic bag until ready to serve. Sprouts will keep several days.
Barbara Ohm
San Joaquin County

WATERGATE SALAD

1 small package Jello Pistachio Pudding Mix
2 cups miniature marshmallows
1 8-ounce container Cool Whip
1 20-ounce can crushed pineapple
1 cup chopped nuts, if desired

Mix all of the above ingredients together. Chill. Can be served as a salad or as a dessert.
Lila Vineyard
Placer County

POPPY SEED DRESSING

½ cup sugar
1 teaspoon salt
1 teaspoon dry mustard
1½ tablespoon grated onion
4 teaspoons poppy seeds
⅓ cup vinegar
1 cup oil

Mix all ingredients and shake well. Good for fruit salads or cold slaw.
Seth Pierce
Marin County

PACIFIC COAST RICE SALAD

1 box M.J.B. chicken rice
3 marinated artichoke hearts
10 green olives, sliced
½ teaspoon curry powder
½ green pepper, diced
4 green onions, chopped
2 tablespoons mayonnaise

Cook rice and let cool. Mix other ingredients and add to rice. Use some of the oil from artichokes to help mix. Make the night before it is to be served.
Ruth Taylor
Santa Barbara County

CALIFORNIA RICE SALAD

3 cups California rice, Calrose or Brown rice, cooked and cooled
½ cup onions, finely chopped
½ cup sweet pickles, finely chopped
1 teaspoon salt
¼ teaspoon black pepper
1 cup mayonnaise
1 teaspoon prepared mustard
1 2-ounce can diced pimentos
4 hard-cooked eggs, chopped
1 4-ounce can cocktail shrimp (optional)

Blend all ingredients thoroughly. Chill. Serve on lettuce leaves if desired. Note: This makes an excellent substitute for the more traditional macaroni salad. Brown rice gives a more "nutty" flavor.
Dona Mast
Yolo County

TEHAMA WATERGATE SALAD

1 small package Instant Pistachio Pudding Mix—Jello Brand
1 15½-ounce can crushed pineapple
1 8-ounce container Cool Whip
1 cup miniature marshmallows
1 cup walnuts, finely chopped

Put the above ingredients into a bowl and mix thoroughly. Set into refrigerator till time to serve.
Note: This recipe takes about 1 minute to make, and it is really delicious.
Beverly Turner
Tehama County

TABOLI SALAD

1 cup hard red winter wheat, cooked
1 cup ripe tomatoes, chopped
1 cup canned garbanzo beans
½ cup green onions, sliced including tops
½ cup parsley, snipped
⅓ cup salad oil
⅓ cup lemon juice
1 teaspoon salt
½ teaspoon garlic powder
½ teaspoon seasoned salt

Soak wheat overnight in salted water; simmer for 1-1½ hours; cool. Mix all ingredients in large bowl. Proportions may be varied according to taste. Chill. When increasing recipe do not add more oil or lemon juice.
Note: This is a "complete protein" dish, good for vegetarian diets or as compliment to meat or sandwiches.
Yvonne Pylman
Yolo County

SACRAMENTO RICE CASSEROLE

2 pounds link pork sausage (cut in small pieces)
2 large onions, chopped
1 green bell pepper, chopped
2 good sized stalks celery, chopped
½ cup butter or margarine
3 packages Lipton's chicken noodle soup
2 cups uncooked rice
9 cups water
1 small bag blanched almonds, chopped

Preheat oven to 350 degrees. Fry pork well, drain off fat, put into roasting pan. Sauté chopped onions, bell pepper and celery in one cube butter. Put in roaster with sausage. In 2 cups boiling water add the 3 packages of noodle soup and boil one minute. Add remaining water and uncooked rice. Combine with ingredients in roaster. Bake 1 hour stirring occasionally. After ½ hour in the oven add the chopped almonds. Do not cover except in electric oven. Stir 2 or 3 times during baking.
Joyce Pappa
Sacramento County

ONION BROWN RICE

1 cube butter
1 can Campbell's onion soup
1 cup rice
1 can Campbell's beef bouillon soup (broth)

Preheat oven to 350 degrees. Melt butter in 2-quart casserole, pour in 1 cup rice, onion soup, beef bouillon soup. Put casserole in oven for 15 minutes with lid on, then 15 minutes with lid off. You may add 1 can of mushrooms if you wish. Serve with chicken, pork or beef.
Mae Wallace
San Luis Obispo County

QUICK RICE PILAF

1 tablespoon butter
½ cup onion, chopped
1 cup raw rice
2 cups chicken broth
1 teaspoon salt
Pinch of white pepper
1 small bay leaf

Sauté onion in butter until golden. Add remaining ingredients and heat until boiling. Turn into 1½-quart casserole. Cover and cook in 350 degree oven for 17 minutes. Stir with a fork and serve. Makes 6 servings.
Vesta Peart
Yolo County

CHILE-CHEESE RICE

1 cup long grain rice
3 cups water
½ teaspoon salt
1 4-ounce can chopped green chiles
1⅓ cups sour cream
2 cups shredded Jack cheese

Preheat oven to 350 degrees. Cook rice in boiling salted water. Combine cooked rice, chiles, sour cream, and 1½ cups cheese. Mix thoroughly. Turn into a greased 1½-quart casserole. Sprinkle remaining cheese on top. Bake for 30 minutes uncovered. Serves 6 to 8.
Mary Louise Naugle
Yolo County

WALNUT RAISIN RICE STUFFING

3 tablespoons butter
1 medium onion, chopped
1 rib celery, chopped
3 cups cooked rice
¼ cup raisins
¼ cup walnuts, chopped
2 tablespoons chopped parsley
1½ teaspoons grated orange rind
Salt, pepper, curry, to taste

Heat the butter in a heavy saucepan over moderate heat. Sauté the onion and celery just until they begin to brown. Add the rice and stir over heat until grains are well coated with butter. Remove from heat and stir in remaining ingredients. Use to stuff Rock Cornish hens or bake with chicken halves. If desired use barley, bulgar or crumbled cornbread in place of rice.
Mary Theiler
Calaveras County

SAVORY WALNUT STUFFING

1 cup butter or margarine
1 tablespoon ground sage
2 teaspoons ground thyme or leaves
2½ cups celery, thinly sliced
1¼ cups onion, chopped
1 chicken bouillon cube
¼ cup boiling water
1¼ teaspoon salt
¼ teaspoon pepper
⅓ cup Parmesan cheese
½ cup parsley, chopped
1½ cups walnuts, coarsely chopped
4 quarts day-old bread cubes (2 loaves—1 pound size)

In a large skillet heat butter until melted. Add sage, thyme, celery and onion, sauté 5 to 7 minutes or until onion is tender. Dissolve the bouillon cube in water and add to vegetables. Stir in salt, pepper, cheese and parsley. In large bowl combine walnuts and bread cubes, stir in the herb and celery mixture, mix well. Makes 2 to 3 quarts of stuffing which is ample for an 18 to 22 pound turkey.
Note: Giblets and the water they were cooked in also may be added.
Rena Swier
San Joaquin County

COUNTRY BRAN MUFFINS

1 cup whole wheat flour
¼ cup brown sugar
2½ teaspoons baking powder
½ teaspoon baking soda
¼ teaspoon salt
1¼ cup bran cereal
1 cup milk or ½ cup powdered milk and water
1 egg
¼ cup oil
1 mashed banana

Blend first five ingredients, set aside. Stir together; bran cereal, milk, egg and oil, beating until blended. Add banana and flour mixture, stirring just until combined; do not overmix. Fill baking cups ⅔ full. Bake for 20 minutes or until done. Makes 12 to 14 muffins.
Madeleine Robinson
Fresno County

BRAN MUFFINS

2 cups of water
2 cups All Bran or Bran Buds
3 cups white sugar
1 cup shortening
1 quart buttermilk
4 eggs, well-beaten
5 cups flour
5 teaspoons soda
2 cups 40% Bran Flakes
2 cups rolled oats

Boil 2 cups water, pour over the All Bran, let cool. In LARGE bowl, put sugar, shortening, buttermilk, eggs and mix well. Add flour, soda, Bran Flakes and oats. Mix well. Add cooled bran mixture. Cover tightly. Refrigerate. Batter will keep for 1 month. To bake, put in greased muffin cups, or paper lined muffin cups. Bake 425 degrees for 15 minutes. Variations: measure out amount to be baked, add raisins, nuts, a little bit of grated apple, or mashed banana.
Louise Correia
Fresno County
County

GRANDMOTHER'S CORN BREAD

1¼ cups flour (part whole wheat if you want)
¾ cup corn meal
4 teaspoons baking powder
1 teaspoon salt
1 to 3 teaspoons sugar (how sweet do you like it?)
¼ cup vegetable oil
Milk
1 egg

Preheat oven to 400 degrees. Mix all dry ingredients together lightly. Add egg and oil to bowl then start to mix in milk. Mix as little as possible and keep adding milk just until batter is a little thicker than pancake batter. Pour into a well greased 8 x 8 inch pan and bake 20 minutes until top springs back when touched. Serve hot with plenty of butter and honey. Serves 4 to 6. This recipe was passed from grandmother to mother to me. This may be the only time it has ever been written down. The amount of milk cannot be measured because it will depend on the size of the egg and the type of flour used.
Sherry Leonhardt
Plumas County

CORN BREAD

3 eggs
1 cup sour cream
⅓ cup vegetable oil
1 cup creamed corn
¼ teaspoon salt
1 tablespoon baking powder
1 cup yellow corn meal

Preheat oven to 375 degrees. Combine eggs, sour cream, vegetable oil and creamed corn and mix well. Grease and heat an 8-inch square baking pan. Combine salt, baking powder and corn meal and stir into egg mixture. Pour into the heated pan. Bake for 30-35 minutes or until well browned. Serve hot.
Judy Sealock
Shasta County

CALIFORNIA NUT LOAF

2 cups flour
¾ cups sugar
1 tablespoon baking powder
1 teaspoon salt
1 teaspoon cinnamon
½ teaspoon baking soda
½ teaspoon nutmeg
¼ teaspoon allspice
1 cup walnuts, chopped
1 cup crushed pineapple
¼ cup reserved pineapple juice
1 egg
2 tablespoons vegetable oil
1 tablespoon lemon peel (optional)

Preheat oven to 350 degrees. Grease 9 x 5-inch loaf pan. Sift dry ingredients into large bowl. Stir in nuts. Mix together pineapple, juice, egg, oil; add to dry ingredients and blend. Pour mixture into pan. Bake for 50 minutes.
Carole Odom
San Joaquin County

MOLASSES NUT BREAD

1 cup sugar
2 eggs well beaten
¼ cup butter melted
⅔ cup molasses
1 cup sour milk
1½ cups flour
1 teaspoon salt
1 teaspoon soda
1½ cups graham or whole wheat flour
1 cup raisiins
1½ cups nuts chopped

Add sugar to eggs and beat until smooth. Add butter and molasses and mix well. Add sour milk, flour sifted with salt and soda, then graham flour. Beat until smooth. Fold in raisins and nuts. Bake in two greased and floured 9 x 5-inch loaf pans at 350 degrees for 50 minutes or until done in the middle. Slice when cool.
Joan Lewis
Santa Clara County

QUICK WALNUT LOAF

3 cups sifted flour
4 teaspoons baking powder
1 teaspoon salt
¾ cup sugar
1 cup walnuts chopped
1 large egg
1½ cups milk
2 tablespoons melted shortening

Preheat oven to 350 degrees. Sift dry ingredients together. Add nuts. Stir in beaten egg mixed with milk. Stir in shortening. Pour into greased bread loaf pan 8 x 4-inch. Let stand 20 minutes before baking. Bake about 70 minutes or until done.
Leora Tower
Calaveras County

YUMMY WHOLE WHEAT PUMPKIN BREAD

1 egg
½ cup honey
½ cup apple juice
½ cup safflower oil
1 cup pumpkin, cooked and puréed
2 cups whole wheat flour
¼ teaspoon salt
¼ teaspoon baking soda
1 teaspoon cinnamon
½ teaspoon cloves
½ teaspoon nutmeg
½ teaspoon baking powder
1 teaspoon vanilla extract
⅔ cup raisins
⅔ cup chopped nuts

Use two mixing bowls. In the smaller, first bowl, blend the egg, honey, apple juice, oil and pumpkin. Beat well. In the second, larger bowl, mix the whole wheat flour (unsifted), salt, baking soda, cinnamon, cloves, nutmeg and baking powder. Stir the contents of the first bowl into the dry ingredients of the second bowl. Next add the vanilla, raisins and chopped nuts. Pour the batter into a greased, standard 3½ x 5 x 9-inch loaf pan and bake it at 350 degrees for 45 minutes. Then turn the oven down to 300 degreesF for another 45 minutes. If you let the bread cool slowly in the pan, it will slice more easily.
Darlene Cole
Kern County

HAWAIIAN SWEET BREAD

¼ cup instant mashed potatoes
⅔ cups boiling water
⅔ cups sugar
¼ cup instant non-fat dry milk
½ cup butter or margarine
2 packages dry yeast
⅓ cup warm water (110 degrees)
4½ to 5 cups all-purpose flour
3 eggs
1 teaspoon salt
½ teaspoon vanilla
¼ teaspoon lemon flavoring

In a small pan, beat instant potatoes into the boiling water. Stir in the sugar, dry milk and butter. Let cool to 110 degrees. Using the large bowl of an electric mixer, dissolve the yeast in the warm water. Blend in cooled potato mixture. Add two cups of flour and beat to blend. Stir in eggs, salt and flavorings until well blended. Then beat in 1½ cups more flour. With heavy mixer or by hand, add more flour to make a stiff dough. Turn dough out onto floured board, knead until smooth and satiny, adding more flour if needed. Turn into well greased bowl and turn over. Cover and let rise in warm place until double in size. Punch down and knead briefly to release air. Let rest 10 minutes. Divide dough in half. Shape each half into a flattened round, about 8-inch across and place in greased 9-inch pie pan. Cover loaves and let rise until almost doubled. Bake at 350 degrees until browned, 25 to 30 minutes.
Wilma Claverie
Imperial County

EASY FRENCH BREAD

4 cups flour
2 teaspoons salt
2 tablespoons sugar
1 package dry yeast
2 cups lukewarm water

Preheat oven to 350 degrees. Sift flour, salt, and sugar into large bowl. Mix yeast and water together and mix into flour mixture. Cover with cloth and let rise double in size. Put on floured board and knead until air bubbles are gone. Place into two buttered bread pans. Let rise one more time, then bake for 1 hour.
Barbara Humphrey
Tehama County

90 MINUTE ROLLS

4 cups warm water
4 tablespoons dry yeast (4 packages)
6 tablespoons sugar
4 tablespoons oil
1 teaspoon salt
8 cups flour

Mix yeast with warm water, add the sugar, salt and oil. Add the flour, one cup at a time mixing well until dough is elastic. It may be a bit sticky, but oil added to hands helps when handling dough. Put in greased bowl and let rise for 30 minutes. Place dough on lightly floured bread board and beat with rolling pin and put back in bowl and let rise another 30 minutes. It may not take 30 minutes so watch it in case it goes over edges. Beat down again, roll out on lightly floured board, cut into rolls, place in PAM sprayed pans or greased pans and bake at 450 degrees for 12 to 15 minutes.
Terry Hartley
Marin County

TASTY BANANA NUT BREAD

½ cup butter
1 cup sugar
2 eggs
1 cup unbleached or wheat germ flour, sifted
1 cup whole wheat flour, stirred
1 teaspoon baking soda
¼ teaspoon salt
1 cup bananas, mashed (3 fully ripe bananas)
1 teaspoon vanilla
½ cup chopped walnuts

Preheat oven to 350 degrees. Cream butter and sugar until fluffy. Add eggs, one at a time, beating well after each addition. Sift dry ingredients together. Mix vanilla with bananas. Add the sifted ingredients in about three parts to the creamed mixture alternating with the banana mixture. Beat the batter smooth after each addition. Add the nuts and mix well. Pour into greased loaf pan 9 x 5 x 3 inches and bake at 350 degrees for about 1 hour, or until center is firm. Cool for 5 minutes in pan, then turn out on rack to finish cooling.
Note: This freezes very well. To slice very thin, wrap loaf in foil after it is completely cooled and store for 24 hours, then slice.
Mona Pankey
Kern County

PROVINCIAL FRENCH BREAD

- **2½ cups warm water (105 to 115 degrees)**
- **2 packages or cakes of yeast, active dry or compressed**
- **1 tablespoon salt**
- **1 tablespoon sugar**
- **1 tablespoon margarine, melted (shortening)**
- **7 cups unsifted flour**
- **Cornmeal**
- **1 egg white, slightly beaten**
- **1 tablespoon cold water**
- **Sesame seeds**

Measure warm water into large warm bowl. Sprinkle or crumble in yeast. Stir until dissolved. Add salt, sugar and margarine. Add flour, a little at a time and stir until flour is well blended. The dough will be sticky. Place dough in a greased bowl. Cover with dish towel. Let rise in warm place, free from draft, until doubled in bulk, about 1 hour. Punch down and turn dough onto lightly floured board. Divide into 2 equal portions. Roll each half into an oblong, 15 x 10 inches. Beginning with the wide side, roll up tightly toward you. Seal edges by pinching together. Taper ends by rolling gently back and forth. Starting at one end, coil tightly each roll of dough on a greased baking sheet sprinkled with cornmeal. Cover. Let rise in warm place, free from draft, until doubled in bulk, about 1 hour. With a sharp knife, score tops of loaves, crisscrossing top 3 times. Bake at 375 degrees 25 minutes. Remove from oven and brush with egg white mixed with cold water. Sprinkle with Sesame seeds. Return to oven and bake 5 minutes longer. Makes 2 loaves.

Lois Hunn
Yolo County

COTTAGE CHEESE PANCAKES

- **1 cup cottage cheese, at room temperature**
- **6 eggs, at room temperature**
- **6 tablespoons whole wheat flour**
- **6 tablespoons butter, melted**

Mix cottage cheese, eggs, flour, and butter in blender. Use ¼ cup batter for each pancake and cook on a hot, lightly greased, griddle. Serve with jelly or syrup. *Note:* This is extremely simple to make and quite high in protein.

Roberta Jones
Orange County

GOLDEN STATE BRAN MUFFINS

5 cups white flour (or part whole wheat)
5 teaspoons soda
2 teaspoons salt
1 cup oil
2 cups honey
4 eggs
1 quart buttermilk
1 15-ounce box Raisin Bran
1 cup chopped nuts

Preheat oven to 350 degrees. In large container mix flour, soda and salt. In separate (2 quart) bowl mix oil, honey, eggs and buttermilk. Add liquid ingredients to dry ingredients and beat well. Then stir in Raisin Bran and nuts. Bake in greased or papered muffin tins for 15 to 20 minutes. Batter may be stored, covered, in refrigerator for up to 6 weeks, and dipped out as needed. *Note:* Do not stir after refrigerating. Tupperware serves well to store batter.
Joan Schramm
Los Angeles County

SHEEPHERDER BREAD

2 packages yeast
3½ cups warm water
2 tablespoon sugar
4 teaspoons salt
8 cups flour

Dissolve yeast in water. In a large pan mix sugar, salt and flour. Pour water mixture over flour mixture and stir with a wooden spoon until "sticky". Add more water if needed. Let rise in same pan until double in size. Knead on floured board, adding small amounts of flour until it can be handled. Divide into three parts; knead well. Put in lightly buttered pans. Use loaf pans or small round aluminum pans. Turn the dough so it is lightly buttered on all sides. Cover and let rise to top of pans. Heat oven to 400 degrees and bake for 55 to 60 minutes. Remove from pans and set aside to cool, if you can keep from eating it long enough to cool.
Note: Substitute 2 teaspoons garlic salt for 2 teaspoons of the regular salt if you like the sour taste.
Josephine Steffanic
Plumas County

COFFEE CAN BREAD

1 package active dry yeast
½ cup warm water
⅛ teaspoon ground ginger
3 tablespoons honey
1 13 ounce can undiluted evaporated milk
1 teaspoon salt
2 tablespoons salad oil
1½ cups whole wheat flour
2½ to 3 cups unsifted regular all-purpose flour

Dissolve yeast in water in a large mixer bowl; blend in ginger and 1 tablespoon of the honey. Let stand in a warm place until the mixture is bubbly, about 15 minutes. Stir in the remaining 2 tablespoons of honey and the milk, salt, and salad oil. With mixer on low speed, beat in whole wheat flour. Beat in all-purpose flour 1 cup at a time, beating very well after each addition. Add the last cup of all-purpose flour beating with a heavy wooden spoon, until dough is very heavy and stiff, but too sticky to knead. Place dough in a well greased 2-pound coffee can, or divide into 2 well greased 1-pound coffee cans. Cover with well greased plastic can lid. Freeze if you wish. To bake, let covered cans stand in warm place until dough rises and pops off the plastic lids, 45 to 60 minutes for 1-pound cans, 1 to 1½ hours for 2-pound cans. (If frozen, let stand in cans at room temperature until lids pop; this takes 4 to 5 hours for 1-pound cans, 6 to 8 for the 2-pound size.) Discard lids and bake in a moderate oven (350 degrees) for 45 minutes for 1-pound cans, 60 minutes for 2-pound cans. Crust will be very brown; brush top lightly with butter. Let cool for 5 to 10 minutes on a cooling rack, then loosen crust around edge of can with a thin knife, slide bread from can, and let cool in an upright position on rack. Makes 1 large or 2 small loaves.
Note: The batter will keep up to 2 weeks in the freezer.
Tressa Connor
Yolo County

OATMEAL TOP FOR PIE

¾ cup rolled oats
¼ cup margarine
½ cup brown sugar
¼ cup whole wheat flour
¼ cup chopped nuts (optional)
1 teaspoon cinnamon (optional)

Put all ingredients in bowl and mix thoroughly, spread on top of fruit pie. Quick pie topping.
Madeleine Robinson
Fresno County

PECAN PIE

4 eggs
2 cups sugar
1½ cups pecans
1 cups raisins (optional)
3 teaspoons vinegar
1 teaspoon cinnamon
1 teaspoon cloves
1 tablespoon butter
1 tablespoon cream

Blend eggs and sugar together. Add rest of ingredients in order. Pour mixture into a 9 inch pie shell and bake in a 350 degree oven until the top of the mixture is crusty - about 45-55 minutes. Walnut meats may be used instead of the pecans.
Inetz Schneck
Shasta County

DAIRY GOOD RICE PUDDING

⅓ cup raw white rice
½ cup sugar
1 quart milk
1 teaspoon vanilla
Cinnamon and raisins to taste (optional)

Preheat oven to 300 degrees. Put all ingredients into heavy crock-bowl or ovenproof casserole. Stir until sugar dissolves. Put into oven and bake for two hours. Turn off heat and leave pudding in oven until cool.
Marlene Martin
Siskiyou County

AUNT IDA'S COFFEE CAKE

2½ cups sifted flour
1 cup brown sugar
¾ cup white sugar
½ teaspoon salt
½ teaspoon nutmeg
¾ cup salad oil
½ cup walnuts, chopped
1 teaspoon cinnamon
1 teaspoon baking powder
1 egg
1 cup sour milk or buttermilk

Preheat oven to 350 degrees. Mix together the first six ingredients, blend well. Take out ¾ cup of this mixture, add nuts and cinnamon, set aside for the topping. To the balance of the mixture, add remaining ingredients. Mix well. Pour into greased baking dish 9 x 13 x 2 inches. Spread reserve sugar mixture on top. Bake in preheated oven for 30 to 35 minutes.
Violet Jensen
Fresno County

DATE-NUT CAKE

1 cup dates, cut in pieces
1½ cups boiling water
1 teaspoon soda
¾ cup shortening
1 cup sugar
2 eggs
1½ cups sifted flour
½ teaspoon soda
¾ teaspoon salt

Preheat oven to 325 degrees. Grease and flour a 9 x 13 inch pan. Combine dates, boiling water, and soda and let cool. Pour into prepared pan. Sprinkle ½ package semi-sweet chocolate bits over raw cake mix and add ½ cup chopped walnuts and ½ cup regular sugar over nuts and bake 50 minutes.
Ruth Taylor
Santa Barbara County

CHERRY-CHEESE-NUT SUPREME

1½ cup flour
4 tablespoons sugar
½ teaspoon salt
2 cups chopped walnuts (fine)
⅔ cup margarine or butter (melted)
1 package 8 ounces cream cheese
2 eggs
1 cup sugar
3 tablespoon cornstarch
2 cups frozen cherries or fresh berries
1 cup sugar
2 tablespoons water
Whipping cream

Preheat oven to 400 degrees. For crust, combine flour, sugar, salt and nuts; blend in melted butter or margarine with a fork. Press mixture on bottom of 9 x 13 inch pan. Bake at 400 degrees for 5 minutes.

For cheese filling, beat cheese, eggs, and 1 cup sugar until mixture is smooth. Pour into crust and bake in 350 degree oven for 20 minutes. Cool.

For cherry top, mix 1 cup sugar and the cornstarch in saucepan. Add cherries and 2 tablespoons of water and mix well. Heat, stirring until mixture is clear and thickened. Cool. Spread on cooled baked cheese cake. Refrigerate. When ready to serve, cut into squares and dab some whipped cream on top. Makes 12 servings.
Diana Machado
San Joaquin County

FAVORITE APPLESAUCE CAKE

2 cups flour
1 cup sugar
1 tablespoon cornstarch
2 tablespoons cocoa or chocolate or one of each
2 teaspoons baking soda
½ teaspoon salt
¼ teaspoon cinnamon
¼ teaspoon nutmeg
½ cup Saffola Oil
1½ cup applesauce
1 egg (optional)
½ cup walnuts, chopped
½ cup raisins

Preheat oven to 350 degrees. Sift flour once and then measure. Sift all dry ingredients together into bowl, add applesauce, oil and egg. Beat for 4 minutes or so with electric mixer. After all the batter has been well mixed, add walnuts and raisins. Pour into an 8 x 12 inch baking dish. Bake at 350 degrees for 45 minutes, or until toothpick comes out dry.
Lorraine Valine
Sacramento County

GOLD RUSH CHOCOLATE SHEET CAKE

½ cup oil
½ cup margarine
1 cup water
2 cups sugar
2 cups flour
½ cup cocoa
2 eggs, beaten
½ cup buttermilk
1½ teaspoons soda
1 teaspoon vanilla

Frosting:

½ cup margarine
½ cup buttermilk
1 box powdered sugar
¼ cup cocoa
1 cup walnuts, chopped

Preheat oven to 350 degrees. Grease and flour a 15 x 10½ x 1 inch jelly roll pan. Bring to boil the oil, margarine and water. Pour over the sugar, flour and cocoa. Add eggs and mix well. Add the buttermilk to which has been added the soda and vanilla. Pour into prepared pan and bake exactly 20 minutes. While cake is baking, make frosting. Melt margarine add add to buttermilk. Pour over the powdered sugar and cocoa. Add the walnuts and stir well. Frost the cake while it is still hot. Makes 18 servings.
Margaret Hagar
San Luis Obispo County

MISSISSIPPI MUD CAKE

2 sticks margarine (1 cup)
½ cup cocoa
4 eggs
2 cups sugar
1½ cups flour
½ teaspoon salt
1½ cups chopped walnuts
1 package miniature marshmallows 10½ ounces

Frosting:

1 pound powdered sugar
⅓ cup cocoa
½ cup margarine, melted
½ cup milk
1 teaspoon vanilla

Preheat oven to 350 degrees. Melt butter, then add cocoa. Beat eggs with sugar. Add flour and salt. Add butter mixture. Mix in the chopped walnuts. Put in 9 x 13-inch baking dish. Bake in 350 degree oven for 30 minutes. Remove from oven and spread marshmallows over top while still hot. Let set until marshmallows melt, then spread on frosting. Let set over night, preferably, before serving.
Elaine Eilers
San Joaquin County

NORTH SAN LUIS OBISPO COUNTY WALNUT DESSERT

3 egg whites
1 teaspoon vanilla
¾ cup graham cracker crumbs
1 cup walnuts, course chopped
1 teaspoon baking powder
¼ teaspoon salt

Preheat oven to 350 degrees. Beat egg whites until stiff. Add vanilla. Fold in dry ingredients until mixed. Put in greased 8 x 8-inch pan. Bake 20 to 25 minutes. When cool cut in squares and top with whipped cream.
Margaret Vandegrift
San Luis Obispo County

NUTTY CARROT CAKE

2 cups sugar
1½ cups oil
4 eggs
2 cups flour
2 teaspoons soda, cinnamon, baking powder
1 teaspoon salt
3 cups grated carrots
1 cup walnuts

Frosting:

1 8-ounce cream cheese
1 pound powdered sugar
1 tablespoon butter
1 teaspoon vanilla

Preheat oven to 350 degrees. Grease and flour 9 x 13 inch pan. Bake at 350 degrees for 40-50 minutes or until done. Cream all frosting ingredients together and frost cake.
Note: Keep refrigerated!
Dede Mariani
Santa Clara County

PARTY ICE BOX CAKE

1 6-ounce package raspberry jello
1 cup sugar
¼ cup butter
1 egg yolk
1 cup chopped nuts
1 15½ ounce can crushed pineapple, drained
1 egg white
½ pound vanilla wafers

Dissolve jello with water, cool to slightly jell. Mix sugar with butter, add egg yolk, nuts and pineapple. When mixed well, add stiffly beaten egg white. Place a layer of wafers close together in bottom of 12 x 8 inch baking dish. Cover with pineapple mixture, alternating each layer with wafers and mixture. When all is used up, pour jellied jello over top and let stand for 24 hours.
Note: Good served with whipped cream.
Pauline Rohrer
San Luis Obispo County

ROCKY ROAD SKILLET CAKE

1 18½ ounce package chocolate or yellow cake mix
1½ cups miniature marshmallows
1½ cups chocolate morsels
1 cup chopped walnuts

Mix cake according to directions on package. Turn into greased 11-inch electric skillet. Cover (vent closed). Bake at 275 degrees for 25 to 30 minutes, or until done. Immediately, sprinkle marshmallows, chocolate morsels and walnuts in layers over top. Replace cover and let stand for about 10 minutes until chocolate is melted. Swirl top, if desired.
Mildred Peterson
Mendocino County

WALNUT APPLESAUCE CAKE

¾ cup margarine
1½ cups sugar
2 eggs
1 No. 303 can applesauce
½ teaspoon salt
1 teaspoon vanilla
½ teaspoon cinnamon
3 cups flour
1 tablespoon baking powder
1½ teaspoons soda
½ cup flour
1 quart black walnuts

Preheat oven to 300 degrees. Grease and flour bundt or angel food pan. Cream margarine and sugar, then add eggs and beat for a minute. Add applesauce, salt, vanilla and cinnamon, and stir. Add the 3 cups flour, baking powder and soda. Mix well. Coat walnuts with ½ cup flour. Add to mixture, stir with spoon. Pour into pan. Bake for 1 hour and 40 minutes until done. Cool in pan for 30 minutes.
Patricia McPhail
Tehama County

WALNUT CREAM CHEESE CAKE

2 tablespoons butter, softened
⅓ cup walnuts, finely chopped
2 tablespoons sugar
1 cup butter
6 ounces cream cheese
1½ cups sugar
4 eggs
2 cups cake flour
2 teaspoons baking powder
½ teaspoon salt
1 teaspoon lemon rind, grated
1½ cups walnuts, coarsely chopped

Generously butter bundt pan and sprinkle with chopped walnuts and sugar. Set aside. Cake: Cream together butter and cream cheese. Add sugar. Beat eggs well and add to mixture. Sift cake flour, baking powder and salt. Add flour mixture to egg mixture. Add lemon rind and walnuts. Put in prepared pan and bake at 300 degrees for 1 hour and 20 minutes or until done when tested. Let stand 10 minutes in pan and then turn out on rack. Cool.
Note: Chef's secret: Don't skimp on butter or walnuts. It's worth it!
Joan Lewis
Santa Clara County

CARROT FRUITCAKE

1 cup carrots, grated
1 cup raisins
¾ cup honey
1 teaspoon cinnamon
1 teaspoon allspice
1 teaspoon salt
½ teaspoon nutmeg
¼ teaspoon cloves
2 tablespoons butter
1½ cups whole wheat flour
1 teaspoon baking soda
½ cup cup wheat germ
½ cup chopped walnuts

Preheat oven to 300 degrees. Cook carrots, raisins, honey, butter and spices in the water for 10 minutes; allow to cool. Mix together the flour, baking soda, wheat germ and walnuts. Combine with the other ingredients. Pour into two small well greased loaf pans. Bake for 45 minutes.
Nancy Thelander
Imperial County

GOLD MINER'S MUD CAKE

3 cups flour
2 cups sugar
2 teaspoons baking soda
½ cup cocoa
2 teaspoons vinegar
1 cup salad oil
1 teaspoon salt
2 teaspoons vanilla
2 cups cold water
2 eggs

Place all ingredients in one bowl. Mix well. Pour into greased and floured 9 x 13-inch pan. Bake at 350 degrees for 35 to 40 minutes. Cool and frost with your favorite chocolate frosting. Serves 10 to 12.
Note: A very rich, moist cake.
Virginia Larsen
Santa Barbara County

FLAKY PIE CRUST MIX

12½ cups all-purpose flour
2 tablespoons salt
5 cups vegetable shortening

Step 1
Combine flour and salt in large bowl. Mix well. With a pastry blender, cut in shortening until evenly distributed. Place in a large airtight container. Label. Store in a cool dry place. Use within 10 to 12 weeks. Or put 2½ cups mixture into freezer bags. Seal and label. Freeze. Use within 12 months. Makes enough for 6 double-crust pies or 12 single-crust pies.

Step 2
2½ cups flaky pie crust mix
¼ cup ice water
1 egg, well beaten
1 tablespoon white vinegar

Put mix in medium size bowl. In small bowl combine water, egg, and vinegar. Sprinkle a spoonful of water mixture over mix and toss with fork until dough barely slings together in bowl. Roll out dough to desired thickness between 2 sheets of lightly floured wax paper. Place dough in 9-inch pie pan being careful not to stretch dough. For double crust pie, place top crust over filling and press together edges and flute. Makes one double-crust pie or two pie shells.
Note: A great time-saver!
Shawn Brandenberg
Imperial County

PIE CRUST

2½ cups unsifted flour
1 teaspoon salt
1 cup shortening
1 egg
1 tablespoon vinegar
½ cup cold water

Blend flour, salt and shortening. In small bowl mix egg, vinegar and water, then add to flour. Let stand 10 minutes or longer. Note: Double this and have some left for another day. It keeps several days in the refrigerator.
Helen Roberti
Plumas County

RAISIN ORANGE CAKE

1 large orange
⅓ cup milk
2¼ cups all-purpose flour
1¼ cups sugar
⅔ cups butter or margarine
2 eggs
1 teaspoon soda
1 teaspoon baking powder
½ teaspoon salt
1 cup raisins
1 cup chopped nuts

Topping:

Juice from one orange
3 tablespoons sugar

Preheat oven to 350 degree. Cut unpeeled orange into small chunks and place in electric blender; add milk and whirl until finely chopped. Pour into large bowl. Add flour, sugar, butter, eggs, soda and baking powder and salt. Beat at low speed until well mixed, scraping bowl often. Then beat at high speed for 3 minutes. Stir in raisins and nuts. Mix by spoon. Pour into greased and floured 13 x 9-inch pan. Bake in a preheated oven for 30 minutes, or until toothpick comes out clean. Heat the juice from 1 orange and add 3 tablespoons of sugar, stirring until sugar is dissolved. While hot, poke holes with a large fork all over the cake. Pour orange/sugar mixture over cake.
Anna Brinkman
Imperial County

AUNT RUTH'S ENGLISH TOFFEE

1 pound butter (no substitutes)
2 cups sugar
2 cups almonds, coarsely chopped

Lightly butter two cookie pans. Chop almonds and have at reach near stove. Put butter and sugar into heavy 4 quart pan and put candy thermometer on edge. Cook over high heat until mixture reaches 240 degrees, stirring constantly. Add chopped almonds and continue stirring until mixture reaches 290 degrees. Remove from heat and pour ½ of mixture onto each cookie pan, spreading to about ¼ inch thickness. When toffee is nearly cool, flip to prevent sticking. When cool, break into bite size pieces.
Note: A candy thermometer is a MUST.
Helen Zinck
Riverside County

EASY LOW-SUGAR CANDY

½ cup dark brown sugar
½ cup honey
1 cup peanut butter
½ cup real chocolate chips (optional)
1 cup almonds, chopped
1 3-oz. can chow mein noodles

Combine sugar and honey in heavy 3 quart saucepan. Heat, stirring constantly, until it comes to a boil. Remove from heat at once. Add peanut butter and chocolate chips, stir until well mixed. Add almonds and chow mein noodles. Stir. Place waxed paper on cookie sheet and drop candy onto waxed paper with a teaspoon. Shape lightly with fingers. Makes about 24.
Nini Hofhenke
Tehama County

PASO ROBLES ALMOND BRITTLE

1 cube margarine or butter
1 cup sugar
1½ cups almonds

Combine margarine, sugar and almonds in heavy saucepan and stir constantly until twenty (20) almonds pop. Takes about ten minutes and reaches 300 degrees on candy thermometer. Pour into greased pan.
Margaret Hager
San Luis Obispo County

POPCORN BALLS

3 quarts of popped corn
¾ cup honey
¾ cup sugar
½ cup water
1 teaspoon salt
1 tablespoon butter

Cook sugar and water to crack stage. Add honey, stirring in slowly. Cook again about one (1) minute. Remove from fire. Add salt and butter. Pour over freshly popped corn and form into balls.
Helen Stewart
Shasta County

PEANUT BUTTER CUPS

1 cup butter or Saffola margarine
1 pound package powdered sugar
1½ cups peanut butter, crunchy or creamy
12 ounces Hershey chocolate (1½ large bar)

Melt butter or Saffola margarine and add sugar and peanut butter. Mix thoroughly. Pat mixture in a 9 x 13 inch buttered pan. Melt chocolate bar and spread over the peanut mixture. Chill until firm. Cut into 60 pieces. Makes 5 dozen candies.
Kathie Merwin
Yolo County

FUDGE CANDY

2 cups sugar
½ cup milk
2 tablespoons cocoa
½ cup Karo syrup
1 tablespoon butter
1 teaspoon vanilla
1 cup walnuts

Mix sugar, milk, cocoa and syrup together. Bring to boil and cook to soft ball stage or 234 degrees. Remove from heat and add butter, vanilla and walnuts. Cool a little while and pour into a buttered dish. Cut in squares when cold.

Helen Roberti
Plumas County

HONEY CANDIED NUTS

1½ cups sugar
¼ teaspoon salt
¼ cup honey
½ cup water
½ teaspoon vanilla
3 cups nuts

Combine sugar, salt, honey and water. Bring to a boil and cook, stirring often to 242 degrees. Remove from heat. Add vanilla and nuts. Stir until creamy. Turn out on waxed paper. Separate nuts.

Helen Sewart
Shasta County

NO-COOK DIVINITY

1 package Betty Crocker fluffy white frosting mix
⅓ cup light corn syrup
1 teaspoon vanilla
½ cup boiling water
1 package (16 ounces) powdered sugar
1 cup chopped nuts

Combine frosting mix (dry), corn syrup, vanilla and boiling water in small mixing bowl. Beat on highest speed until stiff peaks form, about 5 minutes. Transfer to large mixer bowl; drop mixture by teaspoonfuls onto waxed paper. When outside of candy feels firm, turn over and allow to dry at least 12 hours. Store candy in airtight container. 5 to 6 dozen.

Note: Divinity can be frozen in airtight container up to 2 months.

Bessu Duncan
Shasta County

MARGE'S PANOCHA

3 cups brown sugar, firmly packed
1 cup rich milk or cream
2 tablespoons white corn syrup
3 tablespoons butter
⅛ teaspoon salt
1 teaspoon vanilla
1 cup chopped nuts

Place sugar, milk and corn syrup in saucepan, cook uncovered over medium heat to the soft ball stage, 238 degrees. Remove from heat, add butter, salt and vanilla. Cool to lukewarm without stirring. Add nuts, beat until it begins to thicken. Pour at once into an 8 x 8 inch buttered pan. Cut into squares while still warm.
Marjorie Clarke
Plumas County

PANOCHA

⅔ cup (6 oz. can) evaporated milk
2 cups C and H Golden or Dark Brown Sugar, firmly packed
⅛ teaspoon salt
1 tablespoon butter
1 cup coarsely chopped pecans or walnuts

In heavy saucepan mix milk, sugar, and salt. Heat slowly to boiling, stirring constantly. Cook to 236 degrees (soft-ball stage) stirring often. Remove from heat; add butter. Cool undisturbed for 20 minutes, then beat until candy thickens and begins to lose its gloss. Quickly stir in nuts and spread in buttered 8-inch square pan. Cool and cut. Makes about 1½ pounds.
Charlotte Humphrey
Tehama County

SAGE HONEY CANDIED WALNUTS

1½ cups granulated sugar
¼ teaspoon salt
¼ teaspoon sage honey
½ cup water
3 cups walnut halves or large pieces

Boil sugar, salt, honey and water together, stirring often, to 242 degrees on a candy thermometer (soft ball stage). Remove from heat and add vanilla and walnuts. Stir until creamy. Turn out on waxed paper; separate walnuts, using two forks.
Anne Leach
Sutter County

SCRUMP DELICIOUS TOFFEE

2¼ cups sugar
1 tablespoon light corn syrup
½ cup water
1¼ cups butter
1 cup unblanched almond, coarsely chopped
1 cup blanched almonds, coarsely chopped and toasted
2 cups walnuts, finely chopped
2 8-ounce milk chocolate bars, melted

Bring sugar, corn syrup, water, and butter to boiling; add unblanched almond meats. Cook, stirring constantly, to hard-ball stage (260 degrees). Remove from heat, and quickly stir in the 1 cup of toasted almonds and 1 cup finely chopped walnuts. Spread into lightly buttered 13 x 9 x 2-inch pan. When cool, brush with half the melted chocolate, and sprinkle with half of remaining finely chopped walnuts. When set; cover pan with waxed paper or foil; invert. Spread with second bar of melted chocolate; sprinkle with walnuts. If necessary, chill to firm. When set, crack into pieces with the tip of a knife. Makes 2 dozen pieces. How to make Toasted Almonds: Place shelled almonds in a shallow pan in a slow oven (300 degrees) 25 to 30 minutes. Stir occasionally, remove from oven and spread on paper to cool.
Note: Candy thermometers are not always accurate and should not be depended upon completely. They give you an approximation of when you should start testing.
Delphina Roza
San Joaquin County

SURPRISE SUGAR NUTS

2 cups sugar
½ teaspoon salt
1 cup sour cream
3½ cups walnut halves
2 teaspoons lemon rind, grated

Thoroughly mix the sugar, salt and sour cream in large saucepan. Bring to a rolling boil on your medium to high heat, stirring constantly. Add the walnut halves and lemon rind and continue cooking to a soft ball stage of 234 degrees. This takes about 3 to 5 minutes. Remove from heat and stir nutmeats until the syrup coating becomes creamy and loses its gloss. Turn out on waxed paper and separate with two forks. Cool.
Note: This is a super recipe and once you taste these nuts you can't stop eating! It is an easy recipe to make and guaranteed a success.
Betty Wenger
Stanislaus County

"THOSE LITTLE WHITE ONES"

1 cup butter (don't substitute)
4 tablespoons sugar
1 cup whole almonds
2 cups flour
1 box powdered sugar

Preheat oven to 275 degrees. Cream butter and sugar. Pulverize almonds in blender, or chop very fine. Add almonds to butter mixture and mix. Add and mix flour, a little at a time. Shape dough into 10-12 inch long rolls about the size of a quarter. Refrigerate on cookie sheets covered with plastic wrap, for a few hours or overnite. Slice into 1/8 inch thick rounds. Bake on ungreased cookie sheet, 40 minutes. While they are baking, sift powdered sugar into paper sack or bowl. Drop warm cookies into powdered sugar and coat. Cool on cake racks.
Note: These freeze very well.
Lenore Carter
Kern County

RED BLUFF ALMOND COOKIES

1/2 cup butter or margarine, melted
1/2 cup sugar
1/2 cup brown sugar
2 eggs, large (not extra large)
1 teaspoon vanilla
1/4 teaspoon salt
3 1/2 to 4 cups almonds
1 teaspoon baking powder
1 tablespoon wheat germ (optional)

Toast almonds in 300 degrees. oven until slightly crisp. Be careful not to scorch them. Grind rather coarse. Combine butter and white and brown sugar; beat. Add eggs, vanilla and salt; beat well. In 3 quart bowl put 3 1/2 cups almonds, baking powder and wheat germ. Mix with mixing spoon. Add butter sugar mixture and mix until all the almonds are moistened. Drop by teaspoon onto greased cookie sheet. Bake in 325 degree oven until pale brown, 12 to 14 minutes. Makes about 4 dozen.
Note: If dough is too soft, add extra 1/2 cup of almonds.

"JAN HAGEL"

1 cup butter
1 cup sugar
1 egg yolk
½ teaspoon cinnamon
2 cups flour
1 egg white
1 cup almonds, finely chopped

Preheat oven to 375 degree. Cream butter, sugar and egg yolk. Add cinnamon and flour to make dough. Use palm of hand to spread out on 12 x 16-inch cookie sheet which has been very lightly greased with butter. Spread slightly beaten white of egg on top. Sprinkle finely chopped or crushed almonds over all. Bake in 375 degree oven until slightly browned. About 15 to 20 minutes. While still warm cut into diamond shapes.
Note: Do not overbake. To cut diamond shapes, cut approximately 2 inches apart across width. Then diagonally starting at right hand corner down to left hand corner. Continue diagonal cuts also approximately 2 inches apart until entire area has been cut. Remove from pan when cooled. This is an authentic Dutch recipe, imported from Holland.
Angelina Van Dyken
San Joaquin County

ALMOND OATMEAL COOKIES

1 cup granulated sugar
1 cup brown sugar, packed
1 cup butter or margarine
2 eggs
½ teaspoon vanilla
1½ cups finely ground natural (unblanched) almonds
1¼ cups all-purpose flour, sifted
1 teaspoon baking soda
1 teaspoon salt
2 cups quick cooking oats
1 cup crushed granola
½ cup raisins (optional)

Preheat oven to 350 degrees. Cream sugars, butter, eggs, and vanilla until fluffy. Stir in the ground almonds. Sift the flour, baking soda, and salt, and add to the creamed mixture. Stir in the oats and the crushed granola. (Put granola in a plastic bag and roll with a rolling pin to crush it). Drop by teaspoonfulls on a lightly greased cookie sheet. Bake until brown, 7 to 10 minutes.
Rose Ellis
Yolo County

SUE'S PLATTER COOKIES

2 cups melted margarine or butter
2 cups brown sugar (packed)
2 cups granulated sugar
4 eggs (beaten)
2 teaspoons vanilla
2 cups oatmeal
2 cups crisp cereal (Wheaties)
4 cups flour
2 teaspoons soda
2 teaspoons baking powder
1½ cups raisins
1 cup shredded coconut

Preheat oven to 350 degrees. Blend butter and sugars. Stir in eggs and vanilla. Add flour, baking powder and soda. Mix in oatmeal and cornflakes. Stir in raisins and coconut. Drop by tablespoons onto *ungreased* sheets. Allow room to spread. Makes 6 dozen cookies.
Susan Righetti
San Luis Obispo County

OATMEAL CRISPIES

1 cup shortening
1 cup brown sugar
1 cup granulated sugar
2 eggs
1 teaspoon vanilla
1½ cups flour
1 teaspoon salt
1 teaspoon soda
3 cups quick oats
½ cup nuts, chopped
½ cup raisins (optional)
½ cup coconut (optional)
½ cup chocolate chips (optional)

Preheat oven to 350 degrees. Thoroughly cream shortening and sugars. Add eggs and vanilla, beat well. Add sifted dry ingredients. Add oatmeal, nuts and raisins. Drop by small spoonfuls on lightly greased cookie sheet. Bake for 10 minutes.
Lorraine Valine
Sacramento County
Pat Repanich
Tehama County

SUNFLOWER SEED COOKIES (Recipe 40 years old)

1 cup shortening
1 cup brown sugar (packed)
1 cup white sugar
2 eggs
1½ cups flour
1½ cups unsalted sunflower seeds
½ teaspoon salt
1 teaspoon soda
3 cups rolled oats
½ cup chopped walnut meats

Preheat oven to 350 degrees. Cream sugars and shortening in bowl. Stir in eggs. Add remaining ingredients; mix well. Drop by spoonfuls onto greased cookie sheet; press down with fork. Bake for 10 to 12 minutes or until done.

Myra Eberspecher
Shasta County

APRICOT DATE BARS

½ cup butter or margarine
1½ cups graham cracker crumbs
1 8-ounce package chopped dates
1 4¾-ounce jar strained apricot baby food
1 14-ounce can sweetened condensed milk
1 3½-ounce can flaked coconut
½ cup walnuts, coarsely chopped

Preheat oven to 350 degrees, (325 degrees if using glass dish). In 13 x 9-inch baking pan, melt butter; sprinkle crumbs evenly over butter. In small bowl, combine dates with baby food; spoon evenly onto crumbs. Pour sweetened condensed milk evenly over dates. Top evenly with coconut and nuts; press down gently. Bake 30 to 35 minutes or until lightly browned. Cool thoroughly before cutting. Loosely cover any leftovers. Makes 24 bars.

Jean Cabral
San Joaquin County

CHEESE CAKE COOKIES

⅓ cup margarine
⅓ cup brown sugar
1 cup flour
½ cup nuts
¼ cup sugar
8 ounce package cream cheese
1 egg
2 tablespoons milk
1 teaspoon vanilla
1 tablespoon lemon juice

Preheat oven to 350 degrees. Cream margarine and brown sugar and add flour. Blend till like crumbs. Reserve 1 cup. Press rest in a 8 x 8-inch pan. Bake this mixture for 12-15 minutes. Combine sugar and cream cheese; beat till smooth. Add egg and milk, lemon juice, and vanilla. Beat well, spread over top. Spread reserved cup of crumbs over the top of this mixture. Bake in 250 degree oven for 25 minutes. Cool and cut into squares.
Dorothy Petrie
Tehama County

WALNUT BAR COOKIES

1 egg
1 cup brown sugar
½ teaspoon vanilla
½ cup flour
½ teaspoon salt
⅛ teaspoon soda
1 cup walnuts, chopped

Preheat oven to 325 degrees. Beat egg until foamy. Beat in brown sugar and vanilla. Stir in flour, salt, and soda. Mix in walnuts. Spread in greased 8-inch square pan. Bake 25-30 minutes. Cool and cut into bars. Makes 24 bars.
Amy McLaughlin
Yolo County

CALIFORNIA WALNUT BARS

1 cup sifted flour
¼ cup brown sugar (packed)
½ cup butter or margarine
2 eggs
¾ cup granulated sugar
½ teaspoon vanilla
⅓ cup flour
2 teaspoons cocoa
½ teaspoon baking powder
1 teaspoon salt
⅔ cup chopped walnuts

Blend flour, brown sugar and butter together until crumbly. Pack firmly in bottom of an 8-inch square pan. Bake in a 350 degree oven for 15 minutes. Prepare walnut layer: Beat in sugar, eggs and vanilla. Sift together ⅔ cup flour, cocoa, baking powder and salt. Fold in sugar mixture. Blend in walnuts. Turn into pan over baked layer and bake 25 to 30 minutes longer. Cool. Cut into bars. Makes 24 bars.
Yvonne Fillmore
Shasta County

CHAPEL WINDOW COOKIES

1 package colored miniature marshmallows
1 cup chopped nuts
2 squares chocolate
2 tablespoons butter
1 cup powdered sugar
1 egg
1 teaspoon vanilla
2 cups coconut

Combine in large bowl, 1 package colored miniature marshmallows, 1 cup chopped nuts. Melt in double boiler - 2 squares chocolate, 2 tablespoons butter, add 1 cup powdered sugar and 1 egg and 1 teaspoon vanilla. Cool and pour over marshmallow and nuts. Form into 2 rolls. Roll in coconut. Chill overnight wrapped in foil or saran wrap. Slice as needed and serve. Note: This is a great party idea or shower treat.
Diana Dennis
Humboldt County

CHOCOLATE MACAROONS

3 eggs
1½ cups granulated sugar
1 teaspoon vanilla
½ teaspoon salt
4 cups walnut meats, ground
3 ounces bitter chocolate, melted
½ cup white flour

Preheat oven to 350 degrees. Beat eggs and sugar for 20 minutes. Add melted chocolate and beat till well blended. Add vanilla, flour and salt and beat. Add ground walnuts and fold in until blended. Bake for 10 minutes.
Gregory Martha
Calaveras County

HUMDINGERS

½ cup margarine
¾ cup sugar
1 8-ounce package chopped dates
1 teaspoon vanilla
1 cup nuts, chopped
1½ cups RICE KRISPIES OR SPECIAL K

In saucepan melt margarine, add sugar and dates then cook 5 to 8 minutes, stirring constantly. Remove from heat, add vanilla, nuts and RICE KRISPIES or SPECIAL K. Mix well. Cool. Roll into small balls, coat with powdered sugar. Makes about 50 balls.
Connie Bebou
Marin County

INTEGRATED BROWNIES

1 cup margarine
2 cups sugar
1½ teaspoons vanilla
4 eggs
2 cups flour
2 cups nuts, chopped
2 squares unsweetened chocolate, melted

Preheat oven to 350 degrees. Cream margarine, sugar and vanilla. Add eggs, one at a time, creaming after each. Add flour and blend. Stir in nuts. Dollop half the batter here and there into a greased 13 x 9 x 2-inch pan. Add melted chocolate to remaining batter. Drop in between the white batter. Run knife through several times to integrate. Bake 45 minutes at 350 degrees. Cool, frost, if you like and cut into squares.
Nancy Hiller
Tehama County

PERSIMMON NUT SQUARES

1 cup walnuts, chopped
¾ cup sugar
1 cup persimmon pulp
1 teaspoon baking soda
1 egg
½ cup salad oil
1¾ cups flour
1 teaspoon salt
1 teaspoon cinnamon
1 teaspoon nutmeg
¼ teaspoon cloves (optional)
1 cup dates, chopped (optional)

Mix pulp with soda and set aside. Lightly beat the egg, and stir in oil and sugar. Combine flour, salt and spices. Add flour alternately with pulp until blended. Stir in nuts and dates. (Chopped dried figs, prunes or raisins can be substituted). Grease a 9 x 13-inch pan and lightly dust with flour. Spread dough evenly. Bake in 350 degree oven 25 to 30 minutes. While still warm, glaze with ¾ cup powdered sugar and lemon juice to make a thin paste. Cut into small squares.
Sylvia Vorhies
San Luis Obispo County

FANCY CHRISTMAS SUGAR COOKIES

2 cups flour
1½ teaspoons baking powder
6 tablespoons butter
6 tablespoons shortening
⅓ cup sugar
1 egg
1 tablespoon milk
1 teaspoon vanilla

Preheat oven to 375 degrees. Combine flour and baking powder; beat butter, shortening and sugar for 30 seconds. Add egg, milk and vanilla to the shortening and sugar mixture. Combine all ingredients together and then refrigerate dough for 3 hours. Roll out dough about ⅛ inch thick, cut to desired shapes. Bake for 20 to 25 minutes. Makes about two dozen cookies.
Millie Ramos
Kern County

PETER'S GOOEY TOLLHOUSE COOKIES

2 cups and 2 tablespoons unsifted flour
1 teaspoon baking soda
½ teaspoon salt
1 cup and 1 tablespoon softened butter
1 cup sugar
1 cup packed brown sugar
1 teaspoon vanilla
1 teaspoon water
2 eggs
1 12-ounce (2 cups) semi-sweet chocolate chips

Preheat oven to 375 degrees. In a small bowl combine flour, soda, salt and set aside. In a large bowl combine butter, brown sugar, sugar, vanilla and water and beat until creamy. Beat in eggs. Gradually add flour mixture; mix well. Stir in chocolate chips. Drop by spoonfulls onto ungreased cookie sheets. Bake at 365 degrees for 8-10 minutes - do not overbake. Makes 100 - 2 inch cookies.
Peter Pankey
Kern County

SURFER BARS

1 12-ounce chocolate chips
1 12-ounce butterscotch chips
½ cup brown sugar
2 eggs
1½ cups flour
2 teaspoons baking powder
½ teaspoon salt
2 cups miniature marshmallows
2 teaspoons vanilla
1 cup walnuts, chopped

Preheat oven to 350 degrees. Melt butterscotch chips, sugar, butter. Remove from heat and let cool, then add eggs and beat well. Add flour, baking powder, salt. Stir in remaining ingredients and spread in 9 x 13-inch pan. Cool and cut in bars. Bake 25 minutes.
Sally Dohr
Solano County

"NUTS TO YOU" WALNUT SQUARES

1 cup brown sugar
1 egg
1 teaspoon vanilla
½ cup flour
¼ teaspoon salt
¼ teaspoon baking soda
1 cup walnuts, chopped

Preheat oven to 350 degrees. Stir together brown sugar, egg and vanilla. Add flour, salt, baking soda and walnuts. Spread in greased 9-inch square pan. Bake 20 minutes. Cut while warm.
Viola Thomas
Sutter County

SWEDISH COOKIES

½ cup butter
½ cup brown sugar
1 egg yolk, beaten
¼ teaspoon salt
1 cup flour
1 egg white
½ teaspoon vanilla
¾ cup pecans, finely chopped

Fill:

Raspberry jam or marachino cherry pieces

Cream butter; add sugar gradually. Add egg yolk and flour. Form small balls. Dip into egg white and roll in nuts. Bake slowly in oven at 300 degrees for 5 minutes. Take out, make a dent in center and fill with jam or cherries. Return to oven and bake 10 minutes longer.
Candy Jones
San Bernardino County

YUMMY GULUMMY

Crust:

1 cup butter softened
1 cup brown sugar (packed)
2 cups flour

Topping:

4 eggs (slightly beaten)
2 cups brown sugar (packed)
1 tablespoon vanilla
¼ cup flour
2 teaspoons baking powder
1 teaspoon salt
2 cups pecans or walnuts (broken)
2 cups rolled oats

Heat oven to 350 degrees. Cream butter, and sugar. Blend in flour. Press evenly in bottom of ungreased baking pan 13 x 9 x 2-inch. Bake 10 minutes. Mix topping ingredients together, spread over baked crust. Bake 25 minutes longer or until topping is golden brown. Turn off oven. Test for firmness. Leave the oven door ajar and leave the YUMMY GULUMMY inside the oven while it cools down. Cut into bars.
Betty Snyder
Calaveras County

DAIRY

The milk for most of California's dairy products is produced by the state's over 800,000 dairy cow population located on approximately 2,400 dairies. These dairy farms are scattered throughout California, with concentration in the San Joaquin Valley, and the Chino Basin in Southern California. The Holstein breed, because of its high level of milk production, dominates the California dairy industry. Other breeds found on dairy farms include: Jersey, Guernsey, and Brown Swiss.

Dairy

. . . the dairy best

SMOKEY CHEESE BALL

2 8-ounce packages cream cheese
1 8-ounce block smoky Cheddar cheese, shredded
½ cup butter, softened
2 tablespoons milk
2 teaspoons steak sauce
1 cup walnuts, finely chopped

Mix together cream cheese, smoky Cheddar cheese, butter, milk, and steak sauce. Beat until fluffy. Chill slightly. Shape into ball and coat with walnuts. Chill.
Amy McLaughlin
Yolo County

DOROTHY'S HA'PENNY SNACKS

¼ pound margarine
1 cup flour
½ pound Cheddar cheese, grated
½ package onion soup mix
½ teaspoon salt

Preheat oven to 375 degrees. Have cheese and butter at room temperature. Mix well, add rest of ingredients, and blend. Shape into 1-inch rolls, and wrap in waxed paper. Chill. Slice into ¼-inch thick pieces, and bake on an ungreased cookie sheet. Bake for 10 to 12 minutes. Drain on paper towel.
Charlyn Connor
Yolo County

CRISPY CHEESE WAFERS

1 cup margarine/butter
2 cups flour
1 teaspoon salt
2 cups Cheddar cheese, grated
2 cups Rice Krispies
Pepper
Dash of Tabasco

Preheat oven to 350 degrees. Let margarine soften to room temperature. Mix all ingredients except the Rice Krispies. When well blended, add Rice Krispies and roll into small balls and press each with a fork after its placed on cookie sheet. Bake for 15 minutes. Makes 5 dozen.
Sean Pierce
Marin County

CHEESE BALLS

1 8-ounce package cream cheese
½ jar Blue Rocka Cheese
½ jar Old English Cheese
½ tablespoon grated onion
½ tablespoon Worcestershire sauce
1 tablespoon parsley
1 cup nuts, finely chopped

Soften the cheeses and mix together with onion and Worcestershire. Roll into balls and roll in nuts. Wrap well and refrigerate. Makes one 4-inch ball.
Rose Kinslow
Shasta County

DAIRYMAN'S DELIGHT (A QUICHE)

Baked pastry shell:

1½ cups flour
⅛ teaspoon salt
½ cup butter
1 egg, beaten

Filling:

10 slices cooked bacon, crumbled
2 tablespoons minced onion
1¼ cups shredded Swiss cheese
4 eggs
2 cups half and half (or 1 cup cream and 1 cup milk)

Preheat oven to 425 degrees. Sift flour and salt into bowl. Cut in butter. Add beaten egg blending well with fork. Form into a ball and roll on floured board. Fit into 10-inch pie or quiche pan. Prick 10 to 12 times with fork. Bake 20 minutes. Turn oven down to 325 degrees. Put bacon and onion on pastry shell. Distribute shredded cheese over bacon and onion. Beat eggs and half and half together and pour over cheese-bacon mixture. Bake about 40 minutes.
Note: Good for main dish or serve cold cut in tiny wedges for hors d'oeuvres.
Emily Kuff
Tehama County

CREAMY FRUIT SALAD

18 large white marshmallows
1 cup milk
1 6-ounce package lime Jello
1 3-ounce package cream cheese
½ pint whipping cream
2½ cups undrained crushed pineapple

Melt marshmallows and milk. Add Jello and mix well. Stir in softened cream cheese until dissolved. Beat the whipping cream. Pour into gelatin mixture. Add the pineapple. Refrigerate.
Note: Another flavor of Jello and any fruit desired may be substituted.
Christine Van Steyn
Sacramento County

COTTAGE CHEESE WHIP

1 large package Jello, any flavor
1 large carton cottage cheese
½ cup walnuts
2 or 3 cups well drained fruit or berries
1 large container Cool Whip

Mix the Jello *dry*, with the cottage cheese, add the well drained fruit and nuts. Fold in the Cool Whip and refrigerate.
Note: An easy dish for children to prepare. Also a great dish for potlucks.
Phyllis Hartley
Marin County

STRAWBERRY PINEAPPLE JELLO SALAD

2 small packages strawberry Jello
1 20-ounce can crushed pineapple
1 pint cottage cheese
1 8-ounce container Cool Whip

Heat Jello and pineapple together in pan to dissolve Jello. Cool. Fold in cottage cheese. Fold in Cool Whip. Fold until just mixed well. Chill in mold.
Candy Jones
San Bernardino County

ROQUEFORT DRESSING

½ pint sour cream
1 cup cottage cheese
Juice from ½ lemon
⅓ cup oil
⅓ cup water
⅓ cup milk
1 minced garlic clove
15 drops Tabasco sauce
1 teaspoon horseradish
½ pound of roquefort or blue cheese or ¼ pound of each, cut in pieces
Salt and pepper to taste

Put all ingredients in blender and mix.
N. Pierce
Marin County

SOUR CREAM-CAPER SALAD DRESSING

¼ cup mayonnaise
¾ cup Real sour cream
1 tablespoon chopped pimiento
4 tablespoons chopped parsley
3 tablespoons capers
½ teaspoon salt
1 teaspoon vinegar

Blend together all the above ingredients. Makes 1¼ cups.
Kathleen Rowen
Tehama County

CALIFORNIA DREAMIN' SALAD

1 large package lemon Jello
1 pint-sized bottle of 7-Up
1 1 pound 4-ounce can Dole crushed pineapple
4 sliced bananas
Miniature marshmallows

Topping:

1 egg, beaten
1 cup pineapple juice
½ cup sugar
3 rounded tablespoons flour
2 tablespoons butter
½ pint whipping cream
Sharp yellow Cheddar cheese

Dissolve Jello in 2 cups boiling water. Add 7-Up; mix well; then add all pineapple that has been well-drained. (Save juice for topping). Add bananas, stir and cover with miniature marshmallows. Chill in 9 x 13-inch flat pyrex pan until firm. Topping: Boil together egg, 1 cup pineapple juice (add ¼ cup first to eggs then add remainder), [mix together sugar, flour] add sugar and flour and butter. Cook until thick. Stir constantly to avoid scorching. Cover with layer of waxed paper so paper is flat on custard to avoid drying out. Chill. When topping is thick, whip cream to stiff peaks. Beat together. Pour over jello layer. Grate cheese with fine grater over layer of custard. Chill several hours or overnight. Serves 16 to 20 people.
Lavonne Righetti
San Luis Obispo County

HUNGARIAN EGG NOODLE COTTAGE CHEESE MEDLEY

1 8-ounce package wide egg noodles
1 cup creamed cottage cheese
4 heaping tablespoons sour cream

Cook egg noodles according to package directions until barely done. Do not overcook. Drain noodles, but do not rinse with cold water. Add the cold cottage cheese and cold sour cream. Stir well into noodles. Cover and return to stove top burner. Heat gently until hot. Serve at once. Do not overcook as the cottage cheese will become tough and stringy.
Olga Rivaldi
Santa Barbara County

MOCK CHEESE BUTTONS

1 large yellow onion
1 bunch of green onions
½ cup margarine or butter
1½ cups sour cream
1½ cups cottage cheese
¼ teaspoon salt
¼ teaspoon pepper
¼ teaspoon garlic salt or powder
1 10-ounce package bow tie macaroni
2 eggs
⅔ cup evaporated milk
Buttered bread crumbs

Preheat oven to 350 degrees. Chop onions fine and sauté in margarine or butter. Mix together sour cream and cottage cheese, with salt, pepper, garlic salt or powder to taste. Add sautéed onions and mix well. Cook macaroni according to package directions. Butter a 9 x 13-inch glass dish, and add a layer of macaroni, then cottage cheese mixture, then repeat until all is used up. This can be made in advance, and just before baking, beat two eggs together with ⅔ cup evaporated milk and pour over the top of casserole. Cover with foil and bake for 30 minutes, or until egg mixture is set. Before serving, top with buttered bread crumbs.
Christine Meier
San Joaquin County

SOUR CREAM BUTTER HORNS

2 cups flour
½ pound butter
1 egg yolk
¾ cup sour cream

Sugar mixture for filling:

1 cup sugar
2 cups finely chopped nuts
1 rounded teaspoon cinnamon

Preheat oven to 375 degrees. Cut butter into flour, add egg yolk and sour cream. Mix with hands. Shape into oblong roll, flour and roll into floured wax paper. Refrigerate at least 2 hours or longer. This may be done the day before. Cut one piece at a time and roll out quite thin on floured board. Sprinkle with generous amount of sugar mixture and cut into 8 triangles. Starting at wide end, roll each into horn or crescent shape. Place on ungreased cookie sheet. Bake until golden brown approximately 20 to 25 minutes depending on your own oven.
Note: If desired, you may mix different kinds of nuts in sugar mixture.
Jo Bruno
San Bernardino County

CHEESE SCONES

3 cups all-purpose flour
3 teaspoons baking powder
¼ teaspoon salt
¾ cup grated white or yellow cheese
½ cup grated Parmesan cheese
Pinch pepper
3 tablespoons butter
1¼ cups milk

Preheat oven to 425 degrees. Sift together the flour, baking powder and salt. Add the grated cheeses and the pepper. Cut in the butter and mix in the milk to make a soft dough. Roll out ½-inch thick, cut into rounds and put on greased baking sheet. Bake for 15 minutes. Makes 15 scones.
Deborah Thompson
Sonoma County

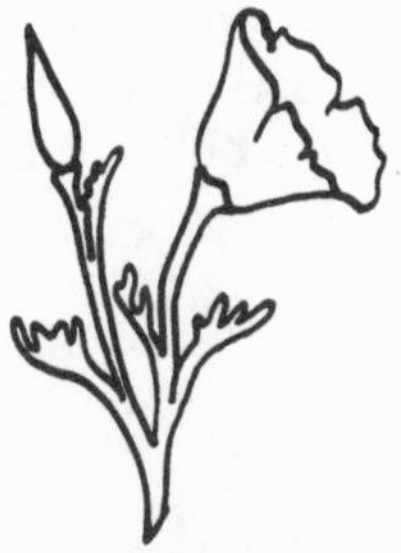

CALIFORNIA BUTTERMILK ANGEL BISCUITS

5 cups flour
1 teaspoon baking soda
3 teaspoons baking powder
1 teaspoon salt
3 tablespoons sugar
¾ cup shortening or oil
2 cups buttermilk
1 yeast cake dissolved in
½ cup lukewarm water

Preheat oven to 400 degrees. Sift dry ingredients together. Cut in shortening until mixed thoroughly. Add buttermilk and dissolved yeast. Work together with large spoon until all flour is moistened. Cover bowl and put in refrigerator overnight or until ready to use as needed. When ready to use, take out as much as needed, roll on floured board to ½-inch thickness and cut. Bake on cookie sheet for about 12 minutes, until brown.
Note: This dough will keep for several weeks in the refrigerator. This recipe makes about 6 dozen light flaky biscuits.
Nell Hughes
San Luis Obispo County

OUR FAVORITE BISCUITS

3 cups self-rising flour
1½ cups buttermilk
3 tablespoons oil

Preheat oven to 425 degrees. Combine buttermilk and oil, pour into flour. Stir just until mixed. Knead on board, floured with self-rising flour (knead only a few times). Roll or pat out till desired thickness (thinner dough will make crisper biscuits). Cut with biscuit cutter, put on ungreased pan. Bake for 10-12 minutes.

Note: Quick cinnamon rolls are possible with this same simple recipe: Add 3 tablespoons sugar and use 5 tablespoons of oil. Roll very thin. Spread with margarine, sprinkle with brown sugar, white sugar, cinnamon, raisins and nuts. Roll the long way, cut, put on baking sheet and bake about 12 minutes at 425 degrees.

Louise Correia
Fresno County

BUTTERMILK COFFEE CAKE

2½ cups flour
1 cup sugar
¾ cup brown sugar
½ teaspoon cinnamon
1 cup buttermilk
2 eggs
1 teaspoon baking powder
1 teaspoon baking soda
¾ cup salad oil
1 teaspoon nutmeg
¼ teaspoon salt

Preheat oven to 350 degrees. Combine flour and sugars. Set aside ½ cup to use as topping. Mix ½ teaspoon cinnamon with topping. Combine dry ingredients with rest of ingredients. Mix thoroughly on medium speed of electric mixer. Pour into greased 9 x 13-inch pan. Bake for 30 minutes.

Louise Correia
Fresno County

BAKED BROWN BREAD

½ cup shortening
½ cup sugar
½ cup light molasses
2 cups graham flour
1 cup white flour
1 teaspoon soda
¼ teaspoon salt
2 cups milk

Preheat oven to 350 degrees. Cream shortening; add sugar and cream again. Add molasses. Sift dry ingredients. Add flour mixture with milk. Put in 2 small bread tins and bake about 20 minutes. Serves 6-8.

Emily Jorstad
Placer County

BLACK BOTTOM CUPCAKES

Cake batter:

1½ cups flour
1 cup sugar
½ teaspoon salt
1 teaspoon baking soda
¼ cup cocoa
⅓ cup oil
1 teaspoon vanilla
1 cup water
1 teaspoon vinegar

Filling:

1 16-ounce package cream cheese
2 eggs
½ cup sugar
⅛ teaspoon salt
1 12-ounce package chocolate chips

Preheat oven to 350 degrees. Combine flour, sugar, salt, baking soda, and cocoa in bowl. Add oil, vanilla, water and vinegar. In *separate bowl*, cream together cream cheese, eggs, sugar, and salt. Add chocolate chips. Fill cupcake papers ⅓ full with the batter mixture, and put one generous tablespoon of the filling mixture on top. Bake for 25-30 minutes.
Note: The cake batter will almost completely cover the filling. Do not frost these cupcakes.
Cyndy Mickelsen
Sacramento County

CHOCOLATE CREAM PIE

3½ cups milk
2 squares (2 ounce) unsweetened chocolate
1 cup sugar
⅔ cup flour
¾ teaspoon salt
1 egg or 2 yolks, slightly beaten
2 tablespoons butter
1 teaspoon vanilla
1 baked 8-inch pastry shell
½ cup heavy cream for topping

Heat milk and chocolate in heavy saucepan over low heat, stirring until blended. Combine dry ingredients; add milk mixture gradually, stirring until smooth. Return to saucepan and cook, stirring, until thickened. Stir small amount of hot mixture into egg. Then stir quickly into remaining mixture in saucepan; cook 2 minutes over low heat, stirring constantly. Remove from heat, add butter and vanilla. Turn into pastry shell; chill. Top with sweetened whipped cream. Yield: 6 servings.
Charlotte Humphrey
Tehama County

CENTRAL COAST PRIZE FROSTING

5 tablespoons flour
1 cup milk
1 cup sugar
½ cup shortening or margarine
½ cup margarine/butter
Flavoring-vanilla or chocolate

Mix flour and milk to a smooth paste is small saucepan. Cook over low heat until very thick, stirring constantly. Remove from heat, set aside to cool. Put sugar and fats into bowl(about 2-quart size) and beat at highest speed for 10 minutes. This is very important; it must be beaten until so smooth that sugar is hardly noticed. When milk and flour paste is cold, beat into sugar mixture until it looks like whipped cream. Beat in flavoring of your choice. I use 1 tablespoon vanilla, or for chocolate, 2 squares melted. Makes 5 cups.
Note: This is a versatile frosting. May be used as a filling for cream puffs, topping for gelatin or desserts, or as cake fillings and frosting. It tastes like whipped cream or ice cream. Will keep several weeks in the refrigerator if covered loosely with waxed paper. It shouldn't be covered tightly.
Margaret Hager
San Luis Obispo County

CHEESE CAKE SUPREME

1¼ cups graham cracker crumbs
3 tablespoons sugar
⅓ cup butter, melted
3 8-ounce packages cream cheese, softened
1 cup sugar
5 eggs
1½ teaspoons vanilla
1 pint sour cream
¾ cup sugar
1 teaspoon vanilla

Preheat oven to 300 degrees. Combine graham crackers and 3 tablespoons sugar in 9 x 13-inch pan. Add melted butter and press firmly into pan. In a large bowl beat cream cheese with mixer until soft. Add 1 cup sugar, eggs one at a time, and 1½ teaspoons vanilla. Mix until thoroughly blended. Pour carefully into crust in pan and bake 30 minutes. Mix until blended sour cream, ¾ cup sugar, and 1 teaspoon vanilla. Very carefully and slowly spoon sour cream mixture over cream cheese mixture. Return to oven. Turn oven OFF and leave in oven 15 minutes or until top is set. Remove from and place in refrigerator. Cool at least 4 hours before serving. Serves 12 to 14.
Ruth Machado
Sacramento County

COFFEE MARSHMALLOW MOUSSE

1 pound miniature marshmallows
1 cup hot, strong, black coffee
1 cup whipping cream, whipped

Combine marshmallows and coffee in a double boiler. Dissolve the mixture over medium heat, stirring it constantly until well blended. Remove from stove, let cool. Place mixture in refrigerator, and chill until firm. Fold in the whipped cream. Return to the refrigerator and chill thoroughly. Yield: 6-8 servings.
Elena Labarthe
Tehama County

DUMP CAKE

1 21-ounce can Comstock cherry pie filling
1 8-ounce can crushed pineapple
1 package yellow cake mix
½ cup butter, melted
2 cups whipping cream, whipped

Preheat oven to 350 degrees. Spread pie filling into a buttered 13 x 9-inch pan. Spread crushed pineapple over the cherries. Put dry cake mix on top of cherries and pineapple, spreading evenly. Slowly pour melted butter over the cake mix. Bake for 50-60 minutes. Serve warm with whipped cream.
Note: This is a very easy recipe for children.
Christina Crayne
Marin County

FRESH CHEESECAKE

Cheese:

4 quarts whole milk
1 quart cultured buttermilk
1 teaspoon salt

Cheesecake:

2 eggs
2 cups fresh cheese (made from above milk)
1 cup sugar
1 teaspoon grated lemon peel
3 tablespoons lemon juice
½ teaspoon vanilla
½ teaspoon salt

In a heavy 6-8 quart kettle, combine milk and buttermilk. To prevent burning place over medium heat (170 degrees). Line colander with 3 or 4 thicknesses of cheesecloth rung out in cold water. Set colander inside a bowl and when thick curds appear, use slotted spoon to scoop into colander. Pour remaining curds and whey in colander and let drain 2-3 hours. Scrape cheese into a bowl and mix in salt, using fork or electric mixer on low speed. Cover and keep in refrigerator. Makes about 4 cups cheese. Use 2 cups for cheesecake and serve rest with fruit. Preheat oven to 325 degrees. Fill large baking pan about ½ inches deep with water and put in oven while preheating. Put eggs, cheese, sugar, lemon peel, lemon juice, vanilla and salt into blender or food processor and whirl until very smooth. Pour in well-buttered 8-inch layer cake pan and set inside pan of hot water in the oven. Bake until knife comes out clean when inserted in center (about 45-50 minutes). Remove from water, cool and turn onto a serving dish. Serve plain or with fruit.
Note: This has a cake-like topping. A dash of nutmeg can be added before baking.
Mildred Filiberti
Tuolumne County

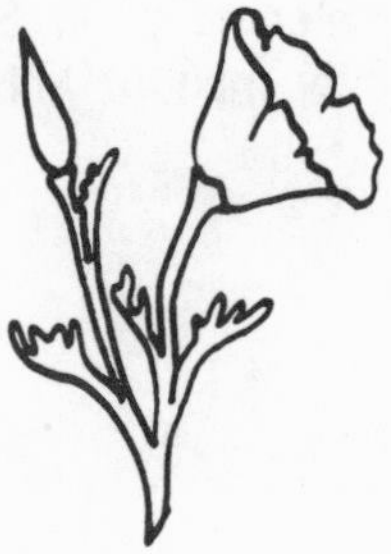

TANGY CHEESE CAKE

⅔ box graham crackers
½ cup butter, melted
1 8-ounce package cream cheese
1 cup sugar
2 teaspoons vanilla
1 3-ounce package lemon Jello
1 cup hot water
1 14-ounce can evaporated milk, chilled

Roll graham crackers fine, add melted butter, mix and spread in 9-inch pie pan, pressing down real well, saving a small amount for topping. Mix cream cheese, sugar and vanilla and set aside. Dissolve lemon Jello and hot water, set aside. Whip milk until stiff, add Jello mix. Fold in cream cheese mix. Pour in pan and sprinkle remaining crumbs on top. Refrigerate. Serves 12-14.
Dorothy McGrew
Placer County

CHERRY CHEESE SQUARES

18 graham crackers
½ cup margarine/butter, softened
1 package Dream Whip
1 cup powdered sugar
2½ teaspoons vanilla
1 8-ounce package cream cheese, softened
1 can cherry pie filling

Crush graham crackers and mix with softened margarine. Press into 9-inch square pan. Chill while making the filling. Prepare Dream Whip according to directions on package. Add powdered sugar, vanilla and cream cheese. Use low speed of electric mixer. Spoon Dream Whip mixture onto graham cracker crust. Cover mixture with cherry pie filling and chill until served. Serves 9.
Pauline Rohrer
San Luis Obispo County

CREAM CHEESE FUDGE BARS

4 tablespoons butter
1 cup brown sugar
1 cup grated coconut
½ cup walnuts or pecans, finely chopped
1 6-ounce can evaporated milk
1 8-ounce package cream cheese, softened
1 egg
2 cups (½ package) fudge frosting mix
1 roll refrigerated chocolate-chip cookie dough

Preheat oven to 350 degrees. Line 13 x 9-inch baking pan with foil. Melt butter in prepared pan. Sprinkle brown sugar, coconut and nuts over butter. Drizzle evaporated milk over all. In small mixer bowl, beat cream cheese and egg until smooth. Add frosting mix to cream cheese mix; mix until well blended. Carefully spread cheese mixture over coconut mixture in pan. Slice cookie dough in ¼-inch thick slices, arrange slices over top of cheese mixture. Bake for 35-40 minutes. Immediately invert on cookie sheet to remove from pan. Chill before cutting into bars. Yield: About 3 dozen bars.
Candy Jones
San Bernardino County

CREAMY CREAM FROSTING

½ cup butter
½ cup sugar
½ cup milk
2½ tablespoons flour
1 teaspoon vanilla

Blend and cream butter and sugar. Set aside. On stove top, heat milk and stir in flour mix with butter and sugar. Beat until very creamy. Add flavoring and also color if desired. Will frost a regular double layer cake.
Alice Bess
Humboldt County

DAIRYMEN'S DELIGHT CHEESE CAKE

16 graham crackers, crushed
4 tablespoons powdered sugar
½ cup butter, melted
3 8-ounce packages cream cheese, softened
5 eggs
2 teaspoons vanilla
1 cup sugar
1 pint sour cream
1 tablespoon sugar
1 teaspoon vanilla
1 can Comstock Cherry Pie Filling (optional)

Preheat oven to 375 degrees. Mix together cracker crumbs, powdered sugar, and melted butter. Pressin bottom of 9-inch spring form pan. Beat cream cheese until soft; add eggs, vanilla, and sugar, beating the mixture until very smooth. Pour into pan and bake for 30 minutes. Beat sour cream, sugar and vanilla for 1 minute. Remove cheesecake and smooth over top of the cake the sour cream mixture. Return to oven and bake for 7 minutes. Remove from oven and cool at room temperature. Refrigerate at least 12 hours. Serve plain or with Comstock Cherry Pie Filling on top of cheese cake.
Janice Corda
Marin County

GRANDMA'S BROWNIES

½ cup butter, melted
1 cup sugar
2 eggs
2 tablespoons cold water
⅔ cup flour
½ cup dry cocoa
½ cup nuts or ½ cup chocolate chips or ½ cup coconut
1 teaspoon vanilla

Preheat oven to 350 degrees. Melt butter, stir in sugar and eggs, and water. Add flour, cocoa and stir until well mixed. Add nuts and vanilla, stir well. Put into an 8 x 8 or 9 x 9-inch pan. Bake for 25-30 minutes. Serve warm or cold.
Tiffany Giacomini
Humboldt County

ITALIAN RICOTTA CHEESE PIE

2 eggs
½ cup sugar
1 pound Ricotta cheese
½ teaspoon lemon extract
¼ teaspoon vanilla
½ cup cream
Dash of cinnamon
1½ tablespoons unsweetened cocoa (optional)
1 tablespoon sugar (optional)
1 9-inch graham cracker crust

Preheat oven to 350 degrees. Beat eggs in mixer until blended. Add sugar and beat a little more. Mix in ricotta and beat slowly until well blended. Add cream, vanilla, lemon, and cinnamon; mix well. At this point, this mixture could be put into crust and baked, or the following may be done: Divide mixture in half. To ½ add the cocoa and sugar and mix well. Layer in graham cracker crust, alternating the two halves until all the mixture is used. Swirl with spatula. Bake for 45 minutes or until toothpick inserted comes out clean. Chill. Pie may be served plain or topped with whipped cream.

Jo Bruno
San Bernardino County

LEMON SUPREME CAKE

1 package lemon cake mix
1 cup milk
1 box vanilla pudding
¾ cup butter or margarine
¾ cup sugar
1 can lemon pie filling or 1 package prepared pudding mix (lemon)
1 large container of Cool Whip or 2 packages of Dream Whip
coconut, nuts, cherries for garnish (optional)

Preheat oven to 350 degrees. Prepare cake mix as directed on package. Pour into jelly roll pan and bake for 20 minutes. Mix milk and pudding, cook and cool. Mix butter and sugar and blend into pudding mixture. Spread on cooled cake. Spread lemon filling over. Top with Cool Whip and sprinkle chopped nuts and or coconut on top and decorate with maraschino cherries. Refrigerate.

Barbara Vineyard
Placer County

MINER'S GOLDEN NUGGETS

2 8-ounce packages shredded coconut
1 15-ounce can (1½ cups) sweetened condensed milk
2 teaspoons vanilla

Preheat oven to 350 degrees. Mix all ingredients. Drop from wet teaspoon onto well greased cookie sheet. Bake 10 to 12 minutes. Cool slightly and remove to rack. Makes 4 dozen.
Patricia Trinkle
Fresno County

OLD FASHIONED CUSTARD

3 or 4 eggs
3 or 4 tablespoons sugar
3 or 4 cups milk
Pinch of salt
1 teaspoon vanilla
Nutmeg to your own taste

Preheat oven to 400 degrees. Beat all of the above ingredients in a bowl. Place bowl with ingredients in a pan of water and bake for about 1 hour, or until knife blade when inserted comes out clean. Chill and serve.
Elaine Dillon
Humboldt County

OLD FASHIONED RAISIN CREAM PIE

1 cup raisins
1 tablespoon cider vinegar
1½ cups cream
½ cup water
2 eggs
¾ cup sugar
½ teaspoon nutmeg
2 tablespoons melted butter
1 unbaked-9-inch pastry shell

Preheat oven to 450 degrees. Bring raisins and water to a boil, reduce heat and simmer 5 minutes. Add the vinegar to cream and let stand for a few minutes to sour. Beat eggs slightly and add sugar and nutmeg. Combine all ingredients together and pour into prepared unbaked pie shell. Place in oven and turn temperature down to 325 degree and bake 35 to 40 minutes.
Janet Van Dam
Kern County

SAUCY CHEESE-CAKE CUPS

⅓ cup sugar
2 tablespoons cornstacrch
¼ teaspoon salt
1½ cup unsweetened pineapple juice
¼ teaspoon grated lemon peel
1 tablespoon lemon juice
1 8-ounce package cream cheese, softened
2 eggs
½ cup sugar
¼ teaspoon salt
½ cup milk
½ teaspoon vanilla
⅓ cup pecans, sliced

Preheat oven to 325 degrees. Mix ⅓ cup sugar, cornstarch, and salt in saucepan; add pineapple juice. Cook and stir till thick and clear. Add peel and lemon juice. Pour into six 6-ounce cups. To cream cheese, add eggs, one at a time, beating smooth after each. Add sugar and salt. Stir in milk and vanilla. Spoon over pineapple layer. Sprinkle with pecans. Bake in slow oven 25 minutes or till set around edge. Cool.
Kimberly Hobbs-Brann
Solano County

UPSIDE DOWN HOT FUDGE PUDDING

1 cup flour
2 teaspoons baking powder
¼ teaspoon salt
¾ cup sugar
2 tablespoons cocoa
½ cup milk
2 tablespoons shortening, melted
1 cup nuts, chopped
1 cup brown sugar
4 tablespoons cocoa
1¾ cups hot water

Preheat oven to 350 degrees. Sift together flour, baking powder, salt, sugar and 2 tablespoons cocoa. Stir in milk and melted shortening; then blend in nuts. Spread in a 9-inch square pan. Sprinkle the mixture of brown sugar and 4 tablespoons cocoa over the top. Then pour over entire batter in pan, 1¾ cups very hot water. Bake for 45 minutes. Serve warm with ice cream or whipped cream.
Nadine Pierce
Marin County

WHIPPED CREAM PINEAPPLE DESSERT

1 cup milk
1 pound marshmallows
1 pint whipping cream
1 large can crushed pineapple
Graham crackers for topping

Cook milk and marshmallows over low heat until melted. Cool. Whip cream until stiff; add well drained pineapple. Fold in the marshmallow mixture and pour into 9 x 13-inch dish. Refrigerate for one hour; then top with crushed graham cracker crumbs.
Martina Galeppi
Plumas County

YUMMY CREAM CHERRY PIE

Pie Crust:

1 cup flour
2 tablespoons powdered sugar
½ cup butter

Preheat oven to 425 degrees. Crust: Crumble together flour, powdered sugar, and butter and pat into pie shell. Bake for 8-10 minutes or until lightly brown. Cool.

Filling:

1 3-ounce package cream cheese
½ cup powdered sugar
½ teaspoon vanilla
1 cup whipping cream
1 cup cherry pie filling

Beat together cream cheese, powdered sugar, and vanilla until smooth. Whip cream and fold into above mixture. Put into baked shell. Spoon cherry pie filling over top.
Candy Jones
San Bernardino County

CALIFORNIA LIVING

We have concentrated on using our edible agricultural products, but California also supports a large nursery stock and cut-flower industry. We would like to share this part of our agricultural life with you.

California growers of nursery stock and cut-flowers not only provide significant enrichment to our environment and personal lives, but they also produce a valuable portion of our farm economy. Nursery and floriculture crops, the production of which is commonly known as environmental horticulture, ranked fifth on the list of the state's top crop and livestock commodities in 1979, with a farm gate value of nearly $785 million.

This prosperous segment of California agriculture has even greater significance at the county level. In many of the coastal counties where these crops predominate, they may represent from 50 to 80 percent of the total crop receipts. For example, in San Mateo County, nursery and flower crops were valued at over $93 million which accounted for nearly 80 percent of that county's agricultural output.

As the California Department of Food and Agriculture said in a recent release, "Flower power is still alive and very big in California."

A home is always enhanced by the beauty of a plant or a bouquet of flowers. In our hurried way of life we need to slow down and see the beauty of nature. An arrangement as simple as a small bouquet of dried wheat can add warmth and dimension to a room. A few bright flowers tucked into some greenery in a vase will add a cheery note to the table. Shrubs and flowers are also the finishing touch to a home, making its appearance warmer and more inviting to all. This is best exemplified by the following thought from one of our Farm Bureau Women:

Flowers are food for the soul!

California Living

. . . the good life

FALSE CAPERS

Green nasturtium buds
1 cup salt
2 quarts water
Distilled white vinegar

Cover buds with salt-water brine. Weight down to keep immersed. Allow to cure 24 hours. Remove buds from brine and soak in cold water for 60 minutes. Drain. Bring vinegar to a boil. Pack buds in hot, sterilized jars. Cover with boiling vinegar. Seal. Process in boiling-water bath 10 minutes.
State Women's Committee

PICKLED PETALS

Flowers and buds of roses, violets, nasturtium, chrysanthemum, calendula, primrose, day-lilies, gladiolus, or geraniums
Sugar
Distilled white vinegar
Mace or mint sprigs

Carefully remove sepals, stems, and stamens from flowers. Layer flowers in jar, covering each layer with sugar. Pour boiling vinegar to fill jar. Add a sprig of mace or mint. Seal. Pickled petals are ready to mix with salads or garnish a relish tray in about 4 to 5 days. Keep refrigerated.
Note: Use flowers that are free from insect damage or garden sprays. Pick in the early morning.
State Women's Committee

ROSE PETAL JAM

8 ounces rose petals, preferably from newly opened roses
1 tablespoon lemon juice
1½ pounds sugar
1 cup rose water (available in pharmacies)

Wash and drain the rose petals. Dissolve the sugar in the lemon juice and rose water. Add the petals and leave in a warm place to steep for a few hours. Put in a saucepan and simmer gently for 30 minutes, stirring frequently, until mixture thickens. Cool slightly and put in glass jars. Cover with parafin.
State Women's Committee

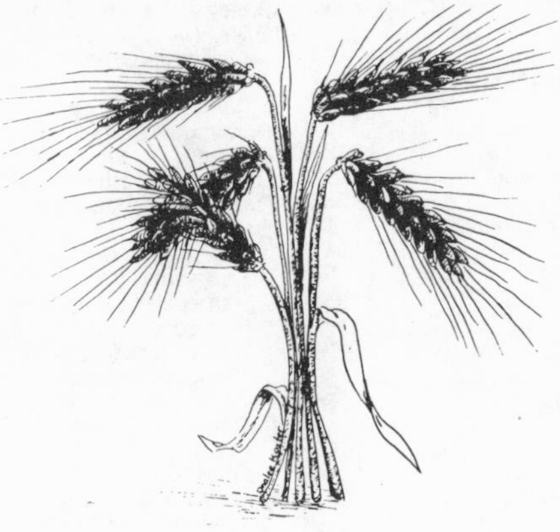

ROSE PETAL POTPOURRI

1 pound rose petals
Salt
Balsam needles
Cloves
Mace
Cinnamon
Allspice
Coriander, crushed
Cardamon seeds, powdered
1 ounce gum benzoin
1 ounce violet sachet
1 ounce brandy

Spread petals on paper, sprinkle lightly with salt and allow to dry. When dry, place in a half-gallon jar that can be tightly covered. Add a sprinkling of balsam needles as well as a pinch of all the spices. Add other ingredients and close jar tightly. Allow to ferment for several weeks, opening occasionally to stir. When desired aroma is attained. place potpourri in open container where desired.
State Women's Committee

INDEX

Re-Order Additional Copies

California Farm Bureau Women
1601 Exposition Boulevard
Sacramento, CA 95815

Please send me_________copies of **COUNTRY COOKING . . . California Style** at $8.50* including tax plus $1.75 shipping and handling.

Enclosed you will find my check or money order for $_________.

Name ____
Address ____
City ______________________________State __________Zip ________

*All prices subject to change without notice.

California Farm Bureau Women
1601 Exposition Boulevard
Sacramento, CA 95815

Please send me_________copies of **COUNTRY COOKING . . . California Style** at $8.50* including tax plus $1.75 shipping and handling.

Enclosed you will find my check or money order for $_________.

Name ____
Address ____
City ______________________________State __________Zip ________

*All prices subject to change without notice.

California Farm Bureau Women
1601 Exposition Boulevard
Sacramento, CA 95815

Please send me_________copies of **COUNTRY COOKING . . . California Style** at $8.50* including tax plus $1.75 shipping and handling.

Enclosed you will find my check or money order for $_________.

Name ____
Address ____
City ______________________________State __________Zip ________

*All prices subject to change without notice.